W9-BWZ-290

DATE DUE

Freud and the Bolsheviks

Freud and the Bolsheviks

Psychoanalysis in Imperial Russia

and the Soviet Union

Martin A. Miller

Yale University Press

New Haven & London

Library of Congress Cataloging-in-Publication Data

Miller, Martin A. (Martin Alan), 1938–
    Freud and the Bolsheviks : psychoanalysis in Imperial Russia and the Soviet
  Union / Martin A. Miller.
        p.   cm.
    Includes bibliographical references (p.   ) and index.
    ISBN 0–300–06810–7 (hardcover : alk. paper)
      1. Psychoanalysis—Soviet Union—History—20th century.
  2. Psychoanalysis—Russia—History—20th century.   3. Freud,
  Sigmund, 1856–1939.   I. Title.
  BF175.M 485   1998
  150.19′5′09470904—dc21   98-3630
                                CIP

A catalogue record for this book is available from the British Library.

The paper in this book meets the guidelines for permanence and durability of the
Committee on Production Guidelines for Book Longevity of the Council on
Library Resources.

10   9   8   7   6   5   4   3   2   1

For Y. N. M., J. L. M. and Z. A. M.

Contents

Preface, ix

Acknowledgments, xv

Part One Before the Revolution

1 Psychiatry in Russia and Its Discontents, 3

2 The Beginnings of Russian Psychoanalysis, 19

3 The Consolidation of a Movement, 30

Part Two Psychoanalysis in the Soviet Union

4 Freud in the House of Lenin: Psychoanalysis Ascendant, 53

5 The Decline and Fall of Soviet Psychoanalysis, 69

6 Killing Freud, 93

7 After Stalin, 114

8 The Rehabilitation of the Unconscious, 139

9   Psychoanalysis and Soviet History, 153

Appendix: Freud's Letters to Osipov, 169

Notes, 175

Bibliography, 211

Index, 231

Preface

And it may have been on the same day, or some other day, we had a long conversation, and he had bitter, harsh words about deadness and lies. Then, frowning, stubbornly—perhaps to himself rather than to me, he said: "And yet there is a grain of truth—of every genuine truth—in all of this. A hating love—this is perhaps the most exact description of my feeling toward Russia."
—*Alexander Blok on Evgenii Zamyatin (1920)*

This book is principally concerned with the importation of the concepts of Sigmund Freud to Russia, the establishment of a psychoanalytic presence there, and the consequences this process had for the country. A century after the publication of *Studies on Hysteria*, which launched Freud's career in the new field he was to name "psychoanalysis," his work has come under attack from many quarters. These arguments revolve around the very serious doubts that have been raised concerning the inability to verify the theory and practice of clinical psychoanalysis by the general standards of modern scientific testing. Moreover, recent work has uncovered mistakes that Freud made in treating his patients, some of which seem to have been at worst damaging or at best unnecessary. Beyond all this, questions have been raised about the usefulness of the entire psychoanalytic enterprise. Even Freud's most passionate defenders are compelled to admit that a crisis is at hand. Training institutes attract fewer candidates than ever before, prestigious psychiatric medical journals rarely publish articles dealing with psychoanalysis, the number of private patients in psychoanalytic treatment has plummeted, and there remain few members of psychiatry departments (and even fewer heads of these departments) who have been trained as psychoanalysts.

Yet at the same time many psychoanalytic institutes, their clinical publications, and their annual professional meetings continue to exist. Moreover, books about Freud and psychoanalysis continue to pour out of publishing houses, both in the United States and abroad. University course syllabi in the humanities and the social sciences still include some psychoanalytic readings (pro and contra) as required material for students. Intimations of great interest in matters psychoanalytic surface in the media on many occasions, sometimes with great dramatic fanfare. One such case was the widespread coverage of the lawsuit filed by Jeffrey Masson against *New Yorker* staff writer Janet Malcolm over her critical observations of his career as the former projects director at the Sigmund Freud archive. Biographies of Freud, of his daughter, Anna, and of his disciples and antagonists are widely reviewed in popular as well as scholarly journals. Even the reaction against Freud attracts great interest, especially when it centers around the feminist critique of psychoanalysis, or events like the cancellation of the Freud exhibition at the Library of Congress in 1995 following the protest against the alleged bias of the curators.

It has long been assumed that, at least as far as the history of psychoanalysis is concerned, the major story had been told. At the time that I began this study I was surprised to learn that neither the main histories of psychoanalysis nor the well regarded books favorable to Freud (from Ernest Jones's *Life and Work of Sigmund Freud* to Reuben Fine's *History of Psychoanalysis*) included anything of significance on Russia. Even the source material was misleading. Witness the observation in the Minutes of the Vienna Psychoanalytic Society that "psychoanalysis was forbidden in Russia after the First World War" (II, 173). More recent work (including Peter Gay's *Freud* and Edith Kurzweil's *The Freudians*) has not altered the portrait painted by the earlier studies in which Russia is simply absent, as though there had been no Freudian community and no serious discussion of psychoanalysis there. In *The Discovery of the Unconscious*, arguably the finest book on the history of psychoanalysis and the development of the concept of the unconscious, Henri Ellenberger was at least able to appreciate the problem when he stated that "the history of psychoanalysis in Russia has yet to be written."

This book is an attempt to correct this omission and to explore the impact of psychoanalysis in Russia. As will be evident, there was (and indeed, once again, is) an active, creative, and vigorous psychoanalytic community in Russia. Moreover, the influence of Freud in Russia can be traced back to the initial development of psychoanalysis in Europe. Freud's works, beginning with his *Interpretation of Dreams* (published in 1899), were translated from German into Russian before they appeared in any other foreign language. Psychiatrists who had traveled to study with Freud, Carl Jung, and Karl Abraham in Western Europe organized a training institute in Moscow years before any existed in London, Paris, New York, or Buenos Aires—all cities that later became flourishing centers of psychoanalysis. Nevertheless, despite these connections abroad and a discourse and institutional structure that in many ways resembled that of European psychoanalysis, the Russians ended up taking a very different professional path.

Part I explores these formative years. The original followers of Freud in Russia were, for the most part, psychiatrists who found that they had run into insurmountable problems in treating their patients. Often referred to in Western Europe as "somatic pessimism," in fin-de-siècle Russia this concept took the form of a combination of two large currents: (1) the exhaustion of the reigning paradigm of organic etiology in which attempts to cure severe psychiatric disorders had led to massive hospital confinement with little improvement in the morbidity rates, and (2) a perception within the psychiatric profession that the government was unwilling to support expanded care. All of this led to a search for new solutions and explanatory frameworks. One alternative which proved vital to a few Russian psychiatrists at this time was being worked out in Vienna by a small group around Sigmund Freud.

Early success led to extraordinary problems as the Russian Freudians learned in their efforts to function in the complex atmosphere following the Bolshevik revolution in 1917. As described in part II, amid these difficulties, during the first half of the 1920s the Freudian community in Soviet Russia managed to establish the first (and to date the only) state-supported psychoanalytic institute in the world. In addition, a therapeutic children's school run on psychoanalytic principles was established with government funding. Moreover, a vigorous debate about psychoanalysis took place throughout the 1920s in the major

Bolshevik party journals. This situation changed decisively at the end of that decade as all matters relating to Freud and psychoanalysis were banished to the exclusionary zone reserved for enemies of the state.

The story of Russian psychoanalysis seemed to stop at this point, with the severe and very public denunciation of Freudianism issued at the Congress on Human Behavior in Moscow in 1930. However, another unusual twist took place. Instead of disappearing, psychoanalysis was transformed into an industry of criticism. Throughout the Stalin era, and well into the postwar period, this critical discourse was sustained by people who were in fact genuinely interested in Freud in spite of the fact that they could neither practice as clinicians nor publish as academics with a psychoanalytic identification. This, in turn, led to the rebirth of a significant interest in Freud and psychoanalysis, most noticeably as a result of the initiatives taken by a group of psychologists in Tbilisi at the Uznadze Institute during the 1970s and the published work of several bold scholars even before the arrival of Gorbachev and his glasnost policies. In the last two decades of the Soviet era, psychoanalysis underwent a genuine revival both as a theory of human motivation emphasizing unconscious forces and as a clinical treatment process seeking to alleviate or understand the symptoms of mental distress. The manner in which these oscillations took place, and their consequences, are described in the pages that follow.

I am well aware of how introductory a study this book is, and I shall consider it a success if others are encouraged to investigate more deeply the fascinating history of Russian psychoanalysis. Unpublished collections of source material are being made available, including individual holdings and state archival files concerned with psychoanalysis, which will permit more thorough investigation of many themes described here than was possible at the time my research was conducted.

Concerning the use of the terms *Freudian* and *psychoanalytic,* I have adapted the usages of my sources in order not to dilute the confusions, distinctions, and distortions that are part of the Soviet discourse on these themes. Thus, during the prerevolutionary period, the two terms were often used synonymously despite the fact that the Russians in Freud's time were also influenced by Adler, Jung, and other members of the original psychoanalytic community. In the Soviet era, supporters and critics of psychoanalysis began to adapt the term *Freudians* to refer to anyone associated with psychoanalysis. From the time of the ideological debates about psychoanalysis in the 1920s, the term *Soviet Freudians* was used as a blanket label for the entire movement, regardless of specific orientation. Much later, the *Large Soviet Encyclopedia* (1978) made a distinction between psychoanalysis as a study of unconscious phenomena and Freudianism as a theory that elevated "the tenets of psychoanalysis to philosophical and anthropological principles." In other instances, *psychoanalysis* was used to refer to the clinical practice of psychotherapy, whereas *Freudianism* signified Freud's theories on subjects as diverse as individual drives and societal conflicts. I have used the terms as they appear in the sources of the time.

Last, a word about the title. I have employed the word *Bolshevik* both literally and metaphorically. It is used to describe the actual name of the ruling political party in Soviet Russia after the 1917 October Revolution (until "Communist" replaced it) and also as a symbolic classification spanning the entire Soviet era. Freud, of course, was never in Russia, but his presence was quite significant, as this book will show.

I have used a modified version of the Library of Congress transliteration system. Also, I have used the prerevolutionary Julian calendar (thirteen days behind the Gregorian), as Russians did, until 31 January 1918, when Russia adopted the Western calendar.

Acknowledgments

Without the help I have received from many quarters, this book could not have been completed. I am deeply grateful for this assistance, and I hope I have not forgotten anyone in the list that follows, in which I offer particular thanks.

An earlier version of this book was read in its entirety by Laura Engelstein, David Joravsky, Philip Pomper, and Richard Wortman. They may not recognize large sections of the complete work, but many of my revisions are largely due to their perceptive critiques. James Rice was helpful throughout the development of this book. In Russia, Aron Belkin, Alexander Etkind, and Valerii Leibin generously shared their work with me, often in manuscript form, and I have learned about Russian psychoanalysis from all of them in various ways.

Sections of the book were presented to audiences at the John J. Gilbride Memorial Lecture at Johns Hopkins University Medical Center, the Third World Slavic Congress of Slavic Studies, the Fishbein Center at the University of Chicago, the Center for International Affairs, the Center for the History of Medicine, and the department of psychiatry at Duke University, the International Affairs Center at Emory University, the Psychoanalytic Society in Atlanta, the American Association for the Advancement of Slavic Studies, the American Academy of Psychoanalysis, and the Duke University–University of North Carolina Psychoanalytic Society, and the Triangle Seminar on Intellectual History at the National Humanities Center. The enthusiastic support and constructive criticism I received at these invited gatherings was of great value in helping me to reinterrogate my materials with fresh perspectives. I also wish to thank the *Slavic Review* for permission to republish in revised form sections of chapter 5, which first appeared there in my article "Freudian Theory Under Bolshevik Rule."

For invaluable bibliographic help, I am especially grateful to the staffs at the Library of Congress, the National Library of Medicine, the Slavic Reference Service at the University of Illinois (Urbana-Champaign), the inter-library loan staff at Duke University, and to Nellie L. Thompson, curator of the archives and special collections at the A. A. Brill Library of the New York Psychoanalytic Institute. Aron Belkin in Moscow made it possible for me to consult the Russian archival materials cited in this book. Orest Pelech, Slavic bibliographer at Perkins Library at Duke, always responded to my requests for sources in addition to reviewing carefully all the Russian and German citations in the book. Dot Sapp and Jenna Golnik typed the manuscript with great competence, and I was fortunate to have had Noreen O'Connor as my manuscript editor. Ron Bobroff's final reading greatly improved the book.

Many years ago when I was an undergraduate, Thelma Levine introduced me to Freud in an indelible manner in her lectures at the University of Maryland on the philosophy of history. As a graduate student on the cultural exchange program at Moscow State University during the 1965–66 academic year, I first learned about the problems of studying psychoanalysis in the former Soviet Union through Vladimir Dobren'kov's work on Erich Fromm, at a time when it was very difficult to conduct such research. The inspiring influence of Leopold Haimson and Michael Confino—both former mentors and contemporary friends—lies "unconsciously" between the lines in much of what I have written.

This project originally took shape during a fruitful two-year fellowship at the Psychiatric Epidemiology Training Program at Columbia University, under the auspices of the National Institute of Mental Health. I was also able to take leave from my teaching responsibilities thanks to grants from the National Endowment for the Humanities, the National Council for Russian and East European Studies, the International Research and Exchanges Board (for travel to Russia), and the Research Council of Duke University. I am grateful for all of this support.

My greatest debt is the unpayable gratitude I owe to my wife, Ylana. Her insightful readings of the many drafts of this book have saved me from numerous errors. She also raised important questions that I would have missed asking. To her, *liubov' navsegda!* In ways perhaps more indirect, my children, Josh and Zina, have also helped me to think out aspects of this project.

Though I bear sole responsibility for the content of this book, the help from everyone mentioned here and in the notes has made it better than it otherwise would have been.

Part One Before the Revolution

Chapter 1 Psychiatry in Russia
and Its Discontents

Nothing is "given" as real except our world of desires and passions, that
we can rise or sink to no other "reality" than the reality of our drives—for
thinking is only the relationship of these drives to one another.
—*Friedrich Nietzsche,* Beyond Good and Evil

FROM ASYLUMS TO HOSPITALS

There are scattered references about treating "disturbances of the soul"
in Russia as far back as the tenth century.[1] In the sixteenth century,
during the reign of Ivan the Terrible, laws were decreed concerning the
care of the insane, who were described as "possessed and deprived of
reason." These individuals were to be placed in specified monasteries
where they would "not be a hindrance to healthy people and would
receive enlightenment and understanding of truth."[2] Responsibility
for the insane on an institutional level rested with monasteries into the
eighteenth century.

Nevertheless, there is little doubt that most of the insane remained
unconfined. The terminology used for mad people is reflective of

widespread attitudes toward insanity. The insane were referred to as "unfortunates," occasionally as "sufferers," and sometimes even as "blessed ones." It was more common for persons considered mad to wander the streets of towns and villages and the nearby forests where legends grew up about them, as long as they were not a danger to society. This makes it difficult to make distinctions between the indigent and the insane because the term *neschastnyi* (unfortunate) was frequently applied to both in contemporary documents.

The gradual shift toward confinement of the insane was the result of several factors. These include the legalization of serfdom (traditionally dated by the 1649 Ulozhenie, or Law Code, which abolished freedom of movement for the peasantry) and the religious schism within the Russian Orthodox Church during the reign of Tsar Alexei (1645–76). Enserfed peasants seeking to escape from their landlords came to Moscow in increasing numbers; whether poor or mad, they were no longer considered as merely "unfortunates" to be pitied, but as a threat to the established order. Regarding the religious issue, in the aftermath of the divisive theological controversy in the church over Patriarch Nikon's reforms in the 1660s, a wide range of "enemies" and "heretics" were identified. In this highly charged atmosphere, religious dissenters and deviants of all categories (primarily peasants fleeing their tyrannical landlords) were swept up in a holy crusade against "immorality."

This important historical development was to haunt the "healers of the soul," as the physicians in the era before psychiatry have been called. Immorality as defined by the church, deviance as defined by the state, and insanity as defined by the medical community were no longer distinct. Indeed, as the state consolidated its authority over the church, powerful aristocrats and local princes, individual deviation was perceived as a danger to be both classified and combatted.

This trend became clear during the reign of Peter the Great (1689–1725), when the secularization of Russian society began in earnest and seriously affected the treatment of the insane. In the modern state forged by Peter, there was no more social space or tolerance for the free insane than there was for free peasants. He announced in a series of legislative decrees that socially "useless," "dangerous," and "threatening" individuals were henceforth to be institutionalized. As Peter mobilized the various sectors of Russian society to create the new imperial state, he instituted stringent state service requirements and an ethos of productivity from which little deviation was permitted. Those who were unable to participate in the state-building enterprise, for whatever reasons, were considered unproductive and idle. A number of correctional institutions were to be designed for "malingerers," "sorcerers," and the large, older category of "unfortunates," whether aristocrat or peasant. Peter's clear intention was to remove the responsibility for institutionalized care of the insane from the monasteries. The new institutions were to be entirely under government auspices and included workhouses as well as hospitals. This corpus of Peter's legislation, most of which was issued in the early 1720s, also included a new legal term (*sumabrodnye*) to designate the insane and distinguish them from other "unfortunates" in Russian society.[3]

Peter the Great's motive for this legislation had far more to do with establishing clear criteria for functioning in state service than in rehabilitating or caring for the ill. None of the proposed institutions, whether corrective or therapeutic, was established during his reign. By using a specific term for insane persons and mandating that they be moved from monastic to secular care, Peter set the stage for an asylum system, but stopped short of creating this system himself. It was to be another half-century before the first asylums for the insane were established in Russia.

The origins of the asylum system in Russia can be traced to 1762 when a government decree by Emperor Peter III, with the sponsorship of the State Senate, proclaimed that "madpeople are not to be sent to a monastery, but rather to a special house, as is the case in foreign countries."[4] Peter III had in mind as a model the German *Tollhaus,* or madhouse, which had been in existence in several German principalities for some time. A lengthy report, commissioned by the Russian Academy of Sciences, provided the framework for the new institution. Four diagnostic categories for the insane were established for treatment purposes: "epileptics, lunatics, melancholics, and maniacs" (*beshenye,* literally, the furious or enraged). Individuals with these disorders were to be housed and treated in separate areas of the asylum. The report also detailed the number of physicians and staff attendants. Everything from the architecture of the building to the treatment modes to be utilized was discussed in the report. It was as though Russia was to move from therapeutic darkness to light in a single historical moment.[5]

Between 1776 and 1779, in an example of state institutional control, the first insane asylums were established in Novgorod, Moscow, and St. Petersburg under Catherine the Great's provincial reform program. The Academy of Sciences in the capital played a key role in setting up these initial asylums, some of which in the provinces, ironically, were housed in existing monasteries for lack of other space.[6] The asylums, known colloquially as "yellow houses" after the paint color frequently used, were created in provinces across the country in the following decades.

However, the asylums were weakened by immense difficulties from the start. Because the criteria for admission were never clarified on a clinical basis, the asylums quickly became a dumping ground for criminals, paupers, and various categories of the "unfortunates" whom the police or members of society wished to have removed from public. As the asylum system preceded a specialized psychiatric profession, no trained personnel supervised and defined the functions of the asylums. Thus, conditions were overcrowded and inmates were ill-treated. Therapy frequently consisted of severe restraints (leather straps and straitjackets) for the "furious," and hot or cold baths for the docile. In addition, the asylums were never provided with funding sufficient to treat the immensely complex problems of such a troubled and varied patient population or to hire quality staff. The asylums, which had been called into being by the state as public institutions, were refused the necessary backing by the state. The modern age of "confinement," as Michel Foucault has termed it, had begun in Russia.

It is not coincidental that the policy for treatment of the insane originated while Russia was exposed to the ideas of the European Enlightenment. Catherine the Great consciously emulated the enlightened despots of Europe—especially Frederick the Great of Prussia—in attempting to bring the new "high culture" to Russia. Among the many reforms initiated during this age of reform were those concerned with the humane treatment of society's unfortunates. Catherine herself was responsible for the establishment of foundling homes, orphanages, and hospitals. The motivation behind this reforming activity has been interpreted either as her sincere desire to ameliorate the plight of the indigent and sick, or as part of her calculated attempt to create a broader base of appeal in order to consolidate her authority.

Often overlooked, however, is the underlying relationship at work here between the politics and aims of the Enlightenment. In a society seeking to refashion itself according to selective perceptions of Western rationalism, those groups which did not fit presented a problem. The world of reason is committed to the mechanics of logic, order, symmetry, and goal-oriented behavior. Just as Peter the Great could not tolerate the idle in his ethos of complete dedication to and participation in the building of the modern nation-state, Catherine could not accept the antithesis of reason—insanity—as part of the Russian Enlightenment. Thus, the institutionalization of the mad in the newly constructed asylums was a direct result of the perceptions and the policies of the Enlightenment. The idle, for Peter, had to be "cured" in order to work to serve the state; the insane, for Catherine, had to be "cured" to regain their reason and contribute to, rather than disturb or threaten, the social order.

During the nineteenth century, a number of advances were made in the treatment of the insane, and psychiatry emerged as a distinct specialization within the medical profession. Alongside the asylum system, a network of hospitals was established to provide care for "mad people." Under Emperor Nicholas I (1825–55), a government department headed by a special council was created to oversee the country's almshouses, orphanages, and hospitals. One of the council's members, Ivan F. Riul' (1796–1846), proved to be a leading psychiatric reformer. His detailed report to the crown in 1832 was an influential statement on treatment of the insane. Riul' proposed the establishment of a specially designed hospital for the insane, where patients diagnosed as curable would be separated from the incurables. Sufficient living space and therapeutic activities would be provided to aid the process of recovery. He also recommended devoting attention to diet, lifestyle, and family background during the examination of patients who were admitted to the hospital. Further, Riul' devised an elaborate patient questionnaire which permitted him to make the first scientific estimates of rates of mental illness in Russia.[7]

The hospital Riul' argued for was approved and constructed in St. Petersburg soon after his report was submitted. The All-Mourners' Hospital (or All-Sufferers'; *Vseskorbiashchie* in Russian) was headed by F. I. Gertsog (1785–1853), one of the country's premier psychiatrists. However, it soon encountered many of the unresolved problems of the asylums and fell far short of the high standards envisioned by Riul'. The quality of treatment suffered as the hospital quickly became overcrowded, and poorly trained attendants were unable to make precise diagnoses. The proportion of incurables was higher than had been anticipated, which had the effect of demoralizing the physicians who worked in the hospital. Funding was at best erratic; in some years the government was generous, and in many others it was not.

The first hospital in Moscow devoted exclusively to the care of the insane, the Preobrazhenskii, opened in 1808 and was headed by Dr. Z. I. Kibal'chich, author of one of Russia's earliest treatises on clinical psychiatry.[8] Conditions at the Preobrazhenskii Hospital in Moscow were similar to those described at the All-Mourners' Hospital in St. Petersburg. Hospital budgets from this period show sizable expenses for chains and iron rods to replace the older wooden gratings for restraining the "furious." In 1828, Dr. V. F. Sabler was appointed chief of the Preobrazhenskii and attempted to humanize treatment there. He abolished chained restraints and introduced his patients to the methods of "moral therapy" used in Western Europe, such as music, crafts, and agricultural work in the hospital garden. He did, however, continue to permit the use of straitjackets and restraining chairs with leather straps for uncontrollable patients.[9] Nevertheless, overcrowding reached unmanageable levels by 1850 when 256 patients were crammed into the hospital. Once again, inadequate funding, a poorly trained staff, and the absence of clear criteria to limit admissions all lessened the effectiveness of the Preobrazhenskii Hospital.

THE FRUSTRATIONS OF REFORM

Russian psychiatry as a modern profession, according to most studies, emerged largely as a result of the work of Ivan Balinskii (1827–1902). He was responsible for establishing the first independent course on psychiatry in a medical facility, the esteemed Medical-Surgical Academy in St. Petersburg, in 1857. He also opened a special clinic for the insane at the academy in St. Petersburg in 1861. At the same time, Balinskii helped form (and later headed) Russia's first professional psychiatric organization, the Society of Petersburg Doctors for the Insane. Having traveled throughout Europe, he was able to bring his perceptions of European psychiatry to the attention of his medical students as well as to achieve a measure of international renown.[10]

During the 1860s, Emperor Alexander II undertook a wide-ranging reform program which had profound implications for Russian society in general and psychiatry in particular. The centerpiece of the reform program, which was set in motion after Russia's unexpected and humiliating defeat in the Crimean War in 1855, was the emancipation of the serfs. In addition, there was legislation on the reform of the army, the judicial system, the educational institutions, and the network of hospitals across the country. Among the many new agencies created by the emperor's reform program were the zemstvos, commissions charged with the mission of ameliorating the near-desperate conditions of the peasantry. The zemstvo boards attracted many students and professionals, inspired by Alexander's bold program for the transformation of the country. They devoted their energies initially to gathering statistical data on rural education, housing, transportation, agricultural production, and health. In their examination of the country's public asylums, they found deplorable conditions in virtually every province. One of the more prominent zemstvo physicians was E. A. Osipov, whose son would later become one of the founders of Russian psychoanalysis.

The elder Osipov was instrumental in establishing a regional health group which served as a model for many provincial health organizations.

The situation was no better in the cities, where medical visitors from abroad corroborated evidence collected in the provinces by the zemstvo groups. In the largest asylum in the capital, according to a visiting British physician in 1867, "many of the unhappy inmates might with equal prospect of benefit be immured in a dungeon, for all the light they receive during the winter." His observations of the asylum attached to the First Military Hospital in St. Petersburg deserve to be quoted more fully:

> The wards devoted to lunatic officers here are simply disgusting, being dark, utterly devoid of pictures, ornaments, plants, or even decent-looking furniture. The sleeping and sitting rooms are used indifferently during the day, and they all bear a cheerless appearance, sufficiently accounting for the discontent and gloom observable among the unhappy inmates, who mope about, partially clad in somber looking grey dressing gowns, apparently without any other means of diversion than smoking. Though hardly thirty in number, they distress the visitor by their very natural clamours and excitement, and painfully impress him with a sense of their forlorn and pitiable condition. There is no book or newspaper to divert their thoughts. . . . [The insane] are confined within-doors with a rigour which must be disastrous in its effects on their mental and bodily health. . . .
>
> The visitor leaves the lunatic department of the First Military Hospital of St. Petersburg with a heavy heart, impressed with a conviction that its managers have ill-prepared themselves for their vocation.[11]

As a result of the zemstvo psychiatric reports and proposals, between 1864 and 1875 more than thirty provincial asylums and many psychiatric sections of general hospitals in the larger municipalities were transferred over to zemstvo supervision. The zemstvo boards recommended new institutions for the insane to ease overcrowding, better trained physicians specializing in psychiatry, and increased government funding for patient treatment. Broadly speaking, the zemstvos were experiments in local self-administration and an effort to correct the abuses and negligence created during years of control by regional authorities.

By 1879, there was reason for cautious optimism. That year the government, responding to repeated requests by the zemstvos for assistance, issued a decree in which the horrendous conditions of the asylums were publicly acknowledged, and increased the level of financial support. The underlying assumption was that "with appropriate care, a significant proportion of the insane can be converted into productive members of society."[12]

In addition, during the last half of the nineteenth century a number of Russian psychiatrists moved into positions of theoretical and clinical authority in relationship to their colleagues, who numbered 180 trained and licensed members by 1890. I. P. Merzheevskii (1838–1908), who succeeded Balinskii at the St. Petersburg Medical-Surgical Academy in 1877, is credited with training over fifty psychiatrists and supervising twenty-six doctoral studies in psychiatry. He also was one of the first Russian psychiatrists to collaborate with colleagues abroad, on a joint neurological project with Valentine Magnan, one of France's leading psychiatrists, and was elected president of the first Congress of Russian Psychiatrists in 1887. Psychiatry developed in Kharkov under P. I. Kovalevskii (1849–1923) and in Kazan under V. M. Bekhterev (1857–1927), who became internationally known as chief of the Neurological Institute in the capital.

In Moscow, there was a succession of important figures in psychiatry during this era, including I. I. Kozhevnikov (1836–1902), who helped establish the new University Psychiatric Clinic in 1887, and, above all, Sergei Korsakov (1854–1900), generally regarded as the outstanding Russian psychiatrist of this era. In the literature, Korsakov is portrayed in virtually legendary terms, occupying the role accorded Philippe Pinel in France and Thomas Kirkbride in the United States as major reformers in the general history of psychiatry. As Pinel had done in France, Korsakov abolished all mechanical restraints on mental patients in Russia, and was responsible for the establishment of an internationally recognized diagnostic classification for alcoholic psychosis.[13]

Theoretically and clinically, Russian psychiatry was more strongly influenced by professional developments in Germany than France during these years, a factor which would be important later for psychoanalysis. Russian psychiatrists accepted the notion that mental illness was primarily a disease of the brain, that there was a somatic (as opposed to a psychological) foundation to brain diseases, and that emphasis should be placed upon classification (nosology) and causation (etiology) in diagnosis and treatment. Although this German influence can be seen even earlier,[14] it is certainly visible in the work of the physiologist Ivan Sechenov (1829–1905). Sechenov is best known for his book *Reflexes of the Brain* (1863), in which he took the position that the psychic activity of the human nervous system is, in large measure, physiologically based and dependent upon external sensory stimuli: "All psychic acts which occur along reflex lines must be studied entirely physiologically because their beginning, the sensory stimulus, and their end, the motor action, are physiological phenomena. Moreover, even their middle, or psychic element is also strictly speaking often, if not always, not an independent phenomenon—as was formerly believed—but an integral part of this whole process."[15]

Sechenov was trained in the laboratory of Carl Ludwig (1816–95), the German physiologist who argued convincingly in his *Textbook of Physiology* (1858) that mental phenomena are the result of conditions contained in the blood and brain of the human organism. This orientation was part of a wider European scientific orientation that involved other fields of knowledge as well. It was, however, fraught with difficulties almost immediately. Sechenov, for instance, was subjected to a lengthy critique by the liberal historian Konstantin Kavelin. In an exhaustive analysis of "German contemporary psychology," Kavelin argued that the problems of Cartesian dualism had not been resolved by Sechenov's work. Kavelin's main point was that the soul, or psyche, remained autonomous from the workings of the body. He made an impassioned plea for greater attention to the individuality of the human personality and believed that psychology should take this on as its primary task. Kavelin remained skeptical of Sechenov's physiological approach as a proper investigation of the nature and functions of the mind.[16]

Korsakov's own investigations were also stimulated by advances in German psychiatric research. He wrote that mental illnesses were, "according to their manifestations, disorders of the personality, and according to localization, diseases of the forebrain."[17] Korsakov's major work was the discovery of the symptoms and causes of "memory illness," which he classified in primarily physiological terms for the first time in 1887 as alcohol-related "polyneuritic psychosis." He also directed attention to the minute functions of the nervous system, suggesting that memory impairment and amnesia may ultimately be the result of molecular or cellular displacement of sensory impressions by the brain.[18] Similar research on the neurological and physiological dimensions of mental illness was carried out by most of Russia's leading psychiatrists, including Bekhterev, Vladimir Serbskii (1858–1917), Vasilii Giliarovskii (1876–1959), and Petr Gannushkin (1857–1933).

In spite of these activities on the part of a growing and increasingly sophisticated psychiatric profession, the crisis in patient care continued to worsen. Moreover, as hospital and asylum conditions once again deteriorated, many psychiatrists searched for new ways to understand the symptoms of their patients in the hope of relieving their distress. Most psychiatrists were in agreement that more money was needed from national and regional authorities to improve the asylums and hospitals, but their critique went beyond government commitment.

A vivid example of this expanding critique was made public in 1887 at the First Congress of Russian Psychiatry in Moscow. The opening address, given by I. P. Merzheevskii, was an effort to clarify the nature of "the conditions favorable to the development of mental and nervous disorders in Russia" and to propose "measures directed toward their reduction." Merzheevskii's argument was based on an environmentalist interpretation which was quite similar to the etiological model used to explain the causes of mental illness in the United States. Many nineteenth-century American psychiatrists were convinced that the rise in the rates of mental illness that they observed was a direct response to the rapid and massive social transformation being experienced by the country. To emphasize their hypothesis of environmental stress causing mental disorders, these psychiatrists argued that rates of psychopathology were lower for blacks than for whites, especially in the antebellum South; the reason cited for this was that blacks living under the plantation system were shielded from the anxieties and stress burdening white Americans in urban areas who had to confront rapid change, geographical dislocation, and decision-making and risk-taking on a daily basis. According to Edward Jarvis, a prominent American psychiatrist at that time, insanity is "a part of the price we pay for civilization."[19]

Similarly, Merzheevskii traced Russia's psychiatric patient care crisis to the emancipation of the peasants in 1861. As a result, former serfs now were compelled to confront the bewildering world of modernity without training and experience in either making decisions or assuming new responsibilities, and were unable to cope. The major consequence of this dilemma over the course of a generation, Merzheevskii argued, was an increase in social stress and anxiety which was manifested in a higher prevalence of alcoholism, deviant behavior, suicide, and severe mental disorders. Rising expectations of achievement, wealth, and social advancement produced by the emancipation were not realized, leading to greater symptoms of mental distress among the general population. To be sure, Merzheevskii held both society and government responsible for this problem; nevertheless, he also suggested that psychiatry, with appropriate financial support, could play a crucial role in alleviating the painful symptoms of these environmentally rooted forms of mental illness by treating a greater number of patients in the country's hospitals and asylums.[20]

A different view of the situation was provided by the Kharkov psychiatrist P. I. Kovalevskii, an organizer of the 1887 congress. Kovalevskii, who founded Russia's first journal devoted to psychiatry, was a university professor as well as a trained physician involved with the leading reforms in his profession. At the congress, he voiced a pervasive fear of the insane when he spoke about an "army of invalids" committing crimes across Russia in ever-increasing numbers. He believed that a kind of contagion of madness was spreading uncontrollably throughout society. He warned that the country was being "enveloped by a pandemonium of insanity" that threatened the foundation of social order. The most vulnerable sector of the population, he argued—Russia's youth—was being drawn to political radicalism, artistic decadence, and criminal deviance. Kovalevskii believed that possibly 90 percent of Russia's mad people were untreated by any institutions and were in some way harming themselves and others.

Kovalevskii proposed joint medical and government action on a number of levels. These included the education of the public about the dangers of tolerating the insane and about the need to confine them, the abolition of marriage among the insane, and a campaign of "material and moral uplifting" in society designed to counter the stress of unrealistic expectations. Further, he emphasized the need to care for the victims of mental exhaustion before they developed severe or chronic disorders.[21]

Perhaps the most comprehensive and radical analysis of the theory of an unchecked and largely untreated insanity epidemic at this time was written by P. I. Iakobii (1842–1913), a physician who spent many years in Western Europe and had been deeply involved in radical politics among the Russian émigrés there. After his return to Russia, he practiced psychiatry in Moscow, and his experience formed the basis of his critique. For Iakobii, there was a direct correlation between the political, economic, and social structure of a society on the one hand and its treatment of and attitudes toward the insane on the other.

In his book, Iakobii used copious sources to show that the institutionalization of the insane was not rooted in ideas of humane treatment but in "class fear of the abstract madman." Frightened by the assumed violence, uncontrolled passions, and incomprehensible motivation they attributed to mad people, ruling social classes supported the building of asylums to remove this threat from society. Iakobii asserted that the emergence of a powerful bourgeoisie in Russia and its concern for the acquisition of private property unobstructed by persons "lacking in reason" coincided with the zenith of asylum construction. If asylums were filled to capacity, this was mainly due to effective psychiatric propaganda and the desire of people from all social classes to rid themselves of people who were perceived as enemies and competitors. It should come as no surprise, according to Iakobii, that asylums and hospitals for the insane had proved to be failures; since they were designed not for cure but for detention, they "lose all of their therapeutic significance and serve as replacements for inexpensive—yet absent—almshouses." Psychiatrists, he concluded, were functioning not as physicians but as wardens and policemen guarding over a captive population of helpless victims.[22]

By 1911, the year the first congress of the Union of Russian Psychiatrists and Neuropathologists was held, it was generally recognized that conditions for the insane had not improved since the alarms had been sounded at the 1887 congress. In spite of Korsakov's efforts to have all mental patients removed from restraints, psychiatrists continued to complain that shackles remained at most institutions. The working conditions of the psychiatrists had become even more difficult than in 1887 because of inconsistent admissions criteria, inadequate staffing, and dismal rates of mortality and morbidity. The overall number of psychiatrists remained very low. By 1914, there were only 350 psychiatrists and neurologists in an empire of 160 million people.

There was still no accepted and tested psychiatric diagnostic classification system. Moreover, as the professions became more international through foreign research journals and annual congresses, existing modes of treatment in Russia seemed to leave much to be desired when compared with hospital facilities and contemporary clinical work in Western Europe. Added to this was the growing discontent among an increasing number of psychiatrists, especially after the 1905 revolution, over what was perceived as a reactionary political regime that could not respond to the crisis at hand with needed reforms. Repression by the tsarist authorities of liberal and radical demands for political liberties produced more widespread despair, pessimism, and resignation in society. The government was blamed for the growing rates of suicide and alcoholism on the eve of the First World War. Psychiatrists began joining the emerging liberal political opposition, many resigned their positions in protest, and others ended up in prison for their anti-regime activities.[23] In their search for alternatives, some of these discontented psychiatrists turned to the theories of Sigmund Freud.

ANXIETIES OF THE AGE

The psychiatrists' reaction to the forces of change was by no means an isolated one. In fact, the country was in the midst of rapid alterations which affected all social classes. Transportation systems, for example, opened up new communications connections that were already profoundly affecting the country. In St. Petersburg, rail lines made it possible to alter the labor force and create entirely new neighborhoods of first-generation urbanites attracted from the country-side by new employment prospects. Migration patterns which uprooted the habitants of other regions of the empire were shaped by the opening of the Trans-Siberian Railroad, the centerpiece of Finance Minister Sergei Witte's plan for the industrialization of the nation at the turn of the century.

These changes were accompanied by a variety of consequences, some of which were perceived as quite threatening. Beneath the statistical counts of hungry peasants moving into cities, and aristocrats slipping into sectors of lower socio-economic status, the anxieties of ordinary people were understandably height-ened.[24] Political terrorism, largely dormant since the aftermath of the 1881 assassination of Alexander II by the People's Will party, re-emerged with a vengeance, largely led by the fanatical members of a breakaway section of the neo-populist Social Revolutionary party. Pogroms against the Jewish community broke out across the Pale of Settlement in western Russia, often with the tacit approval of local officials. In addition, increasing unemployment, homelessness, and lower-class impoverishment produced fears of urban riots, crime, and disease which surfaced in public discussions and the media. Never before had the upper classes been forced to confront the subaltern masses in such close proximity as they did in the last two decades of the Imperial era. The menace of the proletariat, dramatically brought to center stage in the strikes and demonstrations during the 1905 revolution, was extended into frightening and often fantastic images. This, combined with the fears of venereal diseases that the peasants supposedly brought with them to Moscow, St. Petersburg, and smaller industrial areas, led to a resurgence of efforts to control the perceived menace.

The connecting point of these anxieties may have been the extraordinary concern raised by fears of the spread of syphilis, a potentially fatal affliction at this time. The disease also created moral dilemmas since the reputations of respectable families could be ruined by revelations of having contracted symp-toms of syphilis. Once out in the public realm, members of society demanded both explanations and regulations. Illicit brothels were targeted for restrictions and blame. The legal profession drafted codes for the conduct of sexual rela-tions, and newspapers were soon filled with advertisements for "cures" for various sexual difficulties.

Along with the fears and regulations came an intense fascination with the emerging public discourse on sexuality. As had happened so often in Russia's past, literature provided a platform for discussions of subjects that tsarist cen-sorship or social taboos made difficult, if not impossible.

One of the earliest was Anton Chekhov's "A Nervous Breakdown," published in 1888. In this story, a law student, appalled by the degrading conditions he finds at local brothels, attempts suicide and is taken to a psychiatrist to cure his anxiety attacks, delusions (he wants to rescue the fallen women of the streets), and depression.[25]

In 1891, Lev Tolstoy published "The Kreutzer Sonata," which provoked a storm of controversy. The story centered on a man's exoneration by a court, despite the fact that he had killed his wife. Pleading that his wife had been unfaithful, he was freed because the court ruled that he had acted out of honor. In addition to the public discussion carried out in the pages of the major literary journals and newspapers, Tolstoy received a large number of private and anonymous letters, mostly from women, who conveyed some of their deepest sexual anxieties and problems.[26]

More daring was Valerii Briusov's story, "Now When I Have Awakened: Notes of a Psychopath" (1905), a powerful description of a man's struggle with sexual desire, masochism, and rage.[27] Pavel Nilus went even further in his story "Summer Heat" (1907), in which he depicts scenes of incestuous and lesbian love.[28] On a more popular level, the appearance of the novel *Sanin* (1907), with its lust-driven amoral protagonist, led at least to some "eros temples" in St. Petersburg. Another example of the literary fascination with sexual danger can be seen in Anastasiia Verbitskaia's sensual melodrama, *The Keys to Happiness* (1910–13).[29]

Sexual anxieties surfaced in other quarters as well. The most explicit discussions of sex in this prerevolutionary period undoubtedly came from the pen of the uncategorizable philosopher and journalist, Vasilii Rozanov.[30] Also, in a prominent symposium of essays published in 1909 and designed to reassess the significance of the Russian intelligentsia, Alexander Izgoev focused on the decline of moral values among youth. His evidence came from the results of a recently published survey of the sexual attitudes and behavior of Moscow University students which revealed, to Izgoev's evident shock, far more sexual activity and at far younger ages than he had imagined.[31]

Above all, as interest in sexuality advanced, a vast new "scientific" literature was imported to provide the necessary explanations of both permissible and dangerous sexual relationships.[32] Much of this consisted of translations of the new sexology studies from Western Europe, including Richard Krafft-Ebing's *Psychopathia sexualis,* which appeared in Russian in 1887, a year after its initial publication in German, and Havelock Ellis's *Man and Woman: A Study of Human Secondary Sexual Characters,* which was published in Russian in 1898, four years after its first London edition.

One of the most interesting and influential of the sexology texts of this era before psychoanalysis was Iwan Bloch's *Sexual Life of Our Time in Its Relations to Modern Civilization,* a weighty tome originally published in Berlin in 1908 and which appeared in Russian translation two years later. Bloch's purpose was "to write a complete encyclopedia of the sexual sciences" in a scholarly manner which would enlighten his readers on an important subject that was too little understood. He also admitted that he hoped his book would be a contribution to "the campaign against the evils and disharmonies of the sexual sphere." The "need for reform in our entire sexual life, in the sense of a more rational view of that life," was considered essential by Bloch. He had in mind particularly the need to eradicate venereal disease, which he saw as "the central problem of the whole sexual question."[33]

In a special appendix to the section on sexual masochism, Bloch included a document purporting to be the confessions of a Russian anarchist who had participated in the 1905 revolution. Identified only as N. K., the author of the autobiographical essay is introduced dramatically by Bloch as a revolutionary who was arrested in Warsaw in 1906 and saved from certain execution for his rebellious activity as a result of his being identified as "a psychopath" by the commanding officer in charge of his case. Bloch reproduces the document, which N. K. wrote while in prison, "verbatim and without comment."

Entitled (by Bloch) "A Contribution to the Psychology of the Russian Revolution," the memoir is, in effect, an interpretation of recent Western history from the perspective of the forces of human suffering. The author sketched his own childhood, which was filled with domestic violence. As a young boy, he learned from his peers that relationships were established and maintained through mutual tormenting. During his university years, he fell deeply in love and seems to have sensed for the first time the necessity of the painful feelings which are frequently generated in intimate relationships. More important, he experienced the enjoyment of that pain, both in terms of the hurt that is often inflicted on one by another and the hurt that comes from recognizing the inevitable limits that the real world places on desire. N. K. also described the agonizing excitement of participating in "proletarian uprisings" during the 1905 upheaval. He proclaimed that the motivation for rebellion (as well as for state control and the repressive aspects of everyday life) was "a love of cruelty." He described the uprisings of 1905 as a "satanic orgy of suffering" on the part of "*unconscious, instinctive masochists.*" Thus, suffering, he concluded, "is the civilizing factor of mankind," as he gratefully acknowledges the influence of "magnificent Nietzsche." We do not know any more about N. K., but the themes of interest to him would soon be important to Russia's psycho-analysts.[34]

The revolution of 1905 stirred up additional concerns among the mental health professionals themselves. At the 1906 annual meeting of the Moscow Society of Neuropathologists, a report was delivered on the disturbances to the "psychic equilibrium" of both individuals and groups in the heated atmosphere of rebellion. "Current political conditions," according to an article in a Russian medical publication in 1907, "represent a direct threat to the mental health not only of constitutionally unstable people but of completely healthy ones." For some psychiatrists, the collapse of authority during the revolutionary upheaval was responsible for the upsurge in admissions to mental hospitals. Revolution, in other words, was a kind of "psychic epidemic" or "a form of collective psychopathology, involving extreme mood swings, loss of judgment, intense anxiety, and unbridled aggression."[35]

Vladimir Serbskii, a prominent psychiatrist at this time, was also concerned about the correlation between revolution and insanity. He believed that mass movements generally attracted unstable personalities, and that revolutionary situations tended to make worse certain psychotic disorders. He also wrote about the "psychological traumas" experienced at times of combat, pogroms, and executions, but stopped short of declaring a separate clinical category for "revolutionary psychosis."[36] Serbskii, in this way, was able to give rich expression to some of the most fearful anxieties of his age. He also was to play an important role in fostering the development of psychoanalysis.

Chapter 2 The Beginnings of
Russian Psychoanalysis

The senses could refine, and the intellect could degrade. Who could say
where the fleshly impulse ceased, or the psychical impulse began? How
shallow were the arbitrary definitions of ordinary psychologists! And yet
how difficult to decide between the claims of the various schools! Was the
soul a shadow seated in the house of sin?
—*Oscar Wilde,* The Picture of Dorian Gray

THE CONCEPT OF THE UNCONSCIOUS BEFORE
PSYCHOANALYSIS

Historically, whether we are speaking of Russia, Europe, or America,
the relationship of psychiatry to psychoanalysis, and of each to the
larger field of general medicine, has been filled with ambivalence.
After years of struggle, psychiatry gradually became an accepted subspecialty of the larger medical profession during the latter part of the
nineteenth century, but only after its practitioners were able to demonstrate that they were working in an approved scientific framework.
This was accomplished through a difficult process in which psychiatrists adopted the fundamental tenet that mental disorders were em-

pirically provable forms of brain disease. Before the nineteenth century, disserrations and treatises written on melancholia and mania owed more to theologians, philosophers, and poets who had long speculated about the soul of man, than they did to their medical predecessors. However, by the end of the eighteenth century, the "physicians of the psyche" had cut their ties to these discussions and disciplines as they organized themselves into a scientific profession.

As they abandoned concepts such as the divinity of the immortal soul, man's idealist perceptions, and the subjective passions of individuals, nineteenth-century psychiatrists focused instead on the physiology of the brain and its functions to explain the disturbing illnesses of their patients. Their work was strengthened both by the emergence of the field of experimental psychology, in which research on "the mind" was carried on in laboratories with attention to achieving standards of validity, and by neurological research, which dealt with the structure and functions of the brain. Nevertheless, there were always competitive tensions among the new specializations.

Just as psychiatry had reacted against the concept of the soul in establishing itself as a legitimate branch of medical science, psychoanalysis was established in a reaction against the biological model of the diseased brain as the primary explanatory theory of mental illness. This reaction was prompted by unresolved clinical problems in treatment modalities. Mainstream psychiatry was seemingly unable to explain the causes of, and provide cures for, the three main traditionally diagnosed disorders—melancholia, mania, and epilepsy. Beyond this, other chronic symptoms were being brought to the attention of psychiatrists which did not fit into the existing diagnostic categories, such as debilitating phobias in which stricken individuals were rendered dysfunctional or were suffering from unexplainable psychological fears. Such patients were usually hospitalized for long periods of time and, in some cases, never recovered.[1]

Disillusioned by traditional explanations of the causes of mental disorders and the reigning treatment modes, a number of psychiatrists in Europe as well as in Russia chose to seek out new clinical alternatives. A few of these researchers pursued avenues of exploration which, while not explicitly psychoanalytic, allow us to understand more clearly how and when Freud's ideas first made their appearance in Russia.

The new trend centered on the conceptual problem of the divided self. Since the advent of Cartesian philosophy in the seventeenth century, the earlier Copernican revolution in science, and the secular criticism of state and society formulated during the eighteenth-century French Enlightenment, Western society had undergone a profound transformation in collective self-identity. Instead of being perceived as sinful creatures enduring the agonies and seductions of this earthly existence, members of society were reconceptualized as individuals dominated more by powers of logical calculation than passionate faith. People were, above all, believed to be rational and moral in their judgments, and were to act responsibly on others. It followed, then, that by applying reason to political, economic, and social problems, life on earth could be ameliorated and held unlimited possibilities. If, however, this were established as "normal" behavior, then abnormal or pathological behavior was its opposite. The names given to this behavior varied widely, but the basic concept was irrationality, as in the phrases "lost his reason" or "gone out of her mind."

The insidious dimension to this labeling process was that behind the constructed opposition of reason against "unreason," there was an implicit distinction made between order and chaos and, beyond that, of good versus evil. This is important to note because the new neurotic patients who came in increasing numbers to the offices of Russian psychiatrists were suffering not only from painful symptoms which required specialists of the mind, but also from the shameful social stigma associated with the symptoms. What ultimately held this positivistic theory together was the notion that individuals with these psychological difficulties were not able to control their emotions and feelings. Furthermore, it was no longer sufficient to hypothesize that an excess of bile or a "weak constitution" or even anatomical "degeneration" accounted for such irrational and sometimes destructive passions. Responsibility was traced to the possible existence of a recently conceptualized part of the mind, namely, the unconscious. Within this "dark kingdom," animal instincts and drives of awesome power were presumed to reside. In certain people, and under certain circumstances, these forces appeared to break through the routine, normal functioning of reason, and take over the entire personality.[2]

The earliest work in Russian on the subject of the unconscious appears to have been published in 1875. It was not written by a psychiatrist, however, and concerned religious and philosophical themes rather than clinical cases.[3] In 1895, still well before anything by or about Freud had appeared in Russian, the topic of the unconscious was exhaustively explored in a lengthy article published in the official government journal dealing with matters concerning education, science, and culture. The author's intention was to test what he called in his title "the hypothesis of unconscious psychic phenomena." The term "psychic" could also be more literally translated as "spiritual" (the Russian word is *dushevnyi*), although there is no satisfactory English equivalent. The point of the article was to review all of the major Western research on behavior and personality rooted in unconscious motivation. The range of research covered the work of leading psychologists in Europe (Wilhelm Wundt) and in America (William James), psychiatrists (Henry Maudsley) as well as physical and social scientists (such as Herbert Spencer, Franz Brentano, and Hermann Helmholtz). The article familiarized Russian readers with current studies of normal mental perception as well as the pathology of the unnatural "states of the mind." The author concluded that nonrational phenomena, whether religious ecstasy, hysterical moods, or fainting, were still best explained by physiological or neurological causes. The most that could be conceded, he added, was that certain individuals may experience "consciousness without self-awareness," or "psychic reflexes in the absence of self-consciousness."[4]

In 1903, N. N. Bazhenov, one of Russia's most prominent psychiatrists, included a discussion of "the psychic unconscious" in his book on psychiatric themes in belles lettres.[5] Discussions about the unconscious continued and even expanded into new areas. For example, a 1912 article rejected the notion of the unconscious as a fearful force from the "dark kingdom within" and, instead, emphasized the role of the unconscious as having a potentially positive influence on individual acts. Among the examples mentioned were the unconscious drives discussed by Augustine in his *Confessions,* which helped him in his effort to overcome agonizing doubts about the existence of God, and those which may have motivated the creative genius visible in the scientific discoveries of Isaac Newton and in the literary work of Ivan Turgenev.[6]

Russian psychiatrists were also exploring other problems favorable to the reception of psychoanalysis. During the 1880s, I. G. Orshanskii, who had been trained by A. U. Freze, one of the country's first psychiatrists earlier in the century, studied the pathological role of feelings in human behavior. He was convinced that in extreme cases, emotions frequently "take over the whole domain of man's psychic existence." He added that every feeling is "above all a reaction of our *Ia,*" a word (literally, "I") that could mean "self," or "personality," and would later be used by the Freudians to mean "ego." Orshanskii also stated that feelings have an enormous influence on the associations of our ideas and thoughts, and that there are often conflicts between our mood and our reason over which we have little control. Although he emphasized that the nervous system and the biology of the body were fundamental to any understanding of the world of human emotions, he did admit that there was an "unconscious region" of the mind. In discussing his patients, he used the term "psychic energy" and wrote about such subjects as "passive imagination" and "delayed infantilism," and situations of "extraordinary stress."

All of these formulations, as is evident, were laced with terms that would later be reformulated by psychoanalysis. Orshanskii employed the word "ego" as Freud would do, and he theorized an internal conflict in which one's emotional desires were in opposition to one's rational notions. Moreover, his term "psychic energy" is close to Freud's later use of the "energy of the libido." In addition, he noticed that survivals of aspects of early childhood traits could be found in the neurotic adult, and understood the impact of highly stressful moments in an individual's life similar to the concept of the traumatic situation later developed by Freud.[7]

Finally, in considering the precedents for psychoanalysis in Russia, mention should be made of the work of Viktor Kandinskii and Sergei Korsakov. Kandinskii (1849–1889) was concerned with the nature of hallucinations, a psychotic symptom that had been discussed in West European psychiatric publications for decades. Kandinskii, however, studied the "pseudohallucination," specific sensory distortions of external reality, which led him into the uncharted realm of dreams, fantasies, and illusions.[8] At the time of Kandinskii's death in 1889, Korsakov was investigating "the region of mental life where ideas are formed, the sphere of unconscious ideas," at the "substratum of the personality," though his work was thoroughly grounded in a physiological and neurological framework.[9]

PSYCHOANALYSIS AS A MOVEMENT

For the Russian psychiatrists who were searching for alternatives to existing psychological theories, psychoanalysis appeared as a challenge to the established modes of patient care. In turning to psychoanalysis, these pioneering Russian physicians were acting with some risk. They were venturing into an experimental and highly controversial field of knowledge which was itself still in the process of professional formation.

The origins of psychoanalysis are, of course, inextricably intertwined with the work of Sigmund Freud beginning in the 1880s. Freud's significance is rooted in his ability, on the one hand, to have synthesized several disparate intellectual traditions, and on the other, to have forged an entirely new clinical discipline out of that synthesis. Perhaps most important for our purposes, however, was the institutional network of clinical institutes and societies that developed internationally into what Freud himself referred to as the "psycho-analytic movement." As his papers and books appeared explaining his new theory of neurosis and the role of the unconscious in personality development, he began to attract a small but dedicated group of disciples, especially following the publication of his *Interpretation of Dreams* in 1899.[10]

The applications of Freud's theory of neurosis were potentially vast, encompassing not only psychiatry, but also the arts, religion, culture, and the social sciences. With the publication of *The Psychopathology of Everyday Life* in 1901, Freud expanded his theory into the realm of ordinary affairs. Phenomena as disparate as the symbolism of dreams, the role of sexuality, self-destructive acts, and relations of children with parents were infused with a new significance that struck a responsive emotional chord in various circles across the European continent and beyond.[11]

Freud's theory and treatment method expanded further in the next decade, when the Russians first began to familiarize themselves with his work. Organized discussions of psychoanalysis began with a small group that met once a week at Freud's home in the fall of 1902, the Wednesday Psychological Society. As the membership enlarged, the name was changed in 1908 to the Vienna Psychoanalytic Society. Detailed minutes of these meetings were taken. At these "scientific meetings," beginning in 1910, the participants included the names of a number of Russians—Leonid Drosnes, Tatiana Rosenthal, Sabina Spielrein, and Moshe Wulff.[12]

Also at this time, a psychoanalytic presence was established in Berlin by Karl Abraham, in Zurich by Carl Jung, and in Budapest by Sandor Ferenczi. In 1909, the first International Congress of Psychoanalysis met in Salzburg. The second congress on the international level met in 1910 in Nuremberg, at which time the International Psychoanalytic Association was officially created, together with two journals devoted exclusively to psychoanalytic papers.

NIKOLAI OSIPOV AND THE RISE OF
PSYCHOANALYSIS IN RUSSIA

In 1904, a Russian translation appeared of Freud's *Interpretation of Dreams,* the first to be made into any language.[13] Apart from this, there is nothing of substance on the subject of psychoanalysis in the Russian psychiatric literature until 1908. Early that year, the first serious review article on psychoanalysis was published in the country's leading psychiatric journal. The author was Dr. Nikolai Osipov, a psychiatrist at the Moscow Psychiatric Clinic. With barely controlled enthusiasm, Osipov celebrated the new therapeutic orientation which Freud was pursuing and felt that this method was important enough to be brought to the immediate attention of the psychiatric community in Russia.

Osipov emphasized several themes in his discussion. He noted that, although trained as a neurologist in the German tradition, Freud had been influenced by the work of the leading French psychiatrists, particularly Hippolyte Bernheim, Jean-Martin Charcot, and (with some degree of exaggeration on Osipov's part) Pierre Janet. Osipov also discussed the "cathartic method" of treating patients suffering from severe symptoms of hysteria, which had been developed by Freud and his colleague Josef Breuer. Osipov emphasized the point that Freud was interested in the significance of the phenomenon of "psychic trauma," and the fact that Freud's new method involved a complex examination of the patient's unconscious through an analysis of his dreams and fantasies, his recollections of childhood and his relationships with his parents and siblings. Most of these conflicts lay buried and repressed deep beneath the patient's conscious awareness because they were too threatening to confront. The task of this new psychoanalytic therapy, Osipov concluded, was to unlock these buried conflicts and to free the patient from the pain and unhappiness they were causing in everyday life.[14]

As a successful physician in a new area of medical specialization, Nikolai Osipov was following a family tradition begun by his father, Dr. Evgraf Osipov (1841–1904). The elder Osipov, who headed the public health zemstvo organization in Moscow province for over twenty years until his retirement in 1895, had established a reputation for himself as one of Russia's most respected medical reformers and administrators.[15] In addition to providing an example of dedicated public service in medicine, Nikolai Osipov's father introduced him to some of the country's important psychiatrists, including Pavel Iakobii and Vladimir Iakovenko, who were among the profession's leading critical voices. Beyond this, Nikolai Osipov's interest in psychiatry was strongly influenced by his mother's life-long suffering from the symptoms of what was diagnosed as hysteria. He received his medical degree from the University of Basel in 1903, and returned to Moscow the following year when his father died, determined "to study in depth the problems of the physiology, pathology, and psychology of the brain."[16] He worked first at the Preobrazhenskii Hospital for the Insane in Moscow under the guidance of N. N. Bazhenov, and in 1906, he was appointed assistant physician in the Moscow Psychiatric Clinic which was headed by Vladimir Serbskii. Bazhenov and Serbskii both seemed to have recognized Osipov's talent and encouraged him to pursue his newly discovered interests in the recent developments in European psychotherapy.

Freud's work was far from the most popular of these currents from Europe. One of the most frequently cited influences on Osipov and a number of his colleagues at this time was the now-forgotten Swiss psychiatrist Paul Dubois (1848–1918). Dubois, who practiced and taught psychiatry in Bern, developed a new approach to treatment which he called "rational psychotherapy," or "persuasive-suggestive therapy." Dubois's method was based on the notion that the "psychoneuroses" could be cured by a form of psychotherapy which was moral in principle, supportive in tone, and clear in content. Nevertheless, as one authoritative source puts it, "today it is difficult to imagine that Dubois was Freud's most serious competitor for the interest of the Russians," who sought to challenge "the great old men of medical 'science'" and their biologically driven etiologies, which were now being seen as "therapeutic nihilism."[17] Dubois's chief rival in Switzerland was Carl Jung, a psychiatrist at the Zurich Burgholzli hospital who had become one of Freud's disciples. In 1908, Osipov visited Dubois and Jung before going to Vienna to study with Freud.

Osipov became deeply committed to the new psychoanalytic method after returning from Basel. Following the publication of his review essay on Freud, Osipov organized a small "little Friday group" at his clinic to read and discuss psychoanalysis. In addition, "a special outpatient facility for neurotics was opened in the clinic based on my initiative" where Freud's treatment method was used.[18] As one of his colleagues noted, Osipov saw in psychoanalysis three intersecting dimensions of significance—"a method of understanding the psychogenesis of neurosis, a method of psychotherapy, and a scientific worldview."[19]

Serbskii, the chief of the Moscow University clinic, personally presided over Osipov's private circle of meetings on Friday evenings during the next several years. It was at these meetings that Osipov presented his earliest papers on psychoanalysis prior to their publication in the country's main psychiatric journal. Copies of these papers were sent to Freud, who wrote of Osipov enthusiastically to Jung:

> Dr. Osipov, assistant at the psychiatric clinic in Moscow, has written to me; his credentials are two thick offprints, in one of which the tangle of Cyrillic signs is interrupted every two lines by the name Freud in European print, while the other makes the same use of the name Jung. The man has two other, original works at the printer's and is planning to compete for the Moscow Academy prize which is being offered specifically for work in psycho-analysis; the jury is meeting in March. Then in May he is coming to Vienna, whence I shall direct him on to Zurich.[20]

Not knowing Russian, Freud learned of the content of these articles by Osipov only through the summaries provided him (probably by Spielrein or Drosnes, who were in Vienna frequently to attend psychoanalytic meetings). In Russia, however, where Osipov's real audience resided, the articles provided further knowledge about the development of psychoanalysis. The first, entitled "The Psychology of Complexes and Association Experiment in the Work of the Zurich School," was a lengthy analysis of the recent work of Jung and his colleagues at the Burgholzli Clinic in Zurich. In his conclusion, Osipov wrote that "the psychology of complexes receives its fullest significance only in those cases where the unconscious realm of psychic life is recognized." The results of the Zurich experiments, according to Osipov, "may turn out to have tremendous use in Freud's psychoanalysis" in that both physiological and psychological symptoms of conflict emanating from a patient's unconscious will now be able to be diagnosed and treated more accurately than was possible before.[21] Although the Zurich school's work could be seen justifiably as being "purely psychological," Osipov wrote, it was important for psychiatry that it be utilized "as a necessary supplement to anatomical and clinical-nosological research investigations."[22]

The second offprint Osipov sent to Freud, "Recent Works of the Freudian School," was an exhaustive review of thirty-three books and articles in German by the founders of the international psychoanalytic movement, including Freud, Jung, Otto Rank, Wilhelm Stekel, and Abraham, among others.[23] Osipov's stated intent went far beyond a mere review essay, however. He clearly wanted to familiarize his readers, in as comprehensive a manner as possible, with the content of the most recent research of Freud and his followers, "and to explain the sufficiently intricate terminology," for purposes of further study and practical application. This also included a discussion of the expansion of psychoanalytic theory from the therapeutic world of medical science to new applications in art, literature, the history of culture, and religion, all with the intention of locating evidence to prove "the importance of the psychic unconscious, repression and the determining power of every psychic act, including the process of fantasy," as Osipov put it.[24]

OSIPOV'S FIRST PSYCHOANALYTIC CASE

The first of the "two other original works at the printer's" Freud referred to in his letter to Jung was Osipov's 1909 article, "On Anxiety Neurosis," the first detailed clinical case study in the history of Russian psychoanalysis.[25] In this paper, Osipov was attempting to demonstrate one of Freud's diagnoses, *Angstneurosis*. The paper is a long and discursive case history, which was designed to shed light on both the origins of the patient's neurotic symptoms and the difficulties involved in the analyst's search for an appropriate treatment. It also is a revealing glimpse into the sexual fears of this era which, thus far, had appeared primarily in novels and scholarly essays but not in the medical literature.

Osipov summarized the clinical characteristics of this disorder as including the following symptoms: (1) general loss of control of one's temper and severe irritability; (2) fearful apprehensiveness, or the constant expectation of dreadful events and consequences, in which family members are perceived to be in danger (the ringing of a doorbell can be a cause for tremendous anxiety as the harbinger of terrifying news, and where hypochondria and pessimism become overwhelming fears; (3) fits or attacks (*pripadki*) of enormous anxiety for which there appears to be no discernible basis in reality, no catalyst or precipitating phenomena; (4) a variety of physiological symptoms, such as a heightened pulse or heart rate, rapid breathing, diarrhea, and excessive perspiration.[26]

Osipov's patient, whom he called N. P., had an "inherited neurotic disposition" because of his father's alcoholism and the fact that his mother suffered all her life from a number of severe phobias, including the inability to walk into her own clothes closet without a servant or family member present. Moreover, the patient's older brother was diagnosed as having "progressive paralysis and acute paranoia." At about the same time that the patient found out about his brother's illness, he learned that one of his closest friends had died. The patient broke down from these "traumatic experiences," his symptoms including shortness of breath and rapid heartbeats, as well as uncontrollable fears and overwhelming depression. Unable to carry on his daily activities and incapable of distinguishing between his mental anguish and his physical symptoms, the patient was placed in the Moscow Psychiatric Clinic, where Osipov treated him.

Osipov reported further that the patient was dominated by "expectations of dread" as his phobic attacks continued to plague him during their early treatment sessions in the hospital. The patient would not let anyone touch him, and his face was a mask of extraordinary fear. He reacted strongly to the slightest pain, spoke in whispers, breathed with effort, had an excessively high pulse rate, and perspired profusely although the room temperature was normal.

For the next three months, Osipov saw the patient on a daily basis and recorded in his diary the symptoms he observed. Osipov noted that the patient frequently regressed into fits of uncontrollable weeping, and that at times he was so weak that his legs collapsed while he was walking in his room. He also refused to leave his room. His self-confidence had all but vanished and he was now unable to sleep through the night without waking suddenly under the impact of frightening dreams.

After months of psychotherapy based on Freud's free association method, Osipov found limited, though gradual, improvement. The patient learned to trust Osipov and began to confront the nature of his phobias. In his effort to locate the etiology of his patient's disorder, Osipov followed Freud's method into the realm of sexuality.[27] According to Osipov, the patient's sex life had been "abnormal." Although married for many years, and "in spite of strong sexual stimulation," the patient chose to abstain from intercourse for long periods of time. He did this, as he told Osipov during one of their analytic sessions, because he feared becoming impotent. Osipov came to the conclusion that the patient's fears of impotence had led him to sexual abstinence because of "psychic traumas" he had experienced. The most significant of these events were not those he had undergone as an adult (his brother's psychotic deterioration and his friend's death) but rather his responses to his father's alcoholism and his mother's hysteria when he was a child. One of the liberating moments in the analytic sessions, Osipov relates, was when the patient realized, through a dream interpretation, how obsessed he was with the unconscious fear of, and guilt-ridden "masked wish" for, his father's death as an escape from the terror he felt when his father would fly into an inebriated rage.

For Osipov, the case illustrated an important message about psychoanalytic treatment. The therapist had to encourage the patient to conquer the symptoms of pain through "the process of catharsis." In this way, the patient was permitted to confront his deepest fears with the careful guidance of the psychiatrist. The establishing of the patient's trust in the doctor was crucial in this process as the latter encouraged the patient to reach deeply into his interior "world of fantasy" and seek to understand the meaning of his fears and nightmares.

This first clinical psychoanalytic article to appear in Russia was, as events were soon to show, the beginning of a wave of a growing interest in this new field, despite continued skepticism in some quarters about the validity of psychoanalysis and the concept of the unconscious. Freud could not have imagined what lay ahead.

Chapter 3 The Consolidation
of a Movement

Almost without exception, philosophers have placed the essence of mind
in thought and consciousness; this ancient and universal radical error
must be set aside. Consciousness is the mere surface of our minds, which,
as of the surface of the earth, we do not know the inside but only the
crust. Under the conscious intellect is the conscious or unconscious will, a
striving, persistent, vital force, a spontaneous activity, a will of imperious
desire.
—*Arthur Schopenhauer (1851)*

The rise of psychoanalysis in Russia before the revolution occurred as
part of a larger interest on the part of educated society in "the knowledge of our buried life," and to find ways to be "no more racked with
inward striving and demand," as Matthew Arnold put it. Curiosity
alone, however, would not have been enough to sustain psychoanalysis; it was the search for relief from the "stupefying power" of the
strife emerging from "the soul's subterranean depth" that created the
basis for Freud's theories to be put into clinical practice in Russia.

Within the context of the psychiatric profession, psychoanalysis held out the promise, at least for a discontented and inquiring minority of clinicians, of a therapeutic treatment process which might help alleviate the distress of a number of patients left untreated or unsuccessfully treated. Despite all the advances of modern scientific medicine, psychiatrists had managed primarily to treat cases of highly disturbed patients. People with symptoms of a less severe kind—who were already being referred to as "neurotics"—did not fall easily into existing diagnostic categories. Their symptoms caused them substantial suffering, often enormous embarrassment, and frequently rendered them incapable of functioning. However, they did not require hospitalization, nor were they able to be referred to either a general physician or a neurologist. They were, truly, patients without doctors, products of a rapidly changing world with emotional ailments for which there seemed to be little medical concern.

There is, however, another way of looking at this situation. The psychiatrists who were turning with enthusiasm to Freud were also redefining what it meant to be a patient. People who would not have been under medical care with their symptoms in earlier times, now were being attracted to the clinics and private offices of a new generation of psychoanalysts. This was the age of the invention of what is now referred to as outpatient therapy. Individuals suffering from symptoms of distress that did not appear to have somatic origins were referred to psychiatrists who were able to provide a diagnosis and a treatment regimen. Questions naturally arise. Were many of the illnesses described by Osipov and the other Russian analysts in fact pathologies subject to empirical confirmation? If they were, does it follow that their recommendations for psychoanalytic therapy were the best available methods to alleviate the symptoms?

There was little doubt in the minds of the analysts themselves on these matters. They were convinced of the necessity and the validity of the Freudian project as a new stage in the development of professional psychiatry. For them, it was the start of a therapeutic dialogue between doctor and patient in which, as Osipov pointed out many times in his papers, the incoherent language of the unconscious was translated into the vocabulary of consciousness. The introduction of medical psychoanalysis also involved the creation of a professional subspecialty which was committed to the use of words rather than confinement or drugs to bring understanding and a measure of control to their patients' inner conflicts. Once it was disseminated into the wider culture, it provided a conceptual map and a social discourse with which people could explain the difficulties of their relationships with themselves and others. It was, as Freud stated, a "a secular cure of souls."[1]

FREUD'S EARLIEST RUSSIAN DISCIPLES:
THE YEAR 1909

The development of psychoanalysis into a movement in Russia along the lines established by Freud and his small circle in Vienna began in earnest in 1909. Osipov's articles on Freud and Jung were joined by many others as interest in psychoanalysis spread further among the psychiatrists. N. A. Vyrubov, a professor of medicine at Moscow University, published three papers that year on psychoanalytic themes. The first was a review essay on the psychological foundation of Freudian theory centering on the formation of neurotic disorders, the second was entitled "Freud's Psychoanalytic Method and Its Therapeutic Significance," and the third was a discussion of a problem that had interested Osipov as well, "The Genesis and Treatment of Angstneurosis with a Combined Hypnoanalytic Method."[2]

Also that year, Moshe Wulff published his first Freudian paper, "The Psychoanalytic Treatment Method."[3] Wulff had studied medicine in Berlin and then did an internship at the newly opened University Hospital there. In 1907, he read Breuer and Freud's *Studies on Hysteria,* which, according to his biographer, "was a revelation to him."[4] Wulff applied for a position at the Berlin-Lankwitz sanatorium to work under Otto Juliusburger, a psychiatrist and founding member of the Berlin Psychoanalytic Society. Wulff was accepted and became Juliusburger's clinical assistant. The following year, Karl Abraham, one of Freud's closest colleagues, returned from Zurich to work at the Berlin-Lankwitz sanatorium and soon became Wulff's teacher and analyst. However, this training was interrupted by an internal professional conflict. In 1909, Abraham wrote to Freud that Wulff had lost his position because of the prejudice against psychoanalysis in the sanatorium and would return to Russia to practice.

> [Wulff], who has been Juliusburger's assistant in a private mental hospital for some time, is now going to settle in Odessa. He is very interested in psychoanalysis and, because of this, lost his job in Berlin. . . . I know him to be a hard-working and reliable man who is unfortunately in very difficult financial circumstances. Perhaps you or one of your colleagues in Vienna might be able to send him some patients. I expect he will write to you personally as he asked me for your address. Juliusburger also tells me that Wulff would like to do translations [of your work] into Russian.[5]

The burgeoning psychoanalytic movement was not without its skeptics and critics. As Alfred Adler and Jung and other followers of Freud in Europe took issue with their mentor on aspects of his theory, some of his disciples in Russia also expressed their doubts about the application of psychoanalysis in their patient practice. One of the earliest critiques by a member of the Russian psychoanalytic community was written by O. B. Fel'tsman in 1909. Fel'tsman's article was one of the clearest portrayals of the competing orientations of Freud and the "rational therapeutic theory" of Paul Dubois. According to the latter, Fel'tsman argued, many of our fears and anxieties were ultimately under the control of our powers of reason. With some patients, it seemed more sensible to avoid searching for unconscious motivations, and, instead, to emphasize "the need to reeducate the patient, reorienting him toward a healthy understanding" of himself and his relationship to the world in which he must function. For this, "a spray of reason, a massage of moral energy" was required.[6]

One of Fel'tsman's most interesting findings in examining his own patients' problems was that sexual issues actually masked the underlying problems responsible for certain symptoms, rather than being their cause. To demonstrate this aspect of the inadequacy of Freud's method, Fel'tsman described a female patient who suffered from acute attacks in which her convulsions were accompanied by hoarseness, frothing of saliva, uncontrollable urine emissions, attempts at biting herself, and the ripping off of her clothing to reveal her sexual organs. After many psychoanalytic sessions, Fel'tsman concluded that even though "the sexual life of the patient played no small role in the origins of her illness," the psychoanalytic treatment method was not helpful in diminishing the symptoms of distress. It proved more useful to direct the patient's attention to the other, nonsexual aspects of her distress, and to appeal to her reason, as Dubois recommended. Fel'tsman even confessed his own discomforts in publishing "the most intimate details of the patient's life," but justified this as a necessity in determining when psychoanalysis was the appropriate treatment method. In this regard, he referred to a statement Freud made in which the psychiatrist is called upon to recognize that beyond his responsibility to his patient is his greater obligation to science.[7]

There were other psychoanalytic developments in 1909. F. Berg, a Russian psychiatrist who had studied with Jung the year before, returned to Moscow and published a report entitled "Impressions at the Zurich Clinic." He had glowing praise for the work he had seen there and was convinced that "psychoanalysis has already become a powerful therapeutic means in the struggle against neuroses and psychoses, which will achieve even wider and greater clinical results in the future."[8] Also, M. M. Asatiani presented a lecture to the

Academic Society for Psychiatry and Neurology in Moscow which dealt with "the theory and practice of psychoanalysis according to Jung." In addition, the prestigious Kozhevnikov prize competition, offered annually by the Neurological and Psychiatric Society of the University of Moscow, emphasized in 1909 the theme of "Psychoanalysis (Freud and others) and the Functioning Illnesses of the Nervous System," which further illustrates the penetration of Freud's ideas into the corridors of Russian medicine.[9]

The most important of these developments, however, was the establishment of Russia's first psychoanalytic journal which, more than anything else, was responsible for widening the interest in, and the influence of, Freud's work there. This was early by any standard, since Freud's own journal, *Jahrbuch für psychoanalytische und psychopathologische Forschungen,* was founded at the same time.

The Russian journal, *Psychotherapy* (*Psikhoterapiia*), was largely the result of the labors of Vyrubov and Osipov. The original idea was that the journal would provide a forum for all contemporary currents in the field of psychotherapy. Moreover, as interest in psychotherapy intensified, the existing psychiatric journals could not handle the mounting overflow of publishable papers in this field. Nevertheless, within a year of its initial volume, the new journal was dominated almost entirely by psychoanalytic approaches.[10] In addition to Vyrubov and Osipov, the original editorial board of the journal consisted of Asatiani, A. N. Bernshtein, and Iu. B. Kannabikh. By 1912, V. N. Likhnitskii and Fel'tsman were added to the board, and, in 1913, the board expanded into an international group which included Alfred Adler and Wilhelm Stekel in Vienna, F. Asnaurov in Geneva, R. Assagioli in Florence, and Vera Eppelbaum in Zurich among the seventeen members listed on the journal's masthead.

The journal published a rich variety of materials. The original articles included examples of the best theoretical and clinical research being done by the psychoanalytic community in Russia. In addition, each issue of *Psychotherapy* contained detailed and informative reviews of recent papers by Freud and Jung, discussions of the research papers published in the leading European psychiatric and psychoanalytic journals, and reports on congresses and meetings both in Russia and abroad dealing with psychotherapeutic issues.

One last Freudian project was launched in 1909—a series of publications of Freud's works in Russian translation called the Psychotherapeutic Library. This was initiated mainly by Osipov, with help from Wulff and Vyrubov. The first volume, *On Dreams,* appeared that year, and was followed by a succession of books including Freud's *Five Lectures on Psychoanalysis* which he had delivered during his recent visit to America, *The Psychopathology of Everyday Life,* and *Three Essays on the Theory of Sexuality.* In no other country had the collected works of Freud been published in translation.[11]

OSIPOV'S EARLY PSYCHOANALYTIC CASE STUDIES

The psychoanalytic work being done at this time in Russia was brought to the attention not only of Freud, but of the international psychoanalytic community as well. The initial report on the emergence of psychoanalysis in Russia appeared in Freud's *Jahrbuch* in 1910, barely a year after the journal's founding.[12] This was followed the next year by Wulff's article, which was the earliest published review by a Russian psychoanalyst on clinical research being conducted there.[13]

Within this growing community, the individual behind much of the development of psychoanalysis in Russia was Nikolai Osipov. Early in January 1910, Osipov wrote to Freud that he was coming to Vienna in May.[14] Osipov did visit Freud, and left a positive impression. After Osipov's departure, Freud wrote to Karl Abraham, who had analyzed Osipov's colleague Wulff: "Yesterday I had lunch with a . . . pleasing visitor, Osipov, from Moscow, who has a good mind and is a convinced follower. He asked for and received permission to publish the Worcester [Massachusetts] lectures in Russian in his journal."[15]

In 1911, soon after his return, Osipov's mentor Serbskii resigned his teaching position at Moscow University following a dispute with the government over an issue concerning academic autonomy. Osipov, who had also been teaching psychiatry at the university, left his job there in support of Serbskii. The resignations altered their career patterns somewhat, permitting more time for research in psychoanalysis in place of the teaching hours. The result was that Osipov set up a series of weekly psychoanalytic research meetings which were chaired by Serbskii. A number of Osipov's colleagues from the psychiatric clinic joined these meetings. At the same time, Osipov was instrumental in setting up an outpatient facility at the clinic, to which he returned, specifically designed to treat neurotics with the new methods discussed by Freud.[16]

The maturing of Osipov's work in psychoanalysis, which took place in tandem with his keen interest in Dubois's "rational therapy," was clearly reflected in his research during the next few years. In the first volume of the

Russian psychoanalytic journal *Psychotherapy,* Osipov published three articles, more than any other single contributor. The first, a two-part essay on the essential aspects of Freud's theory, was the most systematic explanation of psychoanalysis to appear in Russian.[17]

The second article was a related piece based on Freud's 1909 lectures in America, and included a discussion of recent work by Jung and Stekel. Osipov enthusiastically concluded that "with these lectures, Freud has provided us with a sketch of the pathology and the therapy of neuroses," and was moving toward an outline of the nosology and "the psychology of neuroses."[18]

Osipov's third paper in the 1910 volume of *Psychotherapy,* entitled "The Idealistic Mood and Psychotherapy," was originally delivered at a scientific session of Serbskii's Little Friday psychiatric group on October 1, 1910. The paper was actually a Freudian critique of a recent book, *Idealism as a Physiological Factor,* by A. I. Iarotskii, a professor of medicine. Iarotskii argued that there was a large disparity between the great advances having taken place in recent decades in science, medicine, and technology on the one hand, and the impoverished, comparatively primitive and conflicting theories of psychotherapy for the mentally ill on the other. Osipov wrote that Iarotskii was correct in pointing out the recent achievements of science and in criticizing the medical profession for not having devoted sufficient attention to the treatment of the psychological dimension of man until quite recently. However, Osipov believed that Iarotskii was wrong in his criticism of modern methods of psychotherapy largely because he was not conversant with "the major representatives of contemporary psychotherapy," especially Freud.

Osipov further attacked Iarotskii's conception of idealism in medicine. Physicians were not medieval knights battling against disease to save civilization. Moreover, Iarotskii's discussion of psychiatry was mistaken in assuming that most "psychic problems" could be handled by confessional discussions with priests, which were supposed to act as a "conditioning force for the entire cycle of man's physiological existence."[19] Osipov was convinced that the mind and the body, the psychological and physical components of man, acted in functional interdependence. Both had to be taken into account in treatment, rather than emphasizing either individually. While most of contemporary medicine leaned toward physiological determinism, Iarotskii went to the other extreme in recommending spiritual solutions. Iarotskii naively assumed that religious satisfaction and mental health were the same, and ignored the essence of "the extraordinary complexity of psychic life, . . . the struggle for internal survival being fought out in every individual."[20]

At about this time, Osipov started to work in an entirely new area, the application of psychoanalytic theory to literature, which was later to gain a larger following among the Russian Freudians. Motivated in part by the international interest focused then on Lev Tolstoy, who had died the year before, Osipov published the first of what would become a series of papers on the writer's life and work. "Psychotherapy in the Literary Works of L. N. Tolstoy" began with a discussion of the physicians in Tolstoy's novels who, Osipov wrote, were depicted not only as respected healers of illness, but also as scientific practitioners firmly rooted in "the soil of empirical realism."[21] However, Tolstoy's physicians were locked into rigid and limiting professional orientations which prevented them from taking seriously the range of symptoms of particular concern to psychotherapists. In setting up a contrast between the "empiricist-physician and the philosopher-physician," "Tolstoy strongly opposed the philosopher-physician."[22]

To make his case, Osipov summarized the emotional distress of two of Tolstoy's memorable female characters—Natasha Rostova in *War and Peace* and Kitty Shcherbatskaia in *Anna Karenina*—and then showed the response of their doctors to their symptoms. In Osipov's view, the two women suffered deeply from phobias, tortuous dreams, and suicidal urges. The physicians in each novel tended to dismiss these symptoms as romantic excesses of aristocratic women rather than to recognize the possibility of "deep psychic trauma" in an individual who either threatens or attempts to kill herself. Osipov diagnosed the symptoms expressed by Natasha as those resembling hysteria, "which call for a detailed investigation" by a responsible doctor. This medical investigation did not occur in the novel in spite of Tolstoy's utterly clear statements about the seriousness of Natasha's illness.[23] Osipov's conclusion was that Tolstoy was presenting, deliberately or not, realistic emotional and psychological crises in his literary creations, which at the same time demonstrated the absence of appropriate psychotherapeutic care where it was most needed. Osipov does not, however, appear to be aware of his own uncritical acceptance of the controversial model of female hysteria.

In the summer of 1912, Osipov published a case study that was, arguably, his most important clinical contribution to the formation of Russian psychoanalysis. He had become fascinated by the apparent similarity between a case of his own and one which had been published by the Russian neurologist Vladimir Bekhterev. He made a comparison of the two cases and presented his findings in a report at a meeting of the Moscow Society of Neuropathologists and Psychiatrists on October 11, 1912. The report was published later that year with the enigmatic title "On the Compulsive Smile."[24] Formally, it bears a strong resemblance to several of Freud's classic papers in that it is a dramatically contrived argument which draws the reader into a labyrinth of confusion and false leads before providing a diagnostic climax to "resolve" the unexplained difficulties. Also, we should bear in mind that Osipov, like Freud, was not only interpreting a complex case which had significance for the wider application of psychoanalytic treatment, but was simultaneously arguing against competing clinical interpretations. Whereas Freud was challenging the alternative theories of his peers Jung and Adler, Osipov was taking issue with one of his country's leading researchers in psychiatry and neurology.

As interesting as it is to read through, the case in the end raises more problems than it solves. The patient was a twenty-seven-year-old unmarried male student whose "somatic condition appeared in no way to deviate from the norms" of the healthy sector of society except for the fact that he had lost sight in his left eye. This was the result of an accident at the age of two when the patient stabbed himself in the eye with a pair of scissors. The only member of his immediate family with a history of psychiatric disturbances was his sister, thirteen years older, who suffered from what the patient called "religious insanity" following the death of her husband. On the rare occasions the patient drank, he did so in moderation. When asked to explain what he characterized as a "sufficiently nervous" period in his youth, he confessed to having "engaged frequently in onanism" since the age of thirteen. He had casual sexual relations with women but found them unsatisfying. In the two years prior to treatment, he had abstained from sexual intercourse entirely.

At some point during his years in secondary school, a disturbing symptom began to emerge which became uncontrollable during his university years. He called it "a stupid, self-contented smile." The smile was not only "utterly inappropriate" but also disorienting and debilitating. The patient was told by a friend that the smile was so distracting that it prevented the latter from completing his exams. When the patient had to look anyone in the eye, his smile appeared regardless of the situation. When he ran to a mirror to observe the smile, he often found that he could not bear to see it. The patient, always somewhat shy, increasingly retreated into isolation to avoid the pain and embarrassment of the "obtrusive smile." As his ability to engage in constructive work decreased, he began to identify himself as "a superfluous man" in the manner of the useless and anguished protagonists of nineteenth-century Russian literature. Moreover, he found he could not extinguish the frightening thought of suicide, which became more and more a part of his conscious existence. "I feel that I am dying emotionally," he said. He took on a series of manual jobs and, while doing "peasant labor" by himself, felt temporarily relieved. However, when he had to confront anyone or whenever he realized someone else was watching him, the smile reappeared. He returned to his former studies and again went through alternating periods of relief and pain over his compulsive smile. One further symptom developed, in which the patient had difficulty pronouncing certain words in the course of ordinary conversation. The more unfamiliar were the people around him, the harder he found it to express himself correctly.

Osipov noted that his patient shared a number of characteristics with Bekhterev's patient, who also suffered from the main symptom of the compulsive smile. Both patients conceptualized their conditions as "idiotism" in a self-deprecating manner. Neither patient was able to provide a detailed description of the nature and causes of the obtrusive smile. Neither patient could bear to look at himself smiling in the mirror. Both patients had physical deformities (Osipov's patient had only one eye while Bekhterev's suffered from a permanently bent-over posture) and both had trouble speaking in social situations. Perhaps most telling of all, Osipov wrote, both patients blamed their previous "onanistic experiences" for their present problems.

While many of the symptoms were similar, Osipov disagreed with Bekhterev's interpretation of the nature of the disorder. For Bekhterev, the appearance of the compulsive smile and its associated debilitating consequences were rooted in a malfunctioning physiological mechanism. The smile was comparable, therefore, to a nervous twitch in which involuntary muscle contractions occur in peculiar forms. Osipov, while accepting the physiological explanation, believed that one had to probe beneath the symptoms to understand the true nature of the problem. He argued that the physiological response itself was part of a complex defensive mechanism on the part of the patient to conceal his embarrassment over his impotence. The smile was actually playing the role of a betrayer, preventing him from masking his guilt and fear.

Osipov explained (with acknowledged help from Tolstoy, William James, and the French psychiatrist Pierre Janet) that his patient was suffering from a *mental* illness with somatic symptoms. Moreover, it was so pervasive because the causes lay in the patient's feelings of sexual shame, which were aroused with every social encounter. The patient's contrasting of his feelings of satisfaction with himself when alone and his sense of agonized conflict about the external world were interpreted by Osipov as an inner dichotomy between a wish-fantasy of "passion, power, and success" at war with the sense of dread, incompetence, and destruction. Unable to force reality to conform to his fantasies of power and control, the patient's fear led him to "flee to his illness."

The case was left in this incomplete state. Osipov mentioned that the patient had improved at the time he wrote the paper but did not explain how. His conclusion was more convincing as a plea for psychiatrists to treat such cases than it was in actually demonstrating the utility of psychoanalytic therapy. It was not even clear in what way the compulsive smile was a diagnosed disorder that could be applied to other similar cases for purposes of treatment.

As Osipov put it, the case was about the process of "liberation from moral demands," a freeing of the patient from the emotional confinement of guilt over having committed acts he believed were so shameful as to be tantamount to criminal behavior. At best, Osipov could claim that the case showed a man's shame over his "pitiable impotence" could at least be relieved through psychotherapy. Osipov certainly understood the limitations of his powers to cure and of the patient's ability to be cured. His conclusion was that therapists should seek "to stir a patient toward self-awareness, in search of one's limits and possibilities, toward clarity and honesty with oneself."[25]

THE EXPANSION OF RUSSIAN PSYCHOANALYSIS

Throughout 1910 a professional group modeled on Freud's Vienna Psychoanalytic Society was being planned. A year later, this was realized through the efforts of Osipov and his colleagues. On May 2, 1911, Freud received a visit from Leonid Drosnes, a psychiatrist from Odessa with training in psychoanalysis, who reported that the Russian Psychoanalytic Society had been officially founded by the Osipov group in Moscow.[26]

With the launching of the journal *Psychotherapy*, the small but expanding psychoanalytic community in Russia now had a publication entirely receptive to its work. Freud's Russian followers made full use of this opportunity as they sought to fashion a distinctive orientation in their clinical research.

During the journal's first year, 1910, N. A. Vyrubov published a paper on the treatment of neurosis in which he proposed a "hypno-analytic method" which emphasized the use of hypnosis in a psychoanalytic context. He explained that by using hypnotic therapy, the patient came to associate the phenomena of fearful symptoms with the rational explanation of their causes, thereby converting the irrational into the rational. He called this "a process of translating the unconscious into consciousness."[27]

At about the same time, Tatiana Rosenthal, a Russian psychiatrist who had recently become a member of the new psychoanalytic community, was examining a different side of the role of the unconscious in human behavior. Rosenthal was one of the few analysts who had direct experience with Russian opposition politics. Prior to her involvement with psychoanalysis, she had joined the illegal Marxist Social Democratic party in her native St. Petersburg during the revolutionary events of 1905. While in medical school in Zurich, she began reading Freud and decided to become a psychoanalyst. She was accepted into the Vienna Psychoanalytic Society after completing her training. She then returned to St. Petersburg to practice but traveled several times back to Vienna to participate in meetings of the Vienna Society. In January and February 1912, she was accompanied by her colleague Sabina Spielrein at three of these meetings, making these dates one of the few occasions when Russian was spoken in Freud's chambers. Rosenthal commented frequently at the meetings she attended, at times even voicing strong disagreement with members of Freud's circle.[28]

In 1911 Rosenthal published her first major research paper, which remains a pioneering exploration of the relationship between psychoanalysis and literature. In this paper, titled "The Dangerous Age of Karen Michaelis in Light of Psychoanalysis," Rosenthal investigated the turn-of-the-century Danish writer, using Freudian and Jungian concepts as her interpretive tools. In Rosenthal's view, Michaelis's novels and stories are filled with examples of unconscious conflicts in the leading characters. By interpreting Michaelis's characters in this way, Rosenthal argued that the struggles of the characters were more clearly understood, and the realism of the stories and their direct reflection of everyday conflicts came into sharper focus.

Elsie Lindtner, one of Michaelis's characters in her novel *The Dangerous Age*, was a particularly vivid illustration of this interpretation. Lindtner kept a diary that contained a rich portrait of her interior world and the crisis she faced. Her marriage, which was arranged, had become empty, and she herself sank into a state of depression. Rosenthal showed how Lindtner's problems flowed back in time to her mother's early death and the abnormal relationship which developed with her father during her early years. This was the truly "dangerous age" that Karen Michaelis was depicting, when the individual personality was shaped by powerful parental influences at the moment of the child's greatest vulnerability.

For Rosenthal, Michaelis's fictional characters were endowed with rich fantasies, willful, untraditional behavior, and intensely neurotic lives. The writer was, Rosenthal argued, especially sensitive to the struggles of young daughters who competed with their mothers for the love of their fathers. In some instances, as when the mother died or was "defeated," the daughters would then face the cost of their "triumph." Face-to-face with the object of their unconscious incestuous desire—their fathers—Michaelis's women either fell into deep depression or sought to end their agonizing guilt in suicide. For some, the suffering simply went on unchecked as the women gradually became obsessed with "autoeroticism or narcissism," which prevented them from forming meaningful and satisfying relationships of their own.

For Rosenthal, Michaelis had powerfully depicted the connection between problems in marriage and their underlying unresolved conflicts in the earlier "dangerous age." Elsie Lindtner was fleeing from her husband and her marriage because she could no longer engage in an unconscious competitive struggle to gain her father. Her marriage was described as a "transfer of the libido to another person," from her father to her husband, creating extraordinary demands which their relationship could not possibly satisfy.

Rosenthal dealt with one further aspect of Elsie Lindtner's personality. Linked to her complex and conflicted relationship with her father was the rage she felt at having been abandoned by her dead mother. Being motherless not only forced her into an excessive dependence on her father but left her with a lifelong ambivalence about having children. She feared that by becoming a mother, she would then have to confront the anxieties about the possibilities that her child might die as her mother did or be overwhelmed by incestuous feelings as she herself had been.

Elsie's "erotic crisis" was expressed in her remarkably revealing diaries, where she candidly recorded her sexual fantasies and desires. As with many other female characters in Karen Michaelis's fiction, according to Rosenthal, there was no real resolution of the struggle. Instead, forms of conflict emerged in neurotic symptoms which were experienced in conscious activity as well as in unconscious dreams and fantasies. Her life decisions were determined not by conscious thought and will, but by "the unconscious inventory of her neurotic life"; this was in turn shaped by her childhood conflicts, which emerged in "the family constellation" during her early years.

For Rosenthal, the most important aspect of Elsie's dilemma in fiction was that it expressed so forcefully the problems facing many women at the time. In the conclusion of her paper, Rosenthal found support for her interpretation in two recently published case studies by Wilhelm Stekel, a member of the Vienna

Psychoanalytic Society. Stekel's cases dealt with women whose age and problems were similar to those of the Elsie Lindtner character. The women were in their early forties with strong, unsatisfied sexual drives. Their erotic obsessions and painful circumstances were described in depth in Stekel's analysis. One patient improved substantially after treatment, but the other committed suicide. Suicide and severe depression, Rosenthal concluded, were also the unfortunate fate of many of Karen Michaelis's fictional characters. Thus, literature and psychoanalysis joined together in revealing the severity of these problems which, she argued, must receive greater attention if such tragic consequences are to be prevented.[29]

The journal *Psychotherapy* also published more pedagogically oriented papers which surveyed the current clinical work of the leading European psychoanalysts. A. A. Pevnitskii, for example, discussed some of the recent cases of Freud, Jung, and Adler in a 1910 paper. His purpose in this paper was to provide information for those interested in, but skeptical of, psychoanalysis as well as to present practical examples of the psychoanalytic method for clinical use by Russian psychiatrists. In addition, Pevnitskii made the point that although psychoanalysis seemed to be an effective form of treatment for some patients, it was still subject to revision and discoveries, as demonstrated by the new work being done by Freud's colleagues.[30]

The work of many of the best known nonpsychoanalytic therapists in Europe appeared in the pages of *Psychotherapy*. These included Dubois and his followers, who were grouped together as the school of "rational psychotherapy." Although the competitors of psychoanalysis were discussed objectively and respectfully, it was clear that their emphasis on the conscious world of the patient was antagonistic to the Freudian concentration on the unconscious.[31] Nevertheless, any reader of this journal would have been brought up to date on the latest clinical and theoretical work in European as well as Russian psychotherapy.

Osipov published a long two-part paper in *Psychotherapy* in 1912 in which he tried to demonstrate the role of psychoanalysis in the context of recent debates in European psychiatry over the notion of inherited degeneration. Titled "Thoughts and Doubts About a Case of 'Degenerative Psychopathy,'" Osipov's paper included a discussion of psychiatry as a "cultural science" which, unlike the rest of medicine, made use of disparate fields of knowledge from anatomy and physiology to anthropology and sociology. Psychoanalysis, as an ally of psychiatry in caring for patients suffering from symptoms of psychic distress, had the responsibility of uncovering the psychological factors in the patient's condition, regardless of the state of any biological degeneration. Most important for Osipov was the doctor's relationship to the patient. On this point he quoted his mentor Serbskii, who said that "the doctor's concerns must be not with the illnesses but with the patients, each of whom is ill in his own manner."[32]

Osipov's last major paper prior to the First World War was originally presented as a public lecture at the Russian Society of Neuropathologists and Psychiatrists on October 27, 1913, in Moscow. In this paper, Osipov discussed the theoretical concept and the clinical reality of the "sick soul." His major point was that a large sector of the population which had always suffered from "psychoneurotic illnesses" had gone untreated until the discoveries of Freud and his followers identified these problems as clinical categories and created a treatment mode to help them. Osipov recognized that the insane were in a different category from those patients he called "psychoneurotic." The severely disturbed were incapable of applying reason, had lost contact with reality, and did not have "a critical relationship toward their illness," he wrote. Psychotherapy was less effective for them, consequently. However, for the "sick souls" who were victims of their own distorted and misunderstood wishes, desires, and feelings, the possibilities for improvement through appropriate psychotherapy were boundless. Osipov's main point was that the soul, by which he understood the entire human emotional existence, must be accepted as a legitimate object of medical intervention on an empirical foundation.[33]

ON THE EVE OF WORLD WAR I

During the years before the outbreak of the First World War, the names of two of Russia's leading Freudians are conspicuously absent from the pages of *Psychotherapy:* Moshe Wulff and Sabina Spielrein. Although Wulff had returned to Russia from Berlin in 1911, practicing first in his native Odessa and then in 1914 in Moscow, his orientation remained primarily European. As a member of the Vienna Psychoanalytic Society, he chose to write all his important research papers in German. Thus, since his work was published in Freud's psychoanalytic journals before the revolution, his reputation was better established abroad than it was in Russia.

Wulff's papers clearly reveal that he was, among the Russians, the most accepting of Freud's theory of sexual drives. In the presentation of his cases, he described in great detail the sexual conflicts and fantasies of his patients. In cases ranging from "pregnancy neurosis" in an adult female patient to the dysfunctional autism of a child under his care, Wulff claimed to have uncovered traumatic scenes which his patients had sought to repress. These traumas included a child having witnessed his parents engaging in sexual intercourse at a time when he was in the midst of severe emotional conflicts with them regarding masturbatory prohibitions.[34] Wulff was a master of the Freudian narrative, both in terms of style and content.

Spielrein, meanwhile, was in Europe establishing a reputation for originality within the international analytic community. Spielrein had suffered for years from uncontrollable attacks of hysteria and depression; her parents sent her to Zurich in 1904 to attend medical school and to seek treatment for her mental disturbance. In October 1906, Jung wrote to Freud that he was "currently treating an hysteric with your method. Difficult case, a 20-year old Russian girl student, ill for six years." Indeed, the case was so complex that Jung described to Freud some of the painful sexual problems which emerged in his sessions with Spielrein, with the request that Freud provide some guidance as to treatment. Freud responded with a lengthy interpretation of the patient's illness.[35]

Jung became more deeply involved in the case. In 1907, he published a clinical paper on Spielrein and then had an affair with her that he first concealed and then confessed to Freud.[36] Spielrein nevertheless managed to complete her medical degree in the spring of 1911 with a dissertation, prepared with Jung's aid, called "The Psychological Content of a Case of Schizophrenia." This study, which was published in Freud's *Jahrbuch* that year, was an analysis of the disordered language and thought patterns of one of her own schizophrenic patients. It was also the first research paper in Freud's journal by a Russian contributor.[37]

Spielrein spent almost a year in Vienna in the winter and spring of 1911–1912, at which time she joined Freud's inner circle and produced some of her most creative psychoanalytic papers. The paper for which she is best known is unquestionably her 1912 study, "Destruction as the Origin of Coming into Being." This work has often been cited as having anticipated Freud's formulation of the "death instinct" or the destructive drive which opposes the instincts of preservation and survival. Freud was himself responsible for this view since he drew attention to her paper in one of his own publications. Although some doubt has been cast on this interpretation, Spielrein's paper, based firmly on the work of Freud, Jung, and Otto Rank as well as on her own dissertation, was recognized for its originality and depth of learning by the European analytic community. This opinion was voiced from the moment she delivered her presentation at the Vienna Society's meeting on November 29, 1911.[38]

After leaving Vienna in March 1912, Spielrein moved to Berlin and Munich, then to Lausanne and Geneva (where one of her patients in a training analysis was Jean Piaget). After the First World War, she began to plan her return to Russia, which she discussed with both Jung and Freud.[39]

The war brought an end to the momentum behind the developing psycho-analytic movement in Russia. *Psychotherapy* was unable to survive the exigencies of wartime. Interestingly, the journal was undergoing an important change in 1913, the last year of its regular publication. Although the editors had remained open to the contributions of the entire spectrum of existing psychotherapies, the emphasis had been clearly psychoanalytic. Freud's work was published in the journal with a frequency unmatched by any other theorist.

A shift away from Freud's dominating influence was already evident in 1912. Two lead essays by Alfred Adler were published in Russian translation in this volume. In addition, the journal's fourth issue of 1913 contained an essay by one of Adler's main Russian followers, A. A. Ioffe. Ioffe's paper was an Adlerian analysis of the unconscious motives of a homosexual patient who was suffering from a series of personal tragedies.[40] The fifth and final issue of that year contained three translated papers by Freud under a newly expanded editorial board,[41] which reflected the Russians' attempt to bring under one roof the conflicting orientations of Freud, Jung, and Adler.[42]

The Psychotherapeutic Library series edited by Osipov and Fel'tsman, which was responsible for the publication of most of Freud's books in translation, was also unable to continue its operations in wartime. Osipov, among Freud's Russian followers, defended his mentor in a lecture entitled "Pansexualism in Freudian Theory," which he delivered to the 1913 annual meeting of the Aca-demic Society for Neurology and Psychiatry in Moscow, the last one held before the outbreak of war.[43]

Freud himself was to some extent aware of the developments in Russia. On the eve of the war, he summed up his evaluation with these appreciative but cautious words: "In Russia, psychoanalysis has become generally well known and has spread widely; almost all my writings, as well as those of other adher-ents of analysis, have been translated into Russian. But a really penetrating comprehension of analytic theories has not yet been evinced in Russia."[44] Freud's direct knowledge of the Russian analytic community's work was se-verely limited since he read no Russian. He might have altered his assessment had he read the applications of clinical psychoanalysis to literature in the work of Rosenthal and Osipov.

There was more to Freud's Russian connection than the psychiatrists who had come to meet and train with him. He occasionally received professional referrals from Russia. In 1909, Freud mentioned in one of his letters to Jung that he "received a telegram from Bazhenov in Moscow, announcing that a certain lady, seriously ill, is coming to me for analysis."[45] In the spring of 1914 a Moscow philosopher, Ivan Il'in (1883–1954), came to Freud for treatment. After his return to Russia, he wrote that he learned from Freud the importance of resolving "the mental traumas that are inflicted upon us all in childhood and that live on unhealed the rest of our lives, corroding the soul and throwing many of us into neurasthenia and all manner of morbid deviations."[46]

Freud's most important referral from Russia was the patient known in the clinical literature as the Wolf Man. The analysis of the Wolf Man was important in Freud's own development and in the history of the psychoanalytic movement for a number of reasons. He composed the case study from his notes of the actual analytic treatment sessions during the winter of 1914–15, at the moment when he was not only refining many of his most fundamental concepts but also desperately defending his own method against what he called "the twisted re-interpretations which C. G. Jung and Alfred Adler were endeavoring to give to the findings of psychoanalysis."[47] He had discussed these bitter defections within the movement on a broader level in his essay "On the History of the Psychoanalytic Movement" (1914) but felt he was able to document and demonstrate his arguments from a clinical perspective in the Wolf Man case. Indeed, the case assumed almost legendary proportions as a result of the excessive significance accorded it by Freud's closest associates. The editor of the Standard Edition of Freud's collected works, James Strachey, considered this "the most elaborate and no doubt the most important of all Freud's case histories"; Ernest Jones, Freud's official biographer, spoke admiringly of Freud's "interpretation and synthesis of the incredibly complex material" which he uncovered during his treatment of the Wolf Man.[48]

Perhaps the most compelling aspect of this case grew out of Freud's attempt to grapple in great depth for the first time with a severely disturbed patient from a culture entirely alien to his own. The Wolf Man, whose real name was Sergei Konstantinovich Pankeev (1886–1979), was born into the Russian aristocracy and grew up amid luxury and privilege. His father was a wealthy landowner and a practicing lawyer in the southern port city of Odessa. Pankeev began to experience symptoms of depression while he was a student in St. Petersburg early in 1908. Because of his older sister's recent suicide, his parents decided to provide funds for the establishment of a hospital for nervous disorders in Odessa. The prominent psychiatrist Vladimir Bekhterev got in touch with Pankeev's father when he heard about the proposed hospital and convinced him to make the funds available to create a clinical and research-oriented neurological institute in St. Petersburg.

Using this contact, Pankeev's father asked Bekhterev to examine his son. Bekhterev diagnosed Pankeev as a neurasthenic, a common turn-of-the-century psychiatric classification for depression. Bekhterev used hypnosis on his patient, but neither Pankeev nor his father was a believer in this treatment method. Pankeev then was sent for a consultation with Leonid Drosnes, an Odessa psychiatrist with psychoanalytic experience, who recommended that Pankeev should go abroad for more advanced treatment.[49] Drosnes's first choice was a German sanatorium (where Pankeev's father had gone for some years to treat his own episodes of mania) in order to be seen by Emile Kraepelin and Theodor Ziehen, two of the best-known psychiatrists in Europe.

After Pankeev returned to Russia from his consultations with Kraepelin and Ziehen, who were either uninterested in his case or unable to help him, Drosnes decided that his patient should see Freud and Dubois. He personally accompanied Pankeev to Vienna. After meeting Freud, Pankeev decided to forego the consultation with Dubois. As Pankeev himself put it: "When in January 1910 we arrived in Vienna and met Freud, I was so impressed and inspired by his personality that I told Dr. D. I had definitely decided to be analyzed by Freud, so there was no point in continuing our journey to Dubois in Geneva."[50]

For Freud, the first encounter with Pankeev was hardly taken seriously. He commented to Ferenzci in passing and with evident sarcasm: "As a consequence of your impressive exhortation to allow myself some rest, I have—taken on a new patient from Odessa, a very rich Russian with compulsive feelings, but I am more capable of accomplishment than ever."[51] For Pankeev, however, that first meeting was indeed monumental. Even years later when he recalled the beginning of his treatment with Freud, Pankeev wrote: "During these first months in analysis with Professor Freud, a completely new world was opened to me, a world known to only a few people in those days. Much that had been incomprehensible in my life before that time began to make sense, as relationships which were formerly hidden in darkness now emerged into my consciousness."[52]

The analysis of Pankeev proved to be a major event for both Freud and his patient. For Pankeev, it was the start of a lifelong involvement with psychoanalysis which, though the results were of questionable value in his later opinion, permitted him to function in everyday life, to have some understanding of the nature of his difficulties, and to find a measure of satisfaction in his endeavors and relationships despite the severity of his symptoms. For Freud, the treatment process permitted him to demonstrate the great significance he attached to repressed memories and to sexual fantasies. Freud's analysis of the case centered on Pankeev's recovery of the early memory of having witnessed as his parents engaged in sexual intercourse. On the crucial question of whether this memory could be validated, Freud decided that the patient's fantasy about the event was far more important than proving whether the memory was based on a real event. Freud also used this interpretation of the Pankeev case as further ammunition to argue his general theory about the destructive significance of unconscious drives against his main rivals in the psychoanalytic movement, Jung and Adler.

By 1914, the Russians had developed the necessary components for the training and expansion of psychoanalytic theory and clinical practice to the extent that it was no longer necessary for patients in need of such treatment to be sent abroad, as Spielrein and Pankeev had been. At the historical moment when the next stage would logically have taken place—the spread of psychoanalytic concepts to the culture at large, including new areas of clinical, intellectual, and literary applications—war broke out. As the country mobilized to defend the fatherland, the medical profession felt compelled to join the effort. Hospitals became increasingly absorbed in treating casualties, physicians found their practices filled with larger numbers of soldiers, and the medical school curriculum began to include instruction in "military medicine." Paper shortages and the drafting of the staffs of the editorial boards into the war made the publishing of research in journals more difficult than before.

For psychiatry, both treatment and research became more involved with the neurological and psychotraumatic dimensions of wartime injuries. On the one hand, a great deal of attention was paid to "injuries of the nervous system," "brain lesions" as observed in "mentally deranged" soldiers at the front, and the neurological impact of poisonous gas on the military. On the other hand, the literature of the period was filled with phrases like "war psychosis" and "severe traumatic war psychoneurosis." These wartime studies also described various modes of therapeutic intervention, including hypnosis and psychotherapy. Although Freud was not mentioned explicitly, the influence of psychoanalysis was clearly present in a number of these studies. It had become commonplace, for example, for psychiatric researchers to speak in terminology derived from psychoanalysis, such as the "distinct psychic traumas" emerging from the extreme conditions of war or prior situations of "emotional shock as an etiological factor" in the development of war psychoses.[53]

Russian psychiatric journals also emphasized other wartime research themes. These included the deplorable services of the hospitals, the lack of adequate staffing to accommodate the massive number and acute conditions of the mental casualties in the army, and the large number of mentally ill soldiers who were "overlooked by the psychiatric units at the front."[54] This critique continued to be largely directed against the governing authorities, as had been the case for some years, since the budgets of the hospital services were still controlled by the state ministries. As the country stumbled from war to revolution, this critique faced unexpected challenges in an utterly changed political regime after 1917.

Part Two Psychoanalysis
in the Soviet Union

Chapter 4 Freud in the House of Lenin: Psychoanalysis Ascendant

In front of our eyes, a new and original trend in psychoanalysis is
beginning to form in Russia.
—*L. Vygotsky and A. Luria, preface to the Russian translation of Freud's*
Beyond the Pleasure Principle *(1925)*

In 1917, Russia underwent two political transformations. In February,
Nicholas II abdicated and his autocracy was replaced by a Provisional
Government. Eight months later, the Bolshevik party seized power
and established a socialist government. For the next few years, the new
regime devoted much time to consolidating its power and legitimizing
its authority. During that period, an unusual and conflicting set of
forces commingled. On the one hand, the centralization of power was
accomplished, which included the elimination of competing political
parties and the enforcement of decision making by the party's increasingly authoritarian central committee. On the other hand, as boundaries remained fluid in many areas of society, certain forms of experi-
mentation were tolerated as long as they could be justified as
supportive of the revolution. Thus, until the definition of Bolshevik

legitimacy was completed, questions of collaboration and even survival remained paramount for many professional groups and private individuals. This was especially true for those who thought that political commitments were not required. For their part, the Bolshevik leaders left open the apparent possibilities of competing forms of participation in this process of legitimizing the new order.

By 1922, the ruling Bolshevik party had already taken the name Communist party, and the country was officially renamed the Union of Soviet Socialist Republics (USSR). Having announced exclusive control over political power at the party's tenth congress the year before, the leadership directed its attention in a more focused manner to other sectors of the society. Again, contradictory forces were set in motion at the same time. While Lenin's New Economic Policy permitted the reintroduction of limited forms of capitalist enterprise, the widespread effort to ideologize the entire society went on as well.

For the psychoanalytic community, these new conditions provided an enormous challenge. Survival was not possible without the approval and tolerance of the party. How this approval was to be obtained, and what concessions were necessary, were the most urgent priorities to be confronted. One thing was clear—the followers of Freud had to tackle willingly the problems of everyday life as prioritized by the ruling authorities. Their agenda, in other words, was not entirely their own any longer.

At the same time, many of the difficulties encountered by the psychoanalysts in Soviet Russia were similar to those facing everyone who had lived through the revolutionary era. The situation in Russia was transmitted to the international psychoanalytic community in a report to the Vienna Psychoanalytic Society, which was published in Freud's *International Journal of Psychoanalysis* in 1921. The report was based on information provided by Nikolai Osipov, who had emigrated to Prague, as well as other firsthand data from Martin Pappenheim, a member of the Vienna Psychoanalytic Society who had just returned from a visit to Russia on a medical mission from Vienna.

> Owing to the political state of Russia, it is more than usually difficult to collect facts or to record progress in psychoanalytical circles. Russia has been split asunder by the revolution and the ensuing civil wars, and as there is no communication between the separate parts, it has been impossible to collect and publish accounts either of proceedings of meetings or of papers read and discussed. Scientific journals have entirely ceased to appear during the last three years; the only journal concerning itself with Freudian conceptions, *Psychotherapy,* stopped publication in 1917 [*sic*] owing to financial difficulties.

Such being the conditions, it is only possible to speak or write from personal knowledge of what has transpired in the narrowest scientific circles; thus, although psychoanalytical thought may be making headway in this or that part of Russia, no news has filtered through.[1]

Nevertheless, serious work was under way. The report detailed the efforts of Tatiana Rosenthal, who was most responsible for establishing a base for psychoanalysis in Petrograd (called St. Petersburg before 1914, and renamed Leningrad in 1924 after Lenin's death). "Any headway that psychoanalytic thought may have made in Petrograd during recent years," the reports stated, "is owing in great measure to the steady work of Dr. Rosenthal." In 1919, she was appointed chief physician and supervisor of the clinical section of the Institute of Brain Pathology, which was directed by Vladimir Bekhterev. Although Bekhterev himself does not seem to have been particularly interested in Freud's theories, he obviously was persuaded by Rosenthal to permit the practice of psychoanalysis in his institute, which was a national center for research on the brain and nervous system.

During the winter of 1919–20, Rosenthal gave the first postrevolutionary lecture course on psychoanalysis at the institute. Although at first her emphasis was on Freud's theory, she later revised her lectures to include the work of Adler's individual psychology in presentations at various scientific meetings in Petrograd. In the fall of 1920, she established a separate school for children with neurotic problems and learning disabilities, which was affiliated with the institute and where psychoanalytic psychotherapy was the primary treatment mode. She achieved wider recognition for this effort as a result of a paper she presented at the first national congress of Russian Care Committees for Backward Children, held in Moscow in August 1920, entitled "The Value of Freudian Conceptions in the Education of Children." In addition, she treated patients psychoanalytically at the institute's clinic and trained a number of her colleagues in Freudian principles and techniques.

Rosenthal also continued her research. Building on the original work she had done before the revolution in applying psychoanalytic insights to literature, Rosenthal published a pioneering Freudian study of Dostoevsky's novellas in 1920. She was particularly interested in the connection between creativity and psychopathology. To document the connection, she investigated some of Dostoevsky's descriptions of delusions, hallucinations, fantasies, and phobias in his fictional characters, and tried to connect these to the writer's own suffering and his motivations. In some instances, she tied characteristics described in the stories directly to events in Dostoevsky's life and his mental state. Most significantly, she sought to demonstrate that "the root principle of creative expression lies in the immanent unconscious," particularly in its drives to seek objects and goals irrationally focused rather than rationally calculated in any conscious, deliberate manner. Rosenthal intended to continue her investigations by studying Dostoevsky's major novels, but in 1921, at the age of thirty-six, she committed suicide for reasons which have yet to come to light.[2]

The loss of Rosenthal was made even more painful to the Russian analytic community because it came barely a year after Osipov left the country. Unlike Rosenthal, a Social Democrat who had greeted the revolution with enthusiasm, Osipov was highly critical of the Bolsheviks' seizure of power and of their policies in the aftermath of the revolution. He also was deeply affected by the death in 1917 of his mentor, Serbskii. In Osipov's section of the 1921 report to the Vienna Psychoanalytic Society, he makes clear that Serbskii's passing left the Moscow psychoanalytic community without an influential protector at a particularly vulnerable moment. Fearing the antipathy of Lenin's inner circle to Freud's ideas, Osipov decided to emigrate. Freud personally made arrangements for his Russian colleague in Prague, where Osipov chose to resettle. A small collection survives of previously unpublished letters, written by Freud to Osipov after the latter's arrival in Prague, in which his cordiality and feelings of friendship are clearly expressed. These letters are published for the first time as an appendix of this volume.

In spite of the loss of both Rosenthal and Osipov, the psychoanalytic community began to make significant gains at this time. In March 1921, a psychoanalytic group was formed in Moscow specializing in the study of the principles of artistic creativity. Martin Pappenheim, returning to Vienna from Russia in early October of that year, claimed that there was "considerable interest in Moscow for psychoanalysis." He reported that the new group had eight founding members, three of whom (Ivan Ermakov, Nikolai Bernshtein, and Moshe Wulff) were familiar to European psychoanalysts because their work had been published in Freud's journal. In addition, he mentioned professors A. A. Siderov (aesthetics), A. G. Gabrichevsky (aesthetics), Ivan Il'in (philosophy), and an unnamed professor of mathematics, who was in fact Otto Schmidt. The eighth person was N. E. Uspensky, a physics professor. In addition, Pappenheim listed the titles of the papers read and discussed at the society's initial meetings, most of which were by Ermakov. The topics, ranging from the traditional psychoanalytic to odd and even innovative themes, included symbolism in the statues of river gods and Greek vases, melancholia in Albrecht

Dürer's paintings, characteristics of the sexual differences between boys and girls as evidenced in their drawings, and "relations of tactile eroticism to carpet ornamentation" as a form of psychological expression in observing decorative compositions. Ermakov's course, on the foundations of psychoanalysis, was presented in lectures at the Moscow Psychoneurological Institute. Ermakov also made plans to set up a center for disturbed children below the age of four, which included in its training program an analysis of those responsible for caring for the children in order "to neutralize the potentially damaging impact of their complexes" on their young patients. Wulff, who had accepted a teaching position at Moscow University in 1919, was listed as Ermakov's colleague in running this group.[3] This was the second such children's psychoanalytic institution, as Rosenthal's school in Petrograd was already in existence.

Early in 1922 the Russian Psychoanalytic Society was formed by eight original members, with new members soon joining as well. It was organized into three distinct sections. The first was essentially a continuation of the original group concerned with psychological problems of creativity in art and literature, headed by Ermakov. The second was devoted to clinical analysis, under the direction of Wulff. The third section was concerned with matters of pedagogy, which was of particular interest to the ruling Communist party. The society was seeking to demonstrate the beneficial results of applying psychoanalysis to the educational system, which, if successful, had the potential of bringing their work into the wider social order. This section, run by Otto Schmidt, attracted the attention of some researchers who were working on problems of educational psychology, such as Pavel Blonskii, Stanislav Shatskii, and Lev Vygotsky.

Meanwhile, a second psychoanalytic society was forming in the provincial town of Kazan, on the Volga. The founding group of fourteen declared its formal existence during the summer of 1922 under the leadership of a young psychologist, Alexander Romanovich Luria (1902–1977), who was the president of the Kazan Association for the Social Sciences. He was preoccupied at this time by the desire to find, as he put it, a psychology "that would simultaneously describe the concrete facts of the mental life of individuals and generate general explanatory laws." While engaged in this search he had discovered Freud's early writings which had been translated before the revolution, as well as those of Jung and Adler. "Here, I thought, was a scientific approach that combined a strongly deterministic explanation of concrete, individual behavior with an explanation of the origins of complex human needs in terms of natural science." Luria later recalled his enthusiasm at the time:

To begin with, I established a small psychoanalytic circle. I even ordered stationery with "Kazan Psychoanalytic Association" printed in Russian and German on the letterhead. I then sent news of the formation of this group to Freud himself, and was both surprised and pleased when I received a letter in return addressed to me as "Dear Mr. President." Freud wrote how glad he was to learn that a psychoanalytic circle had been founded in such a remote eastern town of Russia. This letter, written in Gothic German script, as well as another letter authorizing the Russian translation of one of his smaller books, are still in my files.[4]

The list of founding members of the Kazan group of Freudians is noteworthy because of its breadth and because medical professionals were not in the majority. Of the fourteen, half had medical degrees, two were psychologists, three were students of psychology, one was a teacher, and there was one writer who specialized in art and history.

Luria was unquestionably the motivating force. He took the initiative to write to Freud in order to gain official recognition and to link up with the European centers of psychoanalysis in Vienna and Berlin. Also, the report Luria sent to Vienna of his society's activities indicates that he presented bimonthly research papers (more than any other member) on a variety of themes, including comprehensive surveys of the current research literature in psychoanalysis and psychology. However, papers of a more clinical nature, including discussions of Freud's concept of narcissism, the analysis of dream content, and the role of sexuality in society, were presented by the psychiatrists B. D. Fridman and R. A. Averbukh.

In the spring of 1923, the Kazan group was invited to Moscow to join that city's Psychoanalytic Society, which was about to expand its activities significantly. One of the Kazan Society's last acts was to elect seven additional members. This was an exclusively medical group, and would certainly have altered the previous even balance between psychiatrists and social scientists. In any event, the society in Kazan came to an end as its leading members—Luria, Averbukh, and Fridman—moved to Moscow, where they took part in the next phase of the psychoanalytic community's development there.[5]

Luria and his colleagues were also exploring other psychologies. In 1922, for example, Luria visited Bekhterev's Brain Institute in Petrograd where Rosenthal had worked, but ended up accepting an invitation to join the Moscow Institute of Psychology and work under the newly appointed director, K. N. Kornilov, a specialist in experimental psychology. This staff appointment at the Institute of Psychology with its government salary made it financially possible for Luria to settle in Moscow, where he also became a member of the Psychoanalytic Society. In fact, there was considerable overlap between these two organizations as at least eight individuals belonged to both at this time.[6]

By the fall of 1922, Wulff and Ermakov announced in Moscow that they were forming the country's first Institute for Psychoanalysis. The shift from society to institute was an important upgrading to the highest professional status, signifying that the Moscow group was now able to offer psychoanalytic training programs. At this point, there were only two such training institutes in Europe—one in Vienna and the other in Berlin. Moscow, under Communist authority, became the third center.

To accomplish this, the Russians needed to gain approval from Freud's Institute. Among the major requirements for a new institute were the presence of training analysts, a curriculum of courses in psychoanalytic theory and practice, and a clinic. The conditions were met. Wulff and Sabina Spielrein, who returned to Russia from Lausanne early in 1923, were recognized as trained analysts capable of directing a clinical program. Spielrein had been a full member of the Vienna Psychoanalytic Institute while in Europe. Prior to her return, however, she published a paper in which she discussed the history of the psychoanalytic literature in Russia from its origins.[7] In addition to being a useful study which is still worth consulting, the paper is important in showing that Spielrein had given a great deal of thought to the possibility of going home. It is quite unlikely that she would have departed from her clinical studies and devoted so much time to the contributions of the Russian psychoanalytic community unless she were seriously considering joining it.

Further evidence of Spielrein's plan to return to Russia appears in her correspondence with Freud. He supported her intention in a letter to her on February 9, 1923, despite the fact that he had initially recommended that she remain in Europe prior to her departure from Switzerland: "I am in receipt of your letter and really believe that you are right. Your plan to go to Russia seems to be much better than my advice to try out Berlin. In Moscow, you will be able to accomplish important work at the side of Wulff and Ermakov. Lastly, you will be on home ground. These are difficult times for us all."[8]

The course curriculum was arranged by Spielrein, Ermakov, and Wulff, as Freud had assumed. Spielrein taught the courses on the psychology of subliminal thought and on the psychoanalysis of children. The latter course, the largest in the new institute, with thirty members attending, became Spielrein's specialization in her practice. Ermakov taught the basic course of the principles of psychoanalysis, a clinical course on psychotherapy, and one on his specialty, the

psychology of artistic creativity, which concentrated on a psychoanalytic interpretation of the literary writings of Nikolai Gogol and Alexander Griboedov.
Wulff taught the introduction to psychoanalysis and another course on medicine and psychoanalysis. Courses by Luria on oedipal conflicts and by Averbukh on psychoanalysis and religion were announced as "in preparation" for
the coming year.

In addition, under Wulff's direction the institute opened a psychiatric outpatient clinic, which specialized in psychoanalytic treatment. This was important not only because it guaranteed the practice of psychoanalysis to anyone in
the population who volunteered or was referred for the treatment of a disorder,
but also because it permitted analysts in training the opportunity to see patients
under the close supervision of the institute's senior members. Averbukh and
Fridman, from the Kazan Society, were the first two trainees in this clinic,
working under Ermakov, Wulff, and Spielrein.

Most significant, the new institute took over the project, begun in 1921 by
Ermakov and Wulff, to establish a clinical institution for disturbed children in
which psychoanalytic principles could be utilized exclusively in treatment. This
was, in many respects, one of the most original and experimental of the institute's many professional activities in that it sought to deal, in a clinical context,
with the crucial problem of finding a link between the collectivist ethos of a
society committed to Communist principles on the one hand, and the radical
"bourgeois" individualism inherent in Freud's psychoanalytic principles on the
other.

Finally, the institute announced its plans to proceed with a vast publication
project. The intention was to publish all of Freud's most influential works in
Russian translation, followed by volumes with the important papers of Jung,
Sandor Ferenczi, Melanie Klein, and other leading European psychoanalysts.
The editor-in-chief of this project was Ermakov, with most of the translations
to be done by Wulff, in a series called the Psychological and Psychoanalytic
Library. The inaugural work, which appeared in 1922, was, appropriately,
Freud's *Introductory Lectures on Psychoanalysis*, translated by Wulff in two vol-
umes.[9]

ATTEMPTS AT PLEASING TWO FATHERS

Freud was clearly impressed by the activities and plans which the Moscow
Institute reported to him in Vienna. At the congress of the International
Psychoanalytic Association (IPA) which met in Berlin September 25–27, 1922,

Freud proposed "that the group in Moscow should be accepted as a member." However, there was opposition within the international association's leadership. Ernest Jones, who presided at the congress, sought to delay a decision on the Russians for "administrative reasons."

The IPA was concerned about two main problems. One was the comparatively low representation of physicians and psychiatrists in the Russian psychoanalytic groups. In Kazan, the medical component was one-half, but in Moscow the number was far lower. A serious division in the ranks of the IPA appeared over this issue. Although Freud was opposed to requiring medical training for psychoanalytic candidates, a number of the European psychoanalysts in the IPA had a sense of mistrust for psychologists and other nonmedical specialists from the social sciences and humanities practicing psychoanalysis. The idea that a mathematician (Otto Schmidt) was the vice president of the Moscow Institute was inexplicable to the medical people. The IPA also did not put much emphasis at this time on research in applied psychoanalysis by scholars in social psychology, philosophy, aesthetics, or history, fields in which the Russian were already making contributions.

The second problem concerned the political world in which the Russian analysts had to function. There was little understanding abroad, and much fear, of the new Soviet state and its communist ideology. Although there were individual analysts in Europe who were decidedly interested in socialism (Otto Fenichel, Wilhelm Reich, and Siegfried Bernfeld, among others), most were politically conservative and anti-Marxist.

Largely because of Freud's influence, a compromise was worked out at the Berlin congress. Once the phrase "as soon as the necessary conditions are met" was added to the motion admitting the Russians to the IPA, it was accepted.[10] At the IPA's insistence, an "All-Russian" Psychoanalytic Society was established, which included members from Petrograd, Kazan, Odessa, Kiev, and Rostov, with Ermakov, who was medically trained and not a Marxist, as its head. This permitted a centralization of authority in Moscow under the "orthodox" psychiatric direction of Ermakov and Wulff, who were politically acceptable to the IPA.[11] This "Russian problem," as Jones called it, remained an issue nonetheless. At the 1924 congress in Salzburg, a statement was made welcoming "the new federated group into the IPA," but the Russians would remain isolated in the International Psychoanalytic Association despite the fact that the Russian Institute, with around thirty members in 1922–23, represented one-eighth of the entire active constituency of the association.[12]

While the Russian Freudians were working to satisfy the demands of the IPA abroad, they had a far more daunting task facing them at home—convincing the cultural officials in the ruling Communist party in Moscow of the ideological legitimacy of their enterprise. To put it starkly, having won Freud to their side, they now needed Lenin's approval. The Moscow Psychoanalytic Institute could not have functioned so visibly without either tacit or explicit support from the party. Despite the comparative openness of this era and the acceptance (if not encouragement) of experimental trends in the arts which bloomed, albeit briefly, the fact that the psychoanalysts were publishing Freud's works in the press of the State Publishing House and operating a children's school in the capital at a time when most educational activities were already under party control suggests that more than mere tolerance was involved. There have also been indications in various published documents that certain key party leaders were favorably disposed toward psychoanalysis. This has been successfully demonstrated in the case of Trotsky (which I shall examine below), and suggested without evidence in the cases of Nikolai Bukharin, Karl Radek, and Adolf Ioffe.[13] Newly available archival materials from Moscow, however, make it clear that the involvement of the party occurred earlier and was far more widespread than had been assumed.

By the summer of 1922, negotiations were well under way between the Moscow psychoanalytic group and the presidium of the scientific-pedagogical section of the State Scientific Soviet. The section of the Soviet reported directly to Anatoly Lunacharsky, Commissar of Enlightenment and Education, who had very close ties to Lenin. Each side was seeking something rather concrete from the other. The Freudians wanted official approval as well as financial support from the Communist authorities, without which it would have been virtually impossible to function. The government was in the process of formulating its ideological position regarding the field of psychology in general, and in addition, needed practical guidance in coping with the large problem of the homeless and orphaned children who had been victimized by the violence of the civil war. Because the psychoanalysts had already started an experimental school for disturbed children, party officials were willing to listen to a proposal which included that institution as part of its overall activities.

The psychoanalysts brought their intentions directly to the government on September 16, 1922, in a carefully worded report. It began with a statement about the growing international success of the psychoanalytic movement, "in the fields of both the theoretical and the applied sciences," as evidenced by the activities of the existing psychoanalytic societies abroad. In Russia, by contrast, such a society could not be formed until the required knowledge about psychoanalysis had been absorbed and understood. The absence of such knowledge meant that it was impossible to prevent the spread of erroneous and doubtful interpretations of psychoanalytic theory.

Psychoanalysis is, the report continued, "one of the methods of the study and the education of humanity in its social milieu," in which the individual can be helped in the struggle against obstacles in daily life. The applications of psychoanalysis extend from medicine to pedagogy, from psychology to sociology, and include problems of "artistic creativity, labor relations, religious, and philosophical formulations; and in psychiatry, psychoanalysis provides new and fruitful possibilities in its applications."

To accomplish these tasks, the report concluded, a State Psychoanalytic Institute was being established under the directorship of Ermakov. Although a larger staff was needed, "fortunately in Russia there is no shortage of qualified scientists, who are recommended to us by virtue of their accomplished work in various fields of science allied with psychoanalysis." The authors of the report stated that their intention was "to participate in the progressive development of psychoanalysis abroad, which until now has known little of Russian clinicians and researchers who work in this field." They also acknowledged that "working in isolation, without the possibility of making use of their specialization and its literature," has been deleterious from a professional standpoint. To counteract this trend and to disseminate information about psychoanalysis, the State Publishing House agreed to sponsor a series of books by Freud under the imprint "The Psychoanalytic and Psychological Library." The most crucial clause came at the end, with the signers of this document agreeing that the Psychoanalytic Society would abide by agreed upon rules as stipulated by the government. Fourteen signatures followed, including those of Ermakov and Wulff.[14]

About a week later, Ermakov submitted to the government on behalf of his colleagues the "Charter of the Psychoanalytic Society." In this lengthy document, Ermakov set forth the regulations and responsibilities of the new organization. The section on the activities of the Society includes the following topics: the organization of the State Psychoanalytic Institute, arrangement of trips for scientific meetings in other cities, the establishment of an outpatient clinic, the publication of a series of volumes on psychoanalytic themes, presentations in connection with the international psychoanalytic organizations abroad, and courses, lectures, and conferences on psychoanalytic research. In addition, Ermakov stated that the society was obligated to submit annual reports to the State Administration for Scientific Institutions. The last clause, which would later prove to be of great significance, indicated that "in the event of the necessity to liquidate the Society," the government retained the right to control its activities.[15] In this manner, the unique institution of state psychoanalysis was established.

FURTHER EXPLORATIONS

Having gained the approval of the professional leadership in Vienna and the political authorities in Moscow, the Russian psychoanalysts turned their attention to several projects which they hoped would solidify and enhance their reputation in both of the worlds in which they operated. One of their continuing activities, which was watched with interest by clinicians as well as politicians, was the children's school project. Since 1921, Ermakov and Wulff had been listed as the directors of an experimental home for disturbed children, located in Moscow, which was affiliated with the Psychoanalytic Institute. The real head of the school, however, was Vera Schmidt, who was prevented from occupying the title of director only because she lacked a medical degree. She not only ran many of the day-to-day activities but was responsible for the school's theoretical orientation. Schmidt admitted that the school was far from wholly original as an institution in that she had been influenced by the experimental therapeutic kindergartens organized by August Aichhorn and Siegfried Bernfeld in Vienna. Nevertheless, in the uncertain political atmosphere of postrevolutionary Soviet Russia, it was a bold endeavor to assume responsibility for the care of some of the mentally disturbed and homeless young victims of the postrevolutionary era.

The school was financially supported by Lunacharsky's Commissariat of Enlightenment and officially attached to the Institute of Psychoneurology in Moscow. It had opened in 1921 with thirty children between the ages of one and five years, who came from diverse social backgrounds; their parents were workers and peasants as well as intellectuals. The school was openly run according to psychoanalytic principles. Vera Schmidt's report on the school's activities makes clear that an effort was made to apply Freud's ideas to the psychological conflicts of infants and adolescents. Great attention was devoted to the sexual life of the children. Since it was assumed that many of their actions were motivated by the unconscious quest for sexual gratification, the children were permitted to express themselves and interact with others freely, as long as no physical harm was evident. Closely supervised, the children were warmly supported by the staff in the belief that the manner in which the infant experiences his or her "very rich sexual life" will determine to a large extent the presence or absence of serious sexual and sexually derived problems later as adults.[16] "Punishments do not exist in the school," Schmidt wrote. Close relationships between the staff and the children were established in which there was no need even to speak to the children with a tone of severity. The tendency to blame, to foster guilt, to dispense harsh judgments for the children's behavior was to be abolished in favor of supportive examples of tenderness and explanation. Staff members were strictly forbidden to act in any way which would arouse the children sexually and destroy the trust and love that was structured to anchor their sense of self. Similarly, bed-wetting and excretion were to be treated in such a way as to avoid "gravely traumatic experiences" that such activities usually generate from punishing parents.[17]

From the start, the school was plagued by rumors of sexual excesses which were allegedly encouraged by the staff. However, an investigative committee from the commissariat found no evidence to substantiate these charges and even praised the results they saw. By the spring of 1923, however, strong doubts about the school were raised in high government circles. On April 26, party officials responsible for scientific and educational institutions concluded that, after reviewing the functions of the school, there was no longer any basis to continue to support it. The distance that had emerged between the intentions of the party and the Freudians on this matter can be readily seen in the school's very name. The party officials frequently referred to it as the psychoanalytic laboratory called "International Solidarity"; Vera Schmidt used the term "children's home."[18]

The government committee was not unanimous. One member, the well-known educational psychologist Stanislav Shatskii, not only voted against the dissolution of the school, but wrote a minority report that is included in the record in which he bravely defended the mission of the school. From a pedagogical point of view, he wrote, it was undeniable that the relationships with the children in the school were "attentive, cautious, and loving." Educational institutions should be using this as a model to develop a more widespread diffusion of such techniques in Soviet society. At the moment, "the psychoanalytic school is the only place in Russia" where one can find their application in practice, Shatskii concluded.[19]

Debates in government committee meetings continued into the fall of 1923. An investigative commission was set up specifically to oversee the functions of the school, inspect its activities, and make final recommendations. The psychologist P. P. Blonskii and two leading Freudians, Sabina Spielrein and Alexander Luria, among others, were brought in to advise the commission and to present their own views on the fate of the school.[20] With the support of these experts, and with at least one of the five members of the commission definitely in favor of the school (Otto Schmidt), the commission on September 17 concluded that it recognized "the necessity of preserving the children's home as a result of its progressive, extraordinary, and valuable work."

However, the commission recommended some serious political compromises. The school was asked to devote itself to "the study of the social origins of child development," by which the commission meant "the problems of social classes" so important to the ideology of the party. More ominous was the proposal "to place the children's home under the scientific leadership of the Psychoanalytic Institute where the leading influence in its functions would be Marxist workers." Furthermore, the commission recommended that an inspection take place to ensure "the strengthening of the proletarian constituency in the children's school" and "to reduce the cost of maintenance for each child."[21] Several weeks later, these recommendations were ratified by the Commissariat of Enlightenment, the highest level of educational policy making, with Chief Commissar Lunacharsky himself present at the meeting, and by the central committee of the party.[22]

Vera Schmidt obviously could not accept these conditions. With this growing resentment in the government facing the school, she and her husband, Otto Schmidt, felt compelled to travel abroad in October 1923, to seek counsel and support. In Vienna they met with Freud, Abraham, Otto Rank, and other leading psychoanalysts from Austria and Germany. They reported on the recent activities of the Russian Psychoanalytic Institute as well as on the developments regarding the experimental school. According to the official report which appeared in Freud's journal, the psychoanalysts "showed great interest in the Children's Home and Laboratory at Moscow" and offered "many valuable hints with reference to the working of the laboratory. In particular, the question of collective education and psychoanalysis (the fate of the Oedipus Complex under conditions of collective education) was discussed."[23] This was recognized as a crucial issue, and one which the Russians were in a singularly appropriate position to observe, given the ongoing consolidation of the Communist regime. However, despite the apparent concern and empathy the Schmidts found for their work, there was little that the analysts abroad could do. Freud agreed to publish Vera Schmidt's report on the school, and the

Schmidts returned home, where they learned of the government's plans to close the children's home.

Meanwhile, the clinical activities of the institute in Moscow continued. Reports from Moscow appeared regularly in the *International Journal of Psychoanalysis,* but revealed little of the political intrusion already at work. In 1923, Wulff lectured on the development of the libido and its connection to "recent biological research" on the psychoanalysis of childhood, Spielrein conducted a seminar on "aphasic and infantile thinking," and Ermakov spoke on "the problem of self-expression in art." The members of the institute also heard addresses by guest speakers, including one of the rising stars in Soviet psychology, Lev Vygotsky, on December 14, 1924, and by G. A. Charasov, a literary scholar who spoke on "Pushkin's Work in the Light of Psychoanalysis" on March 21, 1925. Courses on various aspects of psychoanalysis continued to be offered at the institute each year.

The other important function of the institute was the publication in Russian translation of some of the most influential books and articles by Freud and his followers. This publishing project remained under the direction of Ermakov, who had planned a large series of volumes on psychoanalysis in 1921, and supervised the volumes as they appeared beginning in 1922. Ermakov envisioned thirty-two volumes total, but only fifteen of the projected volumes were actually published, all of them sponsored and financed under the imprint of the State Publishing House.[24] Wulff, the primary translator, wrote that the Ermakov series was the main reason for the unparalleled burst of interest in psychoanalysis during the years 1922–23, enthusiasm which spread to "large circles of the intelligentsia besides the Communist Party, to scientists, educators, jurists and physicians," among others. The most telling piece of evidence of this extraordinary popularity, he added, was the fact that every volume "rapidly sold out."[25]

Clearly the years 1921–1923 were the high tide of the psychoanalytic movement in Russia. Apart from the one major casualty—the closing of the school for disturbed children—psychoanalysis achieved spectacular successes at this time. An institute with a fully recognized training program was inaugurated, an outpatient clinic was established together with the children's home, all functioning on psychoanalytic principles. The extensive publication of psychoanalytic books and articles was proceeding at a level that was difficult to imagine a few years before. All of these activities were in some measure supported by the state. Indeed, it can safely be said (with all the implied ironies, given what was to come later) that no government was ever responsible for supporting psychoanalysis to such an extent, before or after.

It was no accident that all of this occurred during the New Economic Policy era. Lenin's program, which permitted the reintroduction of private enterprise into the Communist experiment on a limited basis, was very beneficial for psychoanalysis. It ensured a certain measure of tolerance for the radical individualism in which Freudian theory was so rooted, at least for the time being.

Chapter 5 The Decline and
Fall of Soviet Psychoanalysis

Theoretical Marxism, as realized in Russian Bolshevism, has acquired the energy and the self-contained and exclusive character of a *Weltanschauung,* but at the same time an uncanny likeness to what it is fighting against. Though originally a portion of science and built up, in its implementation, upon science and technology, it has created a prohibition of thought which is just as ruthless as was that of religion in the past. Any critical examination of Marxist theory is forbidden, doubts of its correctness are punished in the same way as heresy was once punished by the Catholic Church. The writings of Marx have taken the place of the Bible and the Koran as a source of revelation, though they would seem to be no more free from contradictions and obscurities than those older sacred books.
—*Sigmund Freud, "The Question of a* Weltanschauung*" (1932)*

THE GREAT DEBATE: PSYCHOANALYSIS AS IDEOLOGY

By the mid-1920s, the Russian Psychoanalytic Institute had taken its place in the International Psychoanalytic Association alongside member societies in Vienna, Berlin, Budapest, London, and New York.

Although the Russians had indeed met the standards established by the association, one trait distinguished their organization in Moscow from all others. Nowhere else were the institutions of psychoanalysis supported by a national government whose legitimacy was rooted in the enforcement of ideological doctrine. This unique arrangement placed the Russian psychoanalysts in a difficult and complex situation. On the one hand, they were supported by the state financially, which to some extent explains their rapid development in so short a time span. On the other hand, they were, by virtue of that support, subject to a level of state intervention in their professional affairs that was unknown in Western Europe. This intervention was more than an abstract issue for the Russians since the experimental children's school had already been shut down by the authorities. As the theoretical goals and institutional controls of communism became more clearly defined, increasing numbers of people at all levels of society found themselves drawn into an ever-widening net of political demands. For a time, however, it seemed as if psychoanalysis might be able to play an important role in shaping the new postrevolutionary order. This hope rested on the possibility of making some acceptable contribution to the creation of a Marxist psychology, one of the projects called for by the Communist party during the early 1920s.

Soviet psychiatrists and psychologists were attempting to develop "an analysis of the psyche" on an empirical basis acceptable from a scientific standpoint and on an ideological foundation rooted in a Marxist framework. These simultaneous endeavors required integrating biological and neurological science with Marx's historical materialism. The scientific papers of both Ivan Pavlov and Vladimir Bekhterev, though they themselves were in disagreement on many theoretical issues, were used as a kind of exemplary model for others to follow and develop further.[1]

In this area, as in so many others, individuals in positions of authority found themselves forced to define their own professional identity apart from the Western influences (now increasingly regarded as antirevolutionary and corrupting) which had shaped their specialized training and their scientific orientation. The problem was further complicated by the evolving consolidation of a "revolutionary culture" which was cast as a specifically Russian interpretation of Marx's European-based class theory. This new culture was also predicated on an overt rejection of "prerevolutionary" cultural influences and institutions, much of which were designated as bourgeois and individualist. Those structures were in turn to be replaced by others supporting the new proletarian values of collectivism and egalitarianism. In reality, this emerging systematization of a new revolutionary culture was achieved in large measure by sharpening definitions of who or what was to be included and excluded.

These issues did not have an immediate impact on psychiatrists who remained more closely associated with clinical practice. Psychologists, however, were affected because psychology was where the difficulties of working out the theoretical problems of the new Marxist behavioral science were first experienced. Thus, in the early 1920s at the Moscow Institute of Psychology, a number of scholars and intellectuals with established reputations for their work on psychological and philosophical questions (including the development of human values, personality motivation, systems of belief, and individual ethics) were forced out of their positions. Moreover, in 1923, the head of the Moscow Institute was fired from the institution he himself had founded.[2]

The ideological battles were fierce and the consequences were serious and far-reaching. Underlying the theoretical discussions, which revolved around the issue of understanding mass behavior, were the fundamental Bolshevik concerns—the desire for control and the need to construct a comprehensive theory capable of justifying that control. Echoes of this conflict between the interests of an open science and the demands of ideological politics began to appear in the psychoanalytic community at this time as well. Since this community was professionally composed primarily of psychiatrists and psychologists, they tended to respond in a divided rather than united manner.

The entry of the psychoanalysts into the minefield of ideological politics can be traced back to the presentations made by Alexander Luria to the Kazan Psychoanalytic Society in 1922. On September 7, Luria spoke about the recent upsurge of interest in political questions among "the new psychologists." At the December 10 meeting of the society, he reviewed the leading trends in Russian psychology, including the contrast between the outmoded philosophical orientations and the more recent communist schools of reflexology and brain physiology. He extended this analysis at the February 4, 1923, meeting with a presentation on the comparison between psychoanalysis and current Soviet trends in experimental psychology, a theme he would develop in greater detail later.[3]

Meanwhile, other commentators sought to go beyond the specialized areas of discussion to address directly the place of psychological theory in the development of the new Marxist society. The starting point was the appearance of Bernard Bykhovskii's article on Freudian methodology, which shifted psychoanalytic theory from the literary, medical, and academic groups into the realm of politics and Bolshevik party concerns. Bykhovskii, a young Bolshevik philosopher specializing in dialectical materialism, called his article "On the Methodological Foundations of Freud's Psychoanalytic Theory." It was published in *Under the Banner of Marxism,* a major party organ, at the end of 1923 and inaugurated an extraordinary public debate on "Freudian Marxism." Between 1923 and 1930, a number of bold and intelligent theorists sought a common basis for the inclusion of Freudian psychology within a Marxist ideological framework. With this effort they were also attempting to legitimize Freudian theory at the party and state levels. This debate on Freudian-Marxist theory, which was argued out in the party's most important journals, emerged at a critical juncture in the postrevolutionary period. Lenin was still alive, but ailing. The party leadership was divided into numerous factions and without a clearly established ideological direction. It is highly unlikely that Freudian Marxism could have risen to such prominence in Bolshevik journals at any other moment.

Bykhovskii sought to demonstrate in his article that Freud's concepts were in accord with the work being done in neurology and physiology by Bekhterev and Pavlov. Moreover, he argued that psychoanalysis as a theory could potentially contribute to a deeper understanding of man and society in the specific context of a socialist future. As evidence, Bykhovskii presented a systematic exposition of Freudian theory, the fullest that had ever appeared in a major Bolshevik journal. All the citations and quotations were taken directly from Freud's published writings in Russian. Focusing his attention on the concept of the unconscious, which he believed was of paramount significance, Bykhovskii concluded that Freud's concepts were fully compatible with Marxist theory. Though the prose in the article was stilted and full of unclear abstract terminology, no reader could have missed Bykhovskii's favorable attitude toward Freud.[4]

Bykhovskii's article was followed by another on the subject of psychoanalysis, written by M. A. Reisner (1869–1929). His lengthy piece, entitled "Freud and His School on Religion," appeared in *The Press and the Revolution,* another high-level Bolshevik journal, early in 1924. Reisner was an expert in constitutional law and had been active in both the German and the Russian Social Democratic parties before the revolution of 1917. After the revolution, he was responsible for drafting legislation on the separation of church and state under the new communist regime, was one of the principal authors of the first Soviet constitution, and an expert in the philosophy of law, which he taught at the universities in Tomsk and Petrograd. His proximity to Bolshevik power can also be seen in his work with Lunacharsky in the Commissariat of Enlightenment during the early 1920s and in his appointment as head of the division of social psychology in the reorganized Institute of Psychology in 1924. This made him one of the more powerful figures, from the perspective of state authority, associated with the Freudians in this period.[5]

Reisner's article was the first application of psychoanalysis to the study of religion to appear in Russian. His overall intention was to show the points of convergence shared by Marx and Freud in their interpretation of religion. Reisner explored the role of religious belief in the modern world as found in Freud's early works and in his *Totem and Taboo*, which had been published in Vienna two years earlier. He also referred frequently to Theodor Reik's *Probleme der Religionspsychologie*, as well as to the works of Otto Rank and Carl Jung, all of whom made up "Freud's school" for Reisner. A good deal of attention was also paid to William James's influential *Varieties of Religious Experience.*[6]

Reisner began his presentation with a critical reading of the works of Marx and Engels on the subject of religion. After reviewing their general position on religion in capitalist as well as precapitalist societies, Reisner acknowledged that Marx and Engels had not resolved some of the most crucial aspects of the problem of organized religion in the modern world. What they provided, he wrote, was a socioeconomic critique of religion, but they did not treat the "psychology of religion." By this Reisner meant that, from a Marxist perspective, there still was no means of understanding the meaning of religious aspirations and symbols or the sources of their appeal to masses of people over the centuries. The essence of these spiritual forces, Reisner suggested, may in fact lie elsewhere, particularly in the realm of human psychology on the individual level, rather than solely in the social class structure of society, as Marxists had argued. Moreover, noting that while interesting contributions to this problem had been made in previous studies by Herbert Spencer, Lucien Lévy-Bruhl (particularly with his concept of "pre-logical" thought processes), and William James (who discussed the notion of subconscious motivation in religious commitment), he was convinced that the most important work had been done by Freud and his followers.

Freud's contribution to the "scientific study of religion" was an illuminating one for two main reasons, according to Reisner. First, Freud analyzed the hidden sources of social development and discovered them to be centered in the realm of "sexual mentality" (*myshlenie*). Second, he went further by postulating the notion of "displacement" (*vytesneniia*), in which the unresolved sexual conflicts of individuals are transported or "displaced" into the social and cultural milieu. The true "originality of Freud's work" in this area can be seen in his analysis of the process by which unconscious erotic fantasies in childhood can reemerge later in the individual's development in the form of religious commitment. This commitment often assumes a pathological form, in which an extreme and coercive spiritualism may dominate one's personality in the effort to achieve unrealistic goals or fantasies of gratification.

Reisner also discussed Freud's use of the term "sublimation" (according to which repressed internalized conflicts are rechanneled into socially accepted forms of behavior and purposeful labor) and agreed that there was an analogous process at work in the world of religious experience. Conventional, organized religion and religious belief were accepted forms of spirituality that conformed with the values of society at large. Schismatics, dissenters, and advocates of extreme forms of belief have been condemned by that established sector. The point was, however, that there are concealed forces motivating individuals, whether they are acting within or outside the accepted social and spiritual parameters in any society. The question was not who is "correct" or righteous according to the church, but how unconscious conflicts are managed in society.

This, Reisner believed, was a new approach to understanding the role of religion in society, one with particularly fruitful possibilities when joined more explicitly to the philosophy of Marxist historical materialism. Behind the phenomenon of religious commitment lies a complex emotional web, he wrote. Inside this web are conflicting feelings of dependence opposing independence and worth against worthlessness. These feelings are structured by authority figures in the individual's development, in the family as well as in society. Individuals who turn to religion are frequently seeking solace from the burden of ambivalent and often intolerable personal conflicts. When placed beside a Marxist class analysis of society and history, this insight leads to an understanding of how the church has acted as a vital force in maintaining order over freedom. Freud's interpretation, therefore, permits a more complete portrait of "religion as a world order," supporting traditional social class hierarchies with its powerful ceremonies and symbols.

Following Freud, religion could be redefined as "the social organization of the sexual mentality of man and activity associated with it." This system involves the mass "displacement" of unconscious sexual conflicts and instincts and their transformation through symbolic rituals and ceremonies into a rational system that supports the political and economic structure of the state. This permits individuals to accept exploited positions in the workplace since they appear to be approved tacitly by institutionalized religion. Thus we have an explanation for what is in reality the "organization of neuroses and manias on a large scale," in which organized religion solidifies class divisions and accomplishes "the sublimation of the creative forces of man through the power of revelations." Reisner acknowledged in his conclusion that Freud tended to be "schematic and one-sided in his view of the historical process." Nevertheless, he found Freud's study of religion to be fully in accord with the theory of historical materialism.[7]

Reisner's article was a contribution to both applied psychoanalysis and communist social theory. Though it was a subtle and thoughtful study of the social psychology of religion, its real message concerned the ways in which a society is coerced into accepting forms of belief and opinion. Reisner may have been ostensibly dealing with the "bourgeois" West in his discussion of the unconscious motives driving individuals into spiritual institutions, but the manner in which he described the submission to figures of authority and the sacrificing of freedom for order could easily have been read as a warning to any Soviet reader. For Reisner, the blending of the ideas of Marx and Freud meant that individuals anywhere had to beware of the seductive forces of power, regardless of whether they were in control of a spiritual or a secular faith.

The Freudian tide continued to rise in Soviet Russia. In January 1924, a large number of psychiatrists and psychologists gathered in Petrograd for the national meetings of the Psychoneurological Congress. The purpose of the congress was to explore the varying schools of psychology with the intention of finding an acceptable Marxist orientation at the state level. Some of the speeches resounded with the new strident discourse of communism, such as the plenary address by A. P. Nechaev, an educational psychologist in disagreement with the leading ideological "schools," who spoke of the dangers of an "aggressive gentry-bourgeois politics in the domestic relations of [social] classes."[8] There were clashes between Bekhterev, Kornilov, and Pavlov as the search for a common ideological denominator grew more intense. Nadezhda Krupskaia, Lenin's wife, was also addressed the meeting. She directed attention to the "enormous number of orphaned [*besprizornye*] children," the victims of social chaos who remained uncared for.[9] During these discussions, Freud's ideas were invoked on numerous occasions, chiefly by A. B. Zalkind (1888–1936). Zalkind argued that psychoanalysis was particularly useful in treating those individuals suffering from a variety of disorders, from psychotic disturbances emanating from the war period to sexual traumas affecting numerous children in Soviet society.[10]

Zalkind, a medically trained psychotherapist and party member, also published an article in the spring of 1924 called "Freudism and Marxism" in which he expanded on his presentation at the psychoneurological congress. In the article, Zalkind took the process of ideologizing psychoanalysis one step further by directly and publicly associating important Communist party leaders with psychoanalysis for the first time. Zalkind argued in this essay, which he clearly envisioned as a contribution to the formation of a Marxist psychology, that "the human psyche was a biological reflection of man's social existence," and that biology must be joined with the principles of Marxist sociology to mount "a materialist attack on the 'soul.'" This meant that scientists had a responsibility to ensure that the old philosophical and speculative forms of investigating problems of the mind ("idealism") were to be eliminated in the new postrevolutionary order and replaced by "objective experimental studies" in the framework of building an egalitarian communist society. In the terminology of Marxist ideology, "materialism" would triumph over "idealism."

To accomplish this goal, Zalkind cited the reflex physiology of Ivan Pavlov and the psychoanalytic work of Sigmund Freud as "the two central and new biological studies which, in the literal sense of the word, explode all the old notions about our mental functions." To indicate the Communist party's ideological approval of this scientific paradigm, Zalkind quoted from recently published articles and speeches by members of the party's top echelon. For Pavlov, Zalkind referred to Nikolai Bukharin and Gregory Zinoviev, and for Freud, he mentioned Leon Trotsky and Karl Radek, who had written favorably about the benefits of psychoanalysis for the Soviet Union.[11] The bulk of Zalkind's article is a point-by-point discussion of Freud's major concepts, with an appraisal of the degree to which each concept is compatible with Marxist theory.

Zalkind's article is also noteworthy for its transparently political associations. He spoke of the oppressive and painful struggle between an individual's "external reality" and "psychological reality" in the "underground of the unconscious," which was remarkably similar to his frequent references to the Marxist notion of class conflict causing perpetual unhappiness for ordinary people. More significant was Zalkind's description of Freud's concept of the censor mediating between the demands for gratification and the social and ethical restraints that must be imposed against them, which he literally compared to a kind of police action against "an underground, illegal organization."[12]

Zalkind was not uncritical of Freud's work. Several times in the article he spoke about the "errors" and "mistakes" of psychoanalysis, particularly concerning the excessive attention devoted to "the individual" as opposed the collective in psychoanalytic theory, Freud's exaggeration of sexual forces as the causes of human misery, and what Zalkind called Freud's "metaphysical" (or irresponsibly speculative) side.[13] Nevertheless, his conclusion was that psychoanalysis, utilized with appropriate discretion and caution, deserved the attention of psychologists as well as the medical and intellectual communities for its wide-ranging theoretical and practical applications, its convergence with biological science, and its essential agreements with Marxism.

By coining the term "Freudism" in the title of his 1924 article, Zalkind had added another salient characteristic to the evolving politicization of psychoanalysis in the Soviet Union. In a society dominated by political "isms," from the most favorable (Marxism and Leninism) to the least (Menshevism, the defeated Social Democratic Marxist rival to Lenin's Bolshevism, for example), it was not surprising that psychoanalysis would be swept up by the same tendency. As easy as it was to transform Freud's ideas into an approving political category through the term Freudism, it was just as simple for the opposition to appropriate the name in order to make it pejorative. The political counterattack, in the conditions of this overcharged political situation, was not long in coming. With Lenin's death in January 1924, the country was thrown in confusion and doubt as the Bolshevik leaders intensified their deadly battle for control of the Communist party and, therefore, of the country.

POINT-COUNTERPOINT

The counterattack against the supporters of the Freudian-Marxist position came swiftly on the heels of these articles. It was launched by V. Iurinets, a party ideologist, in the fall of 1924 in an article called "Freudism and Marxism."[14] Although neither Bykhovskii, Reisner, nor Zalkind were mentioned by name, there is no doubt that they were the focus of Iurinets's hostile anti-Freudian critique. Iurinets's article appeared in the same journal as Bykhovskii's, took the same title as Zalkind's, and the topics discussed as well as the organization of the article make it clear that he was refuting Bykhovskii and Zalkind almost point by point.

Iurinets's piece was written in a more overtly polemical style than any of the previous articles. The tone was sarcastic and patronizing, full of self-righteousness and moral indignation. In his introduction, Iurinets suggested that he was undertaking a mission on behalf of Marxist philosophy to confront the current wave of Freudian theory, regarded by too many people "as the last word in contemporary psychiatry." Iurinets was not above mixing absurd metaphors. In reading Freud, he wrote, "we are carried off into the semi-oblivion of a modern *Walpurgisnacht,* with its wild cries and frenzied dances, . . . on the waves of the unconscious contours of Prussian logic."[15] "Freudism," for Iurinets, "is today united with the advance of the *ad hoc* Wagnerian epoch, and joined to the restoration of idealism" as it moves almost imperceptibly into the Marxist camp. He also noted that Freudian theory was linked to the tradition of decadence and irrationalism in Western thought, heralded by Nietzsche, Georges Sorel, and Henri Bergson before the world war. Iurinets saw an authentic conspiracy at work. Quietly and with attractive simplicity, he noted, Freud's followers tried to introduce their master's notions in Russia not so much in their own (that is, "bourgeois") context; rather, they sought a legitimacy in the "respected cloak of Marxist historical materialism."

Iurinets categorically rejected this trend, which he feared as a form of ideological colonialism emanating from the West and threatening postrevolutionary Russia. He therefore devoted the core of his article to proving that Freudian theory was utterly incompatible with Marxist philosophy, and made some telling points. He argued that Freud was not a materialist (as Bykhovskii and Zalkind had erroneously stated) and that his work was riddled with paradoxes and unprovable assumptions. Reviewing some of Henri Bergson's philosophical work, Iurinets found many similarities with Freud's writings. Although he did not claim to have proof of Bergson's influence on Freud, he found enough congruities in their work to make the suggestion. The point of this association was to link Freud with a clearly "idealist" and anti-Marxist philosophical school of thought. For Marxists, ideas could not be forces in and of themselves but had to be rooted in the class structure of society. Iurinets argued that Freud cleverly used biological analogies—as Bergson did with physics—to construct a fundamentally nonmaterialist position. Similarly, while Freud was very knowledgeable about physiology, his theory was only a physiological metaphor.

Iurinets also discussed in detail some of Freud's basic concepts, particularly the distinctions among unconscious, preconscious, and conscious phenomena. He found that Freud's efforts to explain the "alogical" nature and the "asocial tendencies" of the unconscious revealed neither new knowledge nor significant discoveries. Finally, Iurinets believed that the larger societal implications of Freud's works were among the weakest aspects of psychoanalytic theory. By attempting to generalize about unresolved sexual conflicts from questionable individual case studies, Freud had merely produced a highly speculative (as opposed to empirical) and reductionist explanation of mass motivation. There was, in the end, no proof of the universal manifestations of these conflicts in Freud's works or those of his followers. Freudian theory, therefore, not only had to be rejected by Marxists because of its incompatibility with historical materialism, but should also be opposed because of its distortions, pretensions, and glaring inadequacies.[16]

Reisner returned to the debate with another long, three-part article that appeared in the middle of 1925 in *The Press and Revolution*. This time he took on a more formidable task in dealing with the relationship of Freudian theory to social psychology. His article was a response to the critical orientation of Iurinets's essay and an attempt to legitimize psychoanalysis by justifying Freud's work in the context of social, rather than purely psychological, problems.

The key section of Reisner's article consisted of an interesting exposition on the social functions of certain psychoanalytic processes. His intention was to show how the concept of a "reality principle" could be interpreted on an aggregate societal level in either healthy, productive, and satisfying terms or in a destructive and pathological manner. Quoting from both Marx's *Kapital* and Freud's *Introductory Lectures on Psychoanalysis,* Reisner discussed the relation between conscious social class conflict and unconscious individual conflicts. His point was that the proletarian class was deeply submerged in a psychological as well as an economic prison under capitalism. Reisner argued that to understand this fully, Freud's description of sublimation and repression in society needed to be added to Marx's "brilliant" characterization of working-class oppression. Workers were mired not only in the despair of wage slavery but also in a psychological situation of illusion and self-deception which was even more threatening precisely because it functioned largely on an unconscious level.

Moreover, governments and ruling classes were adept at manipulating the existing hierarchy of authority by utilizing the appealing symbols of family, religion, and fatherland. Reisner perceptively noted the way in which the mythology of the "patriarchal family" was used before the revolution by the autocracy to reinforce loyalty to the regime. The tsar, the ideal father in official mythology, became an attractive symbol because the people sustained the illusory belief that their own problems, both socioeconomic difficulties and unconscious infantile conflicts, might be mitigated somehow through this symbolic identification process. In making these formulations, Reisner was, in many respects, anticipating Freud's own later concepts in *Civilization and Its Discontents* and the Frankfurt School's explorations in the areas of common ground in the writings of Marx and Freud.[17]

By 1925, the lines of confrontation were clearly drawn between supporters and opponents of the application of psychoanalytic theory to Marxism. At this point two things were noteworthy about the character of the continuing debate. First, the Freudian Marxists seemed to be growing not only in numbers but also in influence.[18] Second, practitioners and clinicians had not yet entered the debate over Freud. Until this time it had been conducted by scholars, writers, and party philosophers. The situation changed in 1925 with the appearance of an important essay in a volume called *Psychology and Marxism,* under the imprint of the ubiquitous Soviet State Publishing House. The essay, entitled "Psychoanalysis as a System of Monistic Psychology," was written by Alexander Luria, who had already been involved with the development of psychoanalysis in Kazan and Moscow.

Luria began his article by explaining that Marxism assumed the world to be "a single system of material processes," devoid of dualism and of nonmaterialist and static phenomena. In terms of psychology, this translated into the postulate that "the human mind is a product of the brain and in the final analysis, of the effects of the social environment and the class relations and conditions of production underlying it on the brain and on each individual human being."[19]

He then surveyed the main trends in the field of psychology up to the present time, offering a critique of what he saw as the inadequacies of both the rationalist and the empirical modes of analysis. Essentially, Luria saw earlier psychology as dualistic, subjective, idealist, and "naively empirical." In his opinion the focus for previous inquiry was in the erroneous direction of proving the existence of the soul, dividing the realms of mind and body, and providing static and isolated categories to define sensation, will, or passion. What was missing, Luria argued, was a dynamic approach in which processes were sought out and fitted into a larger structural and functional framework that would make it possible to understand the whole person in the context of society.

The real contribution of psychoanalytic research, Luria continued, was that it had directly confronted the problem of "the motive forces underlying individual behavior and the interests impelling people to create ideological systems."[20] To find the means to answer this problem, psychoanalysis had focused on unconscious mental activity in an objective manner which closely resembled a purely physiological explanation. Unconscious activity was viewed essentially "as an energy process, not different in principle from somatic processes." "Psychic energy" for Luria was analogous to energy in physics—subject to the same laws governing all forms of physical matter in that "it cannot disappear but can be transformed into other energy, assume other forms, or be channeled in a different direction."[21] Luria gave some examples from the literature of psychoanalysis in which symptoms of mental traumas were shown to convert into somatic symptoms (hysteria), or were rechanneled through sublimation or repression to the external or internal realms of the individual's experience. This principle, Luria stated, demonstrated the essential organic unity of the two kinds of energy and represented "a considerable step on the way to constructing a system of monistic psychology."[22] This would be a major theoretical advance in that it would end the mind-body dualism problem and establish a unified concept of human behavior.

In his conclusion, Luria acknowledged that many of these processes were only in the beginning stages of theoretical formulation and empirical proof. Nevertheless, he was convinced that Freud's theory rested on a sound basis and that it offered a "materialist approach to the whole personality and the motive forces of the individual psyche." It had, furthermore, "opened up an entirely new biology of the mind" in which further advances would be forthcoming.[23]

The psychoanalytic community received unexpected support, albeit from an independent, critical perspective, as Lev Vygotsky (1896–1934) joined the debate. Vygotsky came of age in the decade prior to the revolution when the richness, complexity, and experimental modernism of Russian culture was at its height. Educated at the University of Moscow after spending his early years in the provincial town of Gomel', Vygotsky was a gifted student who possessed a voraciously curious intellect. Although his first publications were primarily in the fields of art and literature, he became a recognized expert in psychology with little formal training, largely as a result of his prodigious reading of both leading Russian researchers such as Bekhterev, and Western psychological theory, including the works of William James and Freud. Vygotsky seems to have burst into the world of professional psychology with his lecture on consciousness and conditioned reflexes at the Psychoneurological Congress held in Petrograd in 1924. The impact of this lecture was recorded by Luria, who invited Vygotsky to join him at the Moscow Institute of Psychology. Years later, Luria wrote that he considered Vygotsky "a genius," who impressed him as no one else in science ever did during five decades of professional work.[24]

In 1925, Vygotsky published a seminal paper, "Consciousness as a Problem in the Psychology of Behavior," in which he tried to recast the theoretical orientation of Soviet psychology. One part of the essay was a criticism of much of the research in the field, both in the Soviet Union and in the West, and included a discussion of psychoanalysis. However, he differed from his colleagues in that he tried to theorize a new orientation for the study of the mind in which Freud's studies of the unconscious would be taken quite seriously. Vygotsky's main charge against Soviet psychology in this regard was that in attacking introspection and subjectivism in psychoanalysis, certain basic functions of the mind were dismissed because of their association with Freud and other discredited schools of thought. "By ignoring the problems of consciousness, psychology has deprived itself of access to the study of some rather important and complex problems of human behavior," he wrote. However, Vygotsky had alternatives to propose. One of these had to do with conceptualizing an interrelationship between consciousness and the unconscious which was expressed in a social, rather than an individual, framework through both language and activity. Individual consciousness, for Vygotsky, was embedded in the larger social fabric and functioned in direct relationship to the external, material world.[25] All of this was written in a cautious style that managed to be simultaneously acceptable to the authorities and challenging to the current Soviet research paradigms.

Articles on psychoanalytic themes continued to pour forth as more individuals took sides in the expanding debate. B. D. Fridman, a psychiatrist and colleague of Luria's from the Kazan psychoanalytic group, published a detailed article on the compatibility of Freud's concepts with Marx's theory of historical materialism. Displaying an arsenal of quotations from the writings of both Freud and Marx, Fridman went further than Luria in his conclusion, in which he stated that historical materialism and psychoanalysis shared interrelated goals—the former seeks to direct society toward the resolution and satisfaction of "social needs," whereas the latter strives to resolve and satisfy individual needs.[26]

Other essays appeared in immediate response which were increasingly critical of Freud's ideas. Some dealt with specialized areas of applied psychoanalysis, such as those dealing with art and literature.[27] Yet, because of the turn toward more overt political attacks, these articles revealed a far more sinister process that overwhelmed the stimulating intellectual debate over the role of psychoanalysis in a communist society. This amounted to an ideological war against "Freudianism" in order to delegitimize it completely. Such combat was a very important aspect of the consolidation of communist authority in the postrevolutionary period. It became increasingly common for the government to sabotage an area of potential competitive power (whether it was an institution, an individual, or a set of ideas), to delegitimize it, and then to incorporate that area for itself. Psychoanalysis was experiencing one of the early waves of that assault, which would later engulf many other professions.

Among the many damaging attacks leveled against what the Soviet authorities now referred to derogatorily as "Freudianism" was an article that appeared in the leading Bolshevik journal, *Under the Banner of Marxism,* at the end of 1926, which presented the most comprehensive and devastating critique to date of Freudism theory from a Marxist perspective. In contrast to the earlier, more polemical argument by Iurinets, I. D. Sapir's "Freudism and Marxism" was written with greater objectivity and with direct reference to the psychoanalytic literature. Sapir (1897–?), a member of the Communist Academy in Moscow, made a distinction in this article between the sociological dimension of Freud's work and the psychological core of his theory. He emphasized the latter because he believed that Freud's clinical investigations were both the most important aspect of psychoanalysis and the points of departure for the generalizations about society that had been advanced by the Freudian school.

The bulk of Sapir's paper was a close analysis of what he saw as the inadequacies and contradictions of Freud's major concepts, particularly the idea of the "reality of the unconscious." He asserted that "psychic mechanisms by themselves" could not explain the material reality of social phenomena. These phenomena emanate from "objective factors in the social order" and can be explained only in that framework. The concept of the unconscious, Sapir reminded his readers, had been discussed by Engels and by Lenin as being the result of "nonexistent, insufficient or distorted knowledge of the objective processes of nature and society." Also, Marxists could posit a collective "unconsciousness" only to the extent that it was subject to and conditioned by the socioeconomic realities and productive forces of a given period of history. "Individual unconsciousness could therefore only be a function of the social, not the reverse," Sapir wrote.[28]

Regarding the evidence underlying psychoanalytic theory, Sapir argued that, on the one hand, Freud used classical and literary sources to document the supposed historical timelessness and universality of his concepts. This, Sapir stated, was unacceptable for any branch of knowledge claiming to be a science in the twentieth century. On the other hand, Freud sought to legitimize his theory by utilizing the case histories of his own patients, an approach that presented two further problems. First, the patients themselves were selected products of the collective mentality and social class structure of their society. Their symptoms were reflections of their culture, but they were not objective observers of it. Second, Freud's patients were suffering from forms of pathology from which it would be difficult to draw any conclusions about the norms, motives, and behavior of conventional society as a whole. Sapir admitted that "class society was the richest source of traumatizing influences on the psyche," but it was the nature of that society which ought to be the focus of inquiries into the etiology of distress, not its individual victims.[29]

Finally, Sapir argued that "sexualism as a universal doctrine of the human psyche" was exaggerated and empirically unfounded in Freud's work.[30] The psychoanalytic concepts of sexual drives and the Oedipus conflict as the motive force of human behavior and pathology could not be sustained on a scientific foundation, in spite of efforts by Freud's followers (here Sapir clearly had Luria in mind) to try to demonstrate that libidinal energy conforms to the same laws as energy in physics. Thus, the overall subjectivity and speculative basis of Freudian theory, Sapir concluded, made it utterly incompatible with both Soviet science and the Marxist philosophy of dialectical materialism.[31]

LENIN AND TROTSKY ON PSYCHOANALYSIS

As Soviet psychoanalysts found themselves being drawn into a high-risk political struggle for which they were ill prepared, they continued to engage in their professional and clinical work. Reports of their meetings and research (written by Luria and Vera Schmidt) appeared each year between 1925 and 1927 in the *International Journal of Psychoanalysis,* alongside those of all the other national members of the International Association. In 1925, the Russian Psychoanalytic Society held thirty-one scientific meetings on subjects ranging from castration complexes in children to comparisons between Freud and Pavlov. That year also, Wulff was elected to the editorial board of Freud's *International Journal of Psychoanalysis.* There were twenty scientific meetings of the society in 1926 in addition to numerous conferences and lectures at various educational and medical institutions in Moscow. Translations of Freud's books in the Psychological and Psychoanalytic Library series, edited by Ermakov, were still being published, even if less frequently than before. Occasionally, the political storm brewing outside these meetings crept into their reports, although it was interpreted in an unthreatening manner. Wulff noted, on one occasion, "that the feeling against Freud which is now manifesting itself in Russia is, in the main, simply a repetition of the controversy long ago concluded in Western Europe, with the addition of some new factors."[32]

The "new factors" to which Wulff alluded were undoubtedly a reference to the extraordinary political crisis confronting the entire Russian psychoanalytic community. Regardless of whether the Freudians argued that their work was compatible with Marxism (as Luria, for example, did) or not (as Wulff continued to believe), their positions were becoming more untenable. Meanwhile, the debates over the ideological "correctness" of psychoanalysis wound their way up to the very top of the party leadership.

What did Lenin himself think of psychoanalysis? Although he apparently wrote nothing specifically on this subject, there is some indirect evidence about his attitudes from his wife and from a conversation he had with a visiting German Marxist which was published after his death. Krupskaia, who may have been speaking only for herself, published an article in 1923 in which she wrote: "Freud does not just take into account the role of sexual attraction in our actions. He inordinately exaggerates that role, while explaining all sub-conscious actions by sexual attraction. Many of his explanations are artificial, stretched out and, besides, are permeated by a bourgeois-philistine attitude towards women."[33]

More substantial evidence for Lenin's own views can be found in Klara Zetkin's memoir of Lenin, where the Soviet leader is quoted as follows:

> Freudian theory is the modern fashion. I mistrust the sexual theories of the articles, dissertations, pamphlets, etc., in short, of that particular kind of literature which flourishes luxuriantly in the dirty soil of bourgeois society. I mistrust those who are always contemplating sexual questions, like the Indian saint his navel. It seems to me that these nourishing sexual theories which are mainly hypothetical, and often quite arbitrary hypotheses, arise from the personal need to justify personal abnormality or hypertrophy in sexual life before bourgeois morality. . . . This masked respect for bourgeois morality seems to me just as repulsive as poking about in sexual matters. However wild and revolutionary the behavior may be, it is still really quite bourgeois. It is, mainly, a hobby of the intellectuals and of the sections nearest them. There is no place for it in the Party, in the class conscious, fighting proletariat.[34]

This is apparently the only statement attributed to Lenin on Freud's ideas. *Pravda* published a posthumous statement of Lenin's in 1925 in which he said he "may sometime deliver a lecture or write on [Freud]; but not right now."[35] However, since he never managed to write such an essay, Soviet opponents of Freudianism frequently used Zetkin's recollection of her conversation with Lenin to document Lenin's opposition to psychoanalysis.

But does the Zetkin conversation provide such clear evidence? Examining the passage in context, we find that Lenin was actually talking about "the pamphlet of a young Viennese woman" (unnamed) which Lenin uses as repre-sentative of articles written by communist women who "discuss sexual prob-lems and the question of forms of marriage in the past, present and future," in order "to enlighten proletarian women on those subjects." He mentions Freud in passing because a section of the pamphlet dealt with "the extension of the

Freudian hypotheses" to these areas in a manner which Lenin found objectionable. However, he was speaking neither about Freud nor of Russia, but about the way people misuse this literature. Moreover, Zetkin's recollections of her conversations with Lenin are questionable since the book is an obvious example of Leninist hagiography.

Additional questions about Lenin's alleged hostility to Freudian ideas in Russia have been raised. It has, for instance, been assumed that Lenin knew little of Freud's work and that his opposition to psychoanalysis was coupled with a lack of real interest. Yet, in Lenin's private library, he owned three volumes of Freud translations from the Ermakov series on psychoanalysis. One of these volumes, *Introductory Lectures on Psychoanalysis,* had marginal notations in Krupskaia's hand. There were also some possible personal connections between Lenin and Freud, though they remain indirect and inconclusive. Trotsky, one of Lenin's closest collaborators, was acquainted with psychoanalysis (as we shall shortly see), and the subject may have come up between them at some point. Another link to Freud is through L. O. Darkshevich (1858–1925), who had worked with Freud in Paris and Vienna in the 1880s and who, as professor of neurology at Moscow State University, was one of the physicians who treated Lenin in 1922 when he suffered a stroke.

More to the point are the many party officials who were sympathetic to psychoanalysis and who had direct contacts with Lenin. Chief among these may have been the prominent mathematician Otto Schmidt, who was director of the State Publishing House during the early 1920s at the time when Ermakov's Psychoanalytic Library series was published. Schmidt, who was simultaneously an officer in Moscow Psychoanalytic Society, obviously arranged and personally approved of the series. No multivolume series under the imprint of the Bolshevik-controlled state press could have been published without approval at the highest level of the party. Lenin must have been aware of Schmidt's involvement with the psychoanalytic project and may have even received from Schmidt Freud's books, which were in the Bolshevik leader's library. In addition, Schmidt's wife, Vera, was the de facto director of the psychoanalytic children's school, which was the subject of intense discussions in the Commissariat of Enlightenment. Lenin regularly received summaries of these discussions. Moreover, if Lenin were as opposed to psychoanalysis as the Zetkin conversation indicates, he would hardly have permitted these activities in an era of communist ideological control and limited capital expenditures for necessities.

In addition to Schmidt, Stanislav Shatskii, leader of the government's pedagogical section, defended the continued survival of the psychoanalytic children's school in private government meetings. Also, Pavel Blonskii, an educational psychologist, was affiliated with the Psychoanalytic Society as well as a founder of the Academy for Communist Education (later named after Krupskaia). Mikhail Reisner, the author of several seminal articles on applied psychoanalysis and a member of the Psychoanalytic Society, was at the same time a ranking government official. Indeed, Blonskii and Reisner organized lectures and seminars on Freudianism at the party's Communist Academy during this period. Finally, Bykhovskii's 1923 article on the potential accord between psychoanalysis and Marxism appeared in the party's theoretical organ, *Under the Banner of Marxism.*[36] Despite the fact that all these individuals may have had their own agendas at work in maintaining positions in the ideological whirlpool of Soviet politics at this time, the fact is that they were involved with psychoanalysis.

The case for Trotsky is far less ambiguous, for his writings contain numerous references to Freud. In 1923 (September 27), Trotsky wrote in a private letter to Pavlov: "During my years in Vienna, I came in rather close contact with the Freudians, read their work and even attended their meetings." He expressed his belief that Pavlov and Freud were working toward a similar theory of the mind from opposite points of departure. The Freudians, he stated, had made "a series of clever and interesting albeit scientifically arbitrary conjectures about the properties" of the human mind.[37] Although he stopped short of an endorsement of psychoanalysis in the letter to Pavlov, he did not hesitate to say in his book *Literature and Revolution* that he believed that "the psychoanalytic theory of Freud . . . can be reconciled with materialism."[38] In another statement on the subject in 1926, Trotsky defended the work of Freud's Russian followers against the growing determination of the party to take action against it.

> It would be too simple and crude to declare psycho-analysis as incompatible with Marxism and to turn one's back on it. In any case, we are not obliged to adopt Freudianism either. It is a working hypothesis. It can produce, and it does produce deductions and surmises which point to a materialist psychology. In due time, experimentation will provide the tests. Meanwhile, we have neither reason nor right to declare a ban on a method which, even though it may be less reliable, tries to anticipate results towards which the experimental method advances only very slowly.[39]

Although Trotsky's interest in maintaining psychoanalysis as part of the continuing debate over the establishment of a Marxist psychology was politically helpful to the Soviet Freudians during the mid-1920s, his association with them (however indirect it was in reality) soon became a fatal liability once Trotsky himself fell into political disfavor.

THE COLLAPSE OF PSYCHOANALYSIS

The published records of regular meetings of the Russian Psychoanalytic Society begin to diminish in the late 1920s. At the business meeting on April 7, 1927, Luria resigned as secretary; this was in part a political decision in response to the growing antipsychoanalytic chorus at the Institute of Psychology where he worked. He was replaced by Vera Schmidt, who continued to report on the society's activities to the *International Journal of Psychoanalysis*. In addition to the regular members' presentations of their research, the high point of the activities in 1927 was the meeting of March 10, at which Lev Vygotsky delivered a paper on "The Psychology of Art in Freud's Works."

The society received a far more severe blow when Wulff, who had traveled to Berlin in the fall, decided not only to resign as president, but also to remain abroad as Osipov had done earlier. Wulff was among those in the society who refused to make ideological compromises with communism and was left with little choice as conditions worsened. Wulff eventually settled in Palestine, where he founded the Israel Psychoanalytic Society. He was replaced by Iuri Kannabikh as head of the Moscow organization, but, as Vera Schmidt mentioned in her final report to the International Society, the Russian group "lacks properly trained [psycho]analysts with whom serious work might be undertaken in various fields of medicine and medical organizations." In part this was a consequence of the government's decision to cease funding the Psychoanalytic Institute in 1926, leaving only the Psychoanalytic Society as a working organization for the Freudians.[40]

One of the most devastating and comprehensive critiques of the Soviet Freudians at this time came from a 1927 literary work entitled *Freudianism*. The author, V. N. Voloshinov (1895–1936), had begun this critique two years earlier in an article, "Beyond the Social," but the earlier argument was included in the book. Voloshinov, a member of the circle around the legendary literary critic Mikhail Bakhtin, examined Freud's concepts in detail and then sought to show the weaknesses and errors in psychoanalysis as a whole.

Voloshinov was particularly concerned with the "subjective nature" of Freud's ideas. Psychoanalysis, he argued, was not an objectively observed and proven set of laws or processes, but was the sum of an individual's perceptions. Moreover, these perceptions had taken place in a specific social context, and were tied to the ideological reflections of the relationship between that context and the individual's consciousness. By this, Voloshinov had in mind "ideology in the literal sense, as the expression of class consciousness."[41] In the clinical microcosm, Voloshinov explained, Freud's postulates about the "mechanisms of the psyche" and the "instinctual drives of the unconscious" were in fact realities of the "social interrelationship between doctor and patient," each of whom represents an important aspect of the "social situation" in terms of class, consciousness, and ideology.

Voloshinov also criticized Freud for not understanding that the very language of psychoanalysis was a function of these variables. "The construct of the Oedipus complex is just such a purely ideological formulation projected into the psyche of a child," Voloshinov wrote.[42] Verbal discourse, like thoughts and desires, was shaped in the context of the objective social milieu from which it emerged. This, then, explained the "overestimation of the sexual" component in everyday life that Voloshinov objected to in psychoanalytic thought. Such concepts were inevitably informed by the values of the capitalist system and the conflicts of its leading social classes.[43] In an appendix at the end of the book, Voloshinov included a chapter he called "A Critique of Marxist Apologies of Freudianism," in which he personally criticized, quite tendentiously, the articles favorable to psychoanalysis by Bykhovskii, Luria, Fridman, and Zalkind. Voloshinov concluded with a triumphant blast: "Psychoanalysis is an intimate part of the decaying ideology of the bourgeoisie. . . . A calm, objective analysis of all facets of Freudianism can surely leave no doubt whatever as to the legitimacy of the Marxist assessment of that doctrine presented here."[44]

Another important sign of the disintegration of psychoanalysis can be seen in the dwindling number of clinical studies appearing in journals and books. I. A. Perepel, a Leningrad Freudian, published the last Soviet book on clinical psychoanalysis in 1927. While the book ostensibly was an examination of the treatment of neurotic disorders, Perepel was quite explicit about his primary agenda, which was a critique of the Soviet health system and a recommendation for a new policy respective of "individual freedom for the masses of Soviet citizens" and the "medicine of capitalist society" as part of the overall improvement of health conditions and needed social reforms.[45] The world around him, needless to say, was moving the other way. Although Perepel was unable to gain approval to publish his book with the State Publishing House, he managed to have it privately printed at a time when the government had a legal monopoly on the publishing industry.

Beyond that book, only a few references to psychoanalytic research still appeared during the late 1920s in the country's main psychiatric journal. Fridman's 1928 article appears to be the last published in a clinical journal by an avowed Freudian in which psychoanalytic terms were a central part of the presentation. His article was also one of the last discussions of ambivalent sexual conflicts involving homosexuality and bisexuality to appear in a Soviet psychiatric journal.[46] Not only were psychoanalysis and Freud were being repressed, but crucial areas of research with which the Freudians were particularly concerned were also abolished. Sexual abuse and sexual crimes continued to exist, but they were no longer permitted to be the subject of research and publication.[47] "A ban was imposed on the study of the sexual development of children" because of its association with the name of Freud.[48]

Other signs of the decline of psychoanalysis were visible. In an unsigned report to the Tenth Congress of the International Psychoanalytic Association, the dilemma of the Russian Freudians was communicated in tragic terms: "We shall all understand that our colleagues there are working under very difficult conditions, and I should like, in the name of us all, to express our deep sympathy with them."[49] Another piece of evidence can be seen in the changing nature of the forewords introducing each volume of Ermakov's Psychological and Psychoanalytic Library series. The earlier volumes, published in the early and mid-1920s, contain enthusiastic forewords, frequently written by Ermakov himself, with lavish praise for Freud as a revolutionary scientist who succeeded in his work against great professional opposition. Indeed, only a few years before, Vygotsky and Luria had written in their preface to the 1925 Russian edition of Freud's *Beyond the Pleasure Principle* that Freud was "one of the most intrepid among the great minds of our times," and that most of the objections against the popularity of psychoanalysis in Soviet Russia "will not stand up to even the slightest touch of critical thinking."[50] Such assessments were no longer printable.

By the end of the decade, the prefaces reflected the political pressures confronting the psychoanalytic community in Russia. A case in point is the foreword to the Russian translation of Freud's *Future of an Illusion* (1930) in which Ermakov wrote about the relationship between psychoanalysis and the middle-class values of Western capitalist societies. The shift in content from the science of psychology to the ideology of politics in those prefaces is unmistakable.[51]

In the midst of these developments, Wilhelm Reich arrived in Moscow in August 1929 for a two-month visit. Reich, a member both of the Vienna Psychoanalytic Society and the Marxist Social Democratic party, had been engaged in disagreements with Freud on theoretical and clinical issues at the same time that he was investigating the theoretical confluence of communism and psychoanalysis.[52] Although other Freudians in the West had similar interests, Reich was the only psychoanalyst from Vienna who came to Moscow to develop his inquiry on communist soil.

Reich presented several lectures, the themes of which were published in an article under the auspices of the Communist Academy.[53] Reich's acceptability in party and government circles in Moscow stemmed directly from his explicit renunciation of several of Freud's central concepts and from his equally explicit embrace of the cause of communism. His lecture at the Communist Academy expressed a somewhat sanguine view of the possibilities of psychoanalysis in the Soviet Union, though at the same time he made his own plea for tolerance of psychoanalysis in the ongoing struggles over psychological orientations. In a later article, Reich stated that the discussion following his lecture at the Academy "made it clear that the Russians have nothing against psychoanalysis as a psychological discipline, but they are opposed only to so-called 'Freudism,' by which they mean a 'psychoanalytic view of the world.' "[54]

The distinction is an important one, but Reich was exaggerating its significance in 1929. Officially, the regime continued to separate the practice of psychoanalytic psychotherapy from Freud's theory, in principle accepting the former and rejecting the latter. Indeed, even the party-sponsored and widely read *Great Soviet Encyclopedia* and *Medical Encyclopedia* articles on psychoanalysis which were written and approved in the 1930s still made this distinction. However, in practice, the condemnation of Freud's works created a chilling effect on the survival of psychoanalysis as a therapeutic practice.

Reich's portrait of psychoanalysis in Soviet Russia as a thriving discipline was inaccurate, and provoked angry responses both at home and abroad. Among these was a revealing article by Moshe Wulff, who had been the country's leading psychoanalyst until his recent emigration from the Soviet Union. From the vantage point of Berlin, he felt able to express his feelings about the role of psychoanalysis in the Soviet Union, and how different that was from Reich's presentation.

> The reader who thinks he will find in [Reich's] article an objective description of the present situation or of the historical development of psychoanalysis in Russia will be heavily disappointed in this expectation. Reich's publication is, basically, only an attempt to adapt psychoanalysis to the wishes and demands of its communist critics in order to make it more acceptable from their point of view. But psychoanalysis has badly suffered from the attempt, and such a great deal of it was sacrificed that the remains hardly deserve the name of psychoanalysis. . . . The real situation in the

Soviet Union is quite simple, and by no means exceptional. The fate of [psycho-analysis] is shared by, for instance, the theory of relativity, quantum theory, phenom-enology, gestalt theory, modern philosophy and psychology, and even biology. . . . Each new thought, each idea, each new theoretical-scientific discovery is being received with the utmost distrust and suspicion . . . and it is not surprising that psychoanalysis, standing trial before this strict Party tribunal, could not be pro-nounced free of all guilt. . . . One can say with certainty that a strong and productive psychoanalytic movement would develop in Russia if it would not meet the authori-ties' energetic opposition. But what Reich has described is the opinion of the ruling Communist Party of the USSR, and this is what the title of his essay ought to have been.[55]

Reich, however, also was severely criticized by a group of specialists from the Communist Academy in Moscow who believed he had both exaggerated the importance and misunderstood the significance of psychoanalysis in commu-nist Russia.[56] The results of Reich's sojourn appear to have been negligible for the declining psychoanalytic community in Moscow. No further discussion about him occurred in the Soviet media. Echoes of his trip were heard in Europe, but they concerned conflicts in the psychoanalytic movement there rather than developments in the Soviet Union.[57]

Soon after the dust settled following Reich's departure, the psychoanalytic community was silenced. The last report from Vera Schmidt on the activities of the Russian Psychoanalytic Society appeared in 1930, with the notation that at the meeting of February 17, Fridman discussed "the criticisms of psycho-analysis" made at the First All-Union Congress of Psychologists in Moscow.[58] This time, there was no one to defend Freud's name among the psychologists. The last translated work of Freud to be published in the Ermakov series appeared in 1930.[59] There was even an obituary notice. The pronouncement of the end of clinical psychoanalysis from within the analytic community was made by a former psychoanalyst from Leningrad in a brief communication published some years later. He wrote that "the psychoanalytic movement slowed down, and about the year 1930 came to a standstill. From this date it officially ceased to exist and all publication of its work ceased likewise."[60]

Chapter 6 Killing Freud

Why does Soviet psychology reject Freud's teaching? Above all, we have the incompatibility of the entire methodology of Freudianism with generally accepted methods for the establishment of scientific data, the arbitrary character of psychoanalytic dogmas, the therapeutic ineffectiveness of the psychoanalytic method, the harm done to public health by psychoanalysis as a result of deflecting attention from the true capacities of medicine and prophylaxis, the demoralizing influences spread by psychoanalysis, especially in the younger generation, which give criticism the place of a leading social principle and encourage the very worst forms of decadent literature and art. Other reasons for our rejection include the nonscientific interpretation of the role which the so-called unconscious plays in normal and pathological behavior, the grossly biological explanation which psychoanalysis gives for sociological problems and the reactionary role which this point of view plays by masking the true causes of social disasters with discussions of "displacement" instead of concentrating on the tasks related to the struggle against class exploitation and other negative aspects of the capitalist system.
—*F. Bassin (1962)*

THE THREAT FROM WITHIN AND FREUD'S
ASSESSMENT OF THE SITUATION FROM
WITHOUT

The silencing of the Soviet Freudians, their institutions, and their ideas at the end of the 1920s was part of a wider political transition which the entire country was experiencing. The open debates over Freud and psychoanalysis during the 1920s had served their purpose. As long as the party leadership felt itself in need of legitimation, it accommodated psychoanalysis as part of the effort to establish a Marxist psychology. Soviet communism was therefore initially receptive to Freudian thought as one possible mode of explaining human behavior. Between 1925 and 1930, however, psychoanalysis was eliminated, together with other unacceptable psychological orientations traceable to Western antisocialist influences. Moreover, the attack on the psychoanalytic community was not an isolated phenomenon. It was part of the intentional shift from a creative period of competitive theories to one in which any concept or organization could be seen as a threat to the hardening doctrine of Stalinism.

As the infrastructure of "socialism in one country" took hold, all aspects of social relations had to be subordinated to the governing whole. During the late 1920s, in the name of "building socialism," surviving modes of private ownership—banks, businesses, schools, or land—were nationalized or abolished. With the collapse of the policies associated with the New Economic Policy and the establishment of the first Five-Year Plan in 1928, the distinction between public and private spheres was obliterated in exclusive favor of the former. What fell outside the approved public realm was relegated to the domain of "counterrevolutionary forces." More to the point, the concept of socialism in a single country at war with the capitalist world meant that internationalist movements like psychoanalysis, with its institutes stretching from America to Europe, were viewed as oppositional and dangerous.

Psychoanalysis was also vulnerable to Bolshevik attack because of its emphasis on sexuality. Part of the ideological and institutional transformation of the late 1920s focused on the problem of sexuality in a revolutionary society. There were many currents of activity on this problem which were of concern to the party. Alexandra Kollontai, party activist and director of the revolutionary Women's Sections (*Zhenotdel*), had stirred emotions on the "sexual question" even before the revolution, but in the 1920s she published a series of articles on the "new morality" which provoked widespread criticism. Her 1923 article, "Make Way for Winged Eros," was particularly challenging in this regard.

Kollontai attempted to conceptualize a new, socialist form of love, named in the title of the article, in which sexual relations would reflect mutual respect among comrades living in conditions of class equality. Rather than being dominated by possessiveness, competition, and hostility—the "wingless Eros" of bourgeois social relationships—love under socialism, according to Kollontai, would be transformed in the following manner: "Respect for the right of the other's personality will increase, and a mutual sensitivity will be learned; men and women will strive to express their love not only in kisses and embraces but in joint creativity and activity. The task of proletarian ideology is not to drive Eros from social life, but to rearm him according to the new social formation, and to educate sexual relationships in the spirit of the great new psychological force of comradely solidarity."[1]

The party's reaction to Kollontai's sexual ideology was clear but cannot be entirely separated from her involvement with the Worker's Opposition groups, whose advocacy of worker autonomy was even more threatening. Still, Kollontai's ideas, published in newspapers as well as in novels, were perceived by her critics to resonate widely in the society as a whole. Moreover, the resumption of prostitution under the less restrictive conditions of NEP, the apparent rise in the rate of suicides, especially high-profile cases like the death of the poet Sergei Esenin,[2] and the presumed excesses of sexual behavior that took place in the student population all fed the flames ignited by Kollontai's very public discussion of the potential values of love and sex for communism. Added to this was the trial in December 1926 of twenty-six defendants charged with gang-raping a young woman in Leningrad, an event which was covered very openly in the press and interpreted as a graphic illustration of the epidemic of sexual depravity against which the party had to take decisive action.[3] The rape case in Leningrad was especially disturbing because the perpetrators were members of the Communist youth organization (Komsomol). Punishment was severe to make an example of the convicted defendants—six were sentenced to death and nineteen others received jail sentences.

These years also produced regulatory legislation on marriage, divorce, and abortion, committees to combat prostitution, and discussions in the press and Bolshevik party meetings about the need for greater moral vigilance. The Freudians became directly involved in this reaction when a member of their own community published a set of essays in which he offered a program to combat the sexual menace. Aron Zalkind hypothesized that sexual desire was a fixed amount of energy in each individual which could either be wasted in acts of depraved, excessive, and self-gratifying sexual relations or be utilized in healthier "collectivist activities" which would benefit the working class and the party. Zalkind took his ideological moralism farther by actually describing communist-approved sexual behavior. In his notorious "Twelve Commandments," he warned against marriage prior to age twenty, asserted that women (but not men) wished to remain monogamous, and believed that interclass sex was a form of "sexual perversion." For interested readers, Zalkind even cited specific cases of "sexual exhaustion" that needed to be brought under control.[4]

A series of legislative acts in this period also attacked homosexuals as further examples of depraved sexuality. In 1934, Maxim Gorky, the Soviet Union's leading exponent of Socialist Realism, stated proudly that "in the land where the proletariat governs courageously and successfully, homosexuality, with its corrupting effect on the young, is considered a social crime punishable under the law." He contrasted this, sarcastically, with the West, where "it is practiced freely and with impunity." In a similar vein, Justice Minister Nikolai Krylenko, in a 1936 speech to the party's Central Executive Committee on amendments to the existing criminal code, equated homosexuality ("pederasty in foul, secret dens") with "counterrevolutionary work," labeling it essentially an act of state treason.[5] As one contemporary observer put it: "No theory, particularly in conditions of the sharpening of the class struggle, could be free of politics."[6] Sexuality, because it represented individual self-expression and had the potential to involve masses of people in a moral issue about human liberty outside the control of the party, clearly posed a particularly fearful challenge to the party.

This atmosphere helps explain why psychoanalysis was assaulted with such force. Despite the efforts of its supporters to prove otherwise, psychoanalysis remained at its core a system of ideas about personality development and a clinical approach to certain mental disturbances that could not be subsumed within a Marxist framework or a Bolshevik polity. Its theoretical foundations were rooted in sexual conflicts operating within the individual's unconscious, whereas Marxism's assumptions centered on class conflicts in the external world of socioeconomic relations of groups. Both psychoanalysis and Marxism were interpreting these respective conflicts with undertones of determinism that made rapprochement between them unacceptable to both. They each had prescriptions for the relief of society's suffering, but whereas Freud sought to mediate the internalized conflict between the individual's instinctual need for both gratification and social adaptation, Marxist-Leninist ideology operated on a terrain of incessant class warfare, which, in theory, would cease to cause oppression and inequality only after the exploitation of labor was terminated. Moreover, while Marxism foresaw an end to conflict through revolution that would empower the underclasses, psychoanalysis was based on the presumption of conflict as inherent to the human condition. Conflict in psychoanalytic theory was repetitive, regardless of the material circumstances of social classes, because the inner drives of the individual seeking gratification stood at odds with society's demands.

Freud himself, though obviously unable to follow the debate about his theory in the Bolshevik journals, was well informed about the demise of psychoanalysis on the clinical level in the Soviet Union. In an unpublished letter of February 23, 1927, he wrote about this situation to Osipov in Prague: "Things are going poorly for the [psycho]analysts in Soviet Russia, by the way. From somewhere the Bolsheviks have gotten it into their heads that psychoanalysis is hostile to their system. You know the truth that our science cannot be placed at the service of any party, but that it needs a certain liberal-mindedness [*Freiheitlichkeit*] in turn for its own development."[7]

During the late 1920s, Freud made further statements on what he saw as the implications of the Soviet experiment with socialism and revolution. In his *Future of an Illusion* (1927) and more directly in *Civilization and Its Discontents* (1930), he expressed serious reservations about the future prospects of a communist society in which private property was abolished and the bourgeois class made into an officially approved enemy. "The psychological premises on which the [communist] system is based," he wrote, "are an untenable illusion." Human aggression has not been altered in its fundamental nature in this process and will probably only be rechanneled into new areas of social conflict. "One only wonders, with concern," he concluded, "what the Soviets will do after they have wiped out their bourgeoisie."[8]

In a 1933 paper "The Question of a *Weltanschauung*," Freud turned his attention to the Soviet Union more extensively than anywhere else in his published writings. Freud defined this German term for "worldview" as "an intellectual construction which solves all the problems of our existence uniformly on the basis of one overriding hypothesis, which, accordingly, leaves no question unanswered and in which everything that interests us finds its fixed place. It will be easily understood that the possession of a Weltanschauung of this kind is among the ideal wishes of human beings. Believing in it, one can feel secure in life, one can know what to strive for, and how one can deal most expediently with one's emotions and interests."[9]

Freud saw great dangers in the seductive power of any system of belief which appealed to what he viewed as universal wishes in this way. In contrast, he saw science as the modern mode of truth-searching whose task was to conduct experiments, unrestricted by any imposed "uniformity of explanation." It is a fact, Freud continued, "that the truth cannot be tolerant, that it admits of no compromise or limitations, that research regards every sphere of human activity as belonging to it and that it must be relentlessly critical if any other power tries to take over any part of it."[10] This is what Freud had in mind when he used the term *Freiheitlichkeit* in his letter to Osipov to describe the conditions necessary for psychoanalysis to flourish. For Freud, psychoanalysis was a science whose contribution "lies precisely in having extended [scientific] research to the mental field." Moreover, "without such a psychology, science would be very incomplete."

On the other hand, Freud continued, the threats to science and to the process of unrestricted truth-searching have come mainly from religion, which derives its notions from "revelation, intuition or divination" rather than through any empirical investigation. "Religion," Freud wrote, "is an attempt to master the sensory world in which we are situated by means of the wishful world which we have developed within us as a result of biological and psychological necessities." By avoiding the need to find solutions in this world and promising illusions of transcendental escape, religion remains a divisive force in the modern world, creating conditions of further unhappiness for mankind. The main hope for Freud was that intellect, or reason, might "exercise a unifying influence on men," who continue to be "held together with such difficulty and whom it is therefore scarcely possible to rule." In a passage that appears to parallel Marx's idea of the dictatorship of the proletariat, he said: "Our best hope for the future is that intellect—the scientific spirit, reason— may in the process of time establish a dictatorship in the mental life of man. The nature of reason is a guarantee that afterwards it will not fail to give man's emotional impulses and what is determined by them the position they deserve."[11]

For Freud, Marxist political ideology played the role of religious commitment in Soviet Russia. While Freud conceded that Marx's ideas had "acquired an undeniable authority" in recent times, he was skeptical of the notion that societies developed through different stages as a "process of natural history," and of the concept of a "dialectical process" of class conflict operating in history with lawful consistency and regularity. In Freud's view, "the class structure of society goes back to the struggles which, from the beginning of history, took place between human hordes only slightly differing from each other. Social distinctions were originally distinctions between clans and races. Victory was decided by psychological factors . . . and by material factors," but not by the latter alone, as Marx had argued.

Freud realized that the "strength of Marxism clearly lies, not in its view of history or the prophecies of the future that are based on it, but on its sagacious indication of the decisive influence which the economic circumstances of men have upon their intellectual, ethical and artistic attitudes." However, these ideas brought with them "a temptation not to leave alterations [in economic relations] to the course of historical development, but to put them into effect oneself by revolutionary action." According to Freud, Bolshevism had come to embody this temptation in Soviet Russia, and, as a result, had "acquired the energy and the self-contained and exclusive character of a *Weltanschauung*." Using merely the name, instead of the method, of science, it had "created a prohibition of thought which is just as ruthless as was that of religion in the past. Any critical examination of Marxist theory is forbidden, and doubts of its correctness are punished in the same way as heresy was once punished by the Catholic church. The writings of Marx have taken the place of the Bible and the Koran as a source of revelation." Thus, in Freud's view, this "practical Marxism" in Russia had, in the course of sweeping away its antagonists, created illusions of its own "which are no less questionable and unprovable than the earlier ones." Human nature was to be fundamentally altered in the "new order of society" under communism where work would supposedly be undertaken without compulsion or oppression.

Such a transformation, Freud wrote, was most doubtful. What would more likely occur was a shifting of the "instinctual restrictions which are essential in society," a diversion of "the aggressive tendencies which threaten all human communities" to enemies elsewhere while encouraging the hostility of the poor against the wealthy and "of the hitherto powerless against the former rulers." Bolshevism had to compensate its believers and followers for suffering in the present by promising a radiant future of complete gratification. Such an emotional paradise cannot exist, and thus new conflicts were bound to emerge. To maintain the illusion, however, Freud argued that doctrinal coercion in education and restrictions on thought and activity were inevitable under men who were "unshakable in their convictions, inaccessible to doubt, without feeling for the suffering of others if they stand in the way of their intentions."

In spite of these concerns, Freud acknowledged the boldness and courage of the country in its efforts to carry out "the tremendous experiment of producing a new order of this kind." It was a departure from the traditional policies of the leaders of great nations who, throughout history, tended to "expect salvation only from the maintenance of Christian piety." Still, Freud worried that the Bolshevik "message of a better future" would fail because it had been undertaken prematurely: "A sweeping alteration of the social order has little prospect of success until new discoveries have increased our control over the forces of nature, and so made easier the satisfaction of our needs. Only then perhaps may it become possible for a new social order not only to put an end to the material need of the masses but also to give a hearing to the cultural demands of the individual. Even then, to be sure, we shall still have to struggle for an incalculable time with the difficulties which the untameable character of human nature presents to every kind of social community."[12]

THE WAR AGAINST PSYCHOANALYSIS

The "sweeping alteration of the social order," as Freud called it, was already moving into high gear at the time that he was formulating his thoughts on the Soviet experiment. With Lenin dead, Trotsky expelled from the country, and the New Economic Policy brought to an end, Stalin felt ready to launch a massive cultural offensive against all sectors of society remaining resistant to the party's dictates. Although the term *cultural revolution* has traditionally been applied to the period of the 1930s to describe the structure of the new socialist order under Stalinism, the real revolution in culture was already over by then. Whereas in the twenties, competing orientations were permitted—indeed encouraged—to make clear their contribution to the emerging postrevolutionary order, the next decade dawned ominously with a congress empowered to establish guidelines for future inquiries into the nature of man and society. The criteria for these new boundaries seemed to be based, more than ever, on political rather than scientific or intellectual grounds.

The 1930 Congress on Human Behavior, where these criticisms of the past and guidelines for the future were presented, differed completely from the 1923 Psychoneurological Congress, which had epitomized the spirit of searching and the pluralism of viewpoints that characterized the twenties. At the 1923 congress, which was covered by reporters from *Pravda* and *Izvestiia,* supporters of introspective psychology and Freudian psychoanalysis vied with adherents of behaviorism, reflexology, and biological psychiatry. The 906 delegates listened to presentations concerned with immediate problems.[13]

By the time the delegates arrived in Moscow for the 1930 congress, Stalin had crushed the remaining sources of opposition in the party and begun his assault on the peasantry with his collectivization program in the countryside. Terms like "enemies of the people," "wreckers," and "bourgeois deviationists" began to appear with increasing frequency in the daily press as well as in various party pronouncements. As proclaimed in the proceedings of the Sixteenth Party Conference: "Every essential element of the Five-Year Plan must deeply penetrate the consciousness of every worker, every peasant"; moreover, the party "must not make the slightest concession . . . to those trends which find their way into our ranks from the petty-bourgeois element."[14]

The political battle within the party quickly spilled over into the trenches of professional organizations. At the 1930 Congress on Human Behavior, the speeches assumed the inflections and metaphors of that battle. The purpose of the congress, convened by the Society of Materialist Psychoneurologists of the Communist Academy of Sciences, was to resolve the disputes among the competing psychological theories and establish an authoritative Marxist psychology. These disputes centered on the battles over psychological methodology, the relationship between psychological and physiological phenomena, the role of the social environment in a communist society and, above all, the importance for psychology of the Bolshevik-inspired concept of consciousness.[15]

Three thousand delegates attended the congress, and 170 speeches were presented. The speakers were not only academics and researchers but Bolshevik party philosophers as well. The highest ranking party official on the program was Lunacharsky, the former Commissar of Education. The week-long meeting was able to define what was to be condemned more effectively than what was to be supported. Many major psychologists of the 1920s were criticized for failing to create a unified psychology that was thoroughly grounded in Marxist principles and completely free of bourgeois influences from the West. The psyche, of such concern to the Freudians in the 1920s, was now to be studied in terms of its "materialist substratum" in the context of biological evolutionary theory and the science of physiology.[16]

What is striking about these papers is how polemical the professional scholarship on human behavior had become. The aggressive style and adversarial content of earlier political struggles, which had characterized the Bolshevik party both before its rise to power and especially since the revolution, were now brought into the domains of science, research, and culture. Not only were theories criticized; they were condemned, which was tantamount to prohibition. To be publicly named as a theorist or researcher who was not working within the narrowing paradigm established by the party was a ticket to professional oblivion fraught with still graver possibilities.

The career of Aron Zalkind, one of the organizers of the congress and its keynote speaker, illustrates this problem. Zalkind had been identified with the Soviet Freudians during the 1920s until the criticism of psychoanalysis reached irreversible levels. By decade's end, he had moved full circle to become one of the party's official critics of psychoanalysis. Zalkind held positions in several high state institutions, including the Institute for Communist Education and the Communist Academy, both of which were organs of the party's Central Committee. At the congress, Zalkind's speech was designed to be the death knell for the Soviet Freudians. His critique, filled with sarcasm and mockery, was meant to transmit the message that any remaining hopes for the survival of psychoanalysis in the Soviet Union were illusory and misguided.

> Suppose we receive the assignment of studying the child or the adult in an institution composed of Freudians. How would this collective of Freudians carry out their assigned task? Now, *for Freud,* man exists entirely in the past. This past is at war with the present, and it is more powerful than the present. *For Freud,* the personality poses an elemental gravitation toward the past, and [all] attempts to fight the past from the standpoint of the present lead to profound tragedy. *For Freud,* the conscious is subordinate to the unconscious. Man is preserved from the demands of society in a private little world in which he constructs a special strategy of behavior. *For Freud,* man is a pawn of internal, elemental forces.
>
> What sort of results will we get . . . ? How can we use the Freudian conception of man for socialist construction? We need a socially "open" man who is easily collectivized, and quickly and profoundly transformed in his behavior—a man capable of being a steady, conscious, and independent person, politically and ideologically well trained. Does the "Freudian Man" meet the demands of the task of socialist construction? . . . From such an institution composed of Freudians, we would get from their study of human behavior such very "significant" statements as that man selects "unconsciously," and that the past directs all of his behavior.[17]

Zalkind's patronizing dismissal of Freud was intended to isolate psychoanalysis from the terrain approved by the party. He emphasized the need for all disciplines concerned with mental health—psychiatry, neurology, and psychology—to form a "united, moral and productive synthesis" in order to combat the problems of a socialist society. This synthesis, according to Zalkind, had to be rooted "in the methodology of dialectical materialism" and dedicated to raising material conditions to the highest possible level for the young generation growing up under socialism and for the "laboring masses" of the whole country. "Questions concerning the psyche" and "the dynamics of human behavior" would be directed to the attention of specialists in the new field of psychopathology, which was called "pedology." Referring to Freud and Bergson in the coded vocabulary of the moment, Zalkind proclaimed that "idealist and vitalist interpretations of the life process" would be incorporated into the empirical methods of neurological and psychiatric research. Furthermore, the "apolitical" attitudes of people seeking to work outside the interpretive structure of social classes as posited by Marx and Lenin were to be "liquidated." Problems once defined as centered on individuals were now to be reconceptualized in the framework of "proletarian collectivism." Zalkind also included a direct attack on "Western bourgeois values" which fostered elitism and racism; he called for new standards in research which would reflect the values of proletarian socialism to be established by Soviet "pedological specialists."[18]

Zalkind, as one of the party's leading activists in psychiatry, was in a favorable position to help formulate a specifically Soviet and socialist concept for the study of "pedology." This term was designed as a classification cutting across professional boundaries in which psychiatrists, neurologists, and psychologists could work jointly on tasks of common social concern that would also further the government's political projects. A significant part of the pedology project involved the testing of children by educational and child psychologists. A journal, *Pedology,* was set up to publish this research, with Zalkind as the editor. The field was to focus on the study of children, with a view to addressing both family problems affecting young children and delinquency problems that became evident during school years. The underlying goal of Zalkind's project was to allow party supervisors to manage the problems which had been defined by the Freudians as crucial to development, while making it clear that all psychoanalytic concepts were to be repudiated.

Thus, the groundwork was established for psychoanalysis to be equated with being anti-Soviet and bourgeois while the state appropriated many psychoanalytic interests in the name of the new Soviet sciences. These were very serious insinuations, since they suggested to the broader public that anyone associated with such ideas was likely to be engaged in antigovernment and counterrevolutionary activities. These exclusionary identifications, repeated by other speakers at the congress, were enforced in a variety of fields after the delegates returned home.

As the policies for acceptable areas of research were being established in the aftermath of the congress, the war against Freud's influence became more intense. Indeed, the crescendo of criticism suggests not only the threat posed by Freud to the new Stalinist psychologists but also the lingering presence of psychoanalytic currents at this time in spite of all the efforts to eliminate them. To the perceptive observer, this continued interest in psychoanalysis was visible at the 1930 congress. One speaker, B. N. Birman, criticized Freud's "pansexualism," but also admitted that psychoanalysis, free of this negative component, contributed to the study of neuropathological behavior, as long as it was used in conjunction with other methods of psychotherapy. Iurii Kannabikh advocated the theories of Alfred Adler over those of Freud in spite of "substantial inadequacies" in psychoanalysis as a whole. The ambivalence in these speeches about psychoanalysis should not detract from the fact that both Birman and Kannabikh were acting with some courage in admitting even the "limited" value of psychoanalysis at the very moment when it was being officially dismantled. Kannabikh served as the last head of the Psychoanalytic Society and wrote objectively of Freud and the psychoanalytic movement—given the politically constraining atmosphere—in his magisterial textbook on the history of world psychiatry.[19]

Nevertheless, the war against Freud went on without any public advocates willing or able to defend psychoanalysis. It was no longer a debate, but a search for the most effective criticism to discredit psychoanalysis. The only question was how devastating the attack would be. The answer came quickly. The first example of this coordinated attack appeared shortly after the 1930 Congress on Human Behavior had completed its deliberations. Titled *Dialectical Materialism and the Mechanists,* by A. Stoliarov, this book went through five editions in a matter of months. In one of its chapters, called "Freudism and the Freudo-Marxists," the author not only criticized psychoanalytic theory, but, more important from the party's point of view, also denounced communists who had been propagators of Freud's work in the Soviet Union. This was a classic Stalin-era witch-hunt, with professional reputations destroyed overnight by publications like this one. The individuals under attack in Stoliarov's book were Reisner, A. Variash, and Zalkind. Reisner, whose articles on religion and social psychology contributed significantly to the diffusion of psychoanalysis in the mid-1920s, was criticized by Stoliarov for his "sympathetic" introduction to the Russian translation of the first biography of Freud, written by Franz Wittels. Stoliarov also "exposed" Variash's "subjective" interpretation of Freud in a lecture Variash had presented at the Communist Academy as well as in several of his articles that had appeared in highly regarded party publications. Above all, however, Stoliarov directed his attention to Zalkind, whom he criticized, together with Reisner and Variash, for having earlier succumbed to the "error" that Freudianism was compatible with Marxism.

According to Stoliarov, "the psychology of Freud was 'anti-social' because of its ultra-individualist character. Freudism had nothing in common with Marxism and materialism." He also mentioned the "antiproletarian character of the ideology of Freudism," which was mired in subjective methods and the satisfaction of erotic impulses. The duty of Marxists, Stoliarov concluded, was to combat this "wave of bourgeois reaction against materialism" in the Soviet Union and bring the spread of Freudian ideas to an end.[20] Thus, Stoliarov was clearly associating his three comrades with these anti-Marxist tendencies simply by virtue of their former sympathy with Freud's ideas.

The technique of attributing political consequences to theoretical positions outside of politics proved to be quite effective. In 1932, the journal *Psychology* published several articles in which the boundaries between ideological politics and scientific scholarship were eliminated entirely. A group of young psychologists at the Moscow Institute of Psychology affiliated with the Communist party, who had begun their ascent into politics at this point, took over the responsibility for the continuing expansion of Stalinist ideology into the psychological professions. In the lead article in the first issue of *Psychology* in 1932, F. Shemiakin and L. Gershonovich published their speech to the Society of Materialist Psychoneurologists at the Communist Academy of Science on "how Trotsky and Kautsky have revised Marxism in problems of psychology." It is a good example of the extreme uses to which ideology was put by Stalin's loyalists in order to consolidate their own political authority and to ensure unchallenged obedience in the professions. The emerging pattern revealed that each time a doctrinal position appeared to be established, it was undermined, leading to the replacement of one set of leading players with another. Just as Zalkind seemed to have achieved a degree of political stability after renouncing Freudianism and championing pedology, pedology itself was attacked, he lost his position and disappeared from sight completely.[21]

The most damaging trend in this official assault on psychoanalytic theory was the association of Freud directly with counterrevolutionary political trends in the Soviet Union. In their article, Shemiakin and Gershonovich referred to a published letter of Stalin's entitled "On Several Problems in the History of Bolshevism." In their view, the letter had "enormous significance" because it not only dealt "a destructive blow" to Trotsky's counterrevolutionary, anti-Marxist, and bourgeois influence, but also "raises to new heights the working out of the problem of our science," psychology. Previously, the "purely empirical and experimental basis of bourgeois schools of psychology" had been accepted by Soviet neurologists and psychiatrists. However, Soviet psychologists had "exposed" the inconsistencies and inaccuracies of those schools, and they had to be rejected in favor of "specifically Soviet theories," as Stalin proposed. No mention was made of the fact that these "Soviet theories" were constantly in flux and changed rather quickly according to the shifting positions of the party leadership.

Trotsky's main difficulty, the authors continued, was his physiological reductionism, the belief that all psychological phenomena were reducible to the laws of physics and biology. Moreover, they argued that Trotsky had obliterated Lenin's notion of "the relative boundary between thought and matter," between mental processes and brain functions. Apart from scoring ideological points, the authors mainly criticized Trotsky's attempt to unify the theories of Freud and Pavlov, as evidenced by Trotsky's letter to Pavlov, and his admission of involvement in Freudian circles while in Vienna before the revolution. Quoting the Klara Zetkin memoir where Lenin mentioned that Freud's theory was a "faddish mode," the authors concluded that Trotsky had "capitulated to bourgeois psychology." Thus, Shemiakin and Gershonovich joined Freud's work and Trotsky's politics as "harmful to Marxism-Leninism," recommending that they both had to be countered vigorously on "the psychoneurological front."[22] The underlying drive to discredit any and all theories with the potential to obtain a measure of independence from the Stalinist school became glaringly clear.

A similar article appeared at the same time written by A. Talankin, another member of this politically oriented group of young psychologists working at the Moscow Institute of Psychology. Talankin's purpose was also to celebrate Stalin and to criticize Freud, except that he chose to accomplish this by attacking one of the most longstanding sources of political opposition to Lenin, the Mensheviks. Although they were Marxists, the Mensheviks had been critical of Lenin's Bolshevik faction ever since the original division within the Russian Social Democratic Labor party at the Second Party Congress in 1903. Despite the fact that the Mensheviks had been suppressed after the 1917 revolution and were no longer a threat to Stalin, the tactic of labeling his enemies as "Mensheviks" was still useful.

Once again, Stalin was cited in this article, but this time for his statement at the recent Sixteenth Party Congress in which he directed attention to the importance of "the psychology of the masses and their relationships to labor." For the successful formulation of a truly Marxist psychology which transcended the unresolved problems of bourgeois psychology, efforts were required to focus on this collective phenomenon, "the psyche of the people," as Talankin put it. This, however, could not be accomplished until the influences of bourgeois trends in Soviet psychology were completely eliminated. Foremost among these remained "the theory of the unconscious," which continued to attract followers. Psychoanalysis, for Talankin, was the anti-Bolshevik enemy in psychology that Menshevism represented in politics.[23]

Talankin's article was followed by a contribution from Alexander Luria. This was a critical point in Luria's professional life, since he had been one of the leading Soviet Freudians during the mid-1920s, and had already endured direct public criticism in Voloshinov's book. Moreover, he had been privately warned by his colleague Vygotsky to be careful. Vygotsky had recently attended a lecture given by Talankin in which the latter stated that "the cultural-psychological conception of Vygotsky and Luria has to be fought seriously." Describing the Talankin attack in a letter to Luria, Vygotsky concluded that the party had decided that they would be "beaten, but not killed."[24]

In his 1932 article, Luria seemed to accept the party's line as espoused by Shemiakin and Talankin, though a careful reading of his article, entitled "The Crisis in Bourgeois Psychology," shows that he chose his words with great care. In reviewing a wide range of recent work in Western psychology, Luria found all of it to be in fundamental opposition to Marxism. The basic dividing point, he argued, was that Marxism "approaches the psyche of contemporary man as a product of development, as a complex process emerging as a result of the development of labor and social relations." Bourgeois psychology, on the other hand, saw the psyche as a "natural product, not linked to the history of society or to any organic ties." Marx knew that man's psyche could not exist without a direct and dynamic connection to society, history, and labor. Bourgeois psychologists, however, continued to speak of "psychological laws emanating from 'the natural characteristics of man'" as though the psyche could be isolated from its social environment by using analogies from biology and physics. Above all, Luria went on, all the variations in Western psychological thought were reflections of "the ideology of moribund capitalism" and of "the internal collapse of the bourgeois worldview. . . . The crisis of bourgeois ideology and bourgeois science was connected to the crisis of capitalism."

In discussing psychoanalysis, Luria's prose was critical but less militant and more respectful. In its focus on the unconscious, psychoanalysis stood "outside the boundaries" of the scientific mainstream, he wrote. The theory, centered on the highly individualized forces of the id and ego, remained inaccessibly mired in the abstract and unverifiable terrain of the unconscious. Instead of relating the psyche of the individual to the social conditions of the external world, psychoanalysis concentrated on "the primitive, prehistorical biological roots of man's personality."

Moreover, according to Luria, Freud had then moved from his early clinically based explorations into the theoretical speculations of "metapsychology," in which he sought to explain large-scale phenomena such as religion, war, and the organization of society in terms of universal patterns of aggression, hostility, and repression. Luria felt that this macroscopic interpretation rested on very soft ground because Freud did not have his own case histories as evidence for these hypotheses and was too removed from the empirical methods inherent in the biological and neurophysiological disciplines of contemporary science. Freud fell into the "Dionysian" tradition of thinkers from Schopenhauer to Nietzsche and Bergson, philosophers of "social pessimism" and the dark forces of the unconscious. Freud's obsessive interest in the irrational aspects of human behavior, Luria concluded, exemplified an important distortion endemic to bourgeois psychological theory.[25] Luria's assessment was comparatively objective, given the strident pronouncements of most of his colleagues who were assigned to write critically on psychoanalysis. Indeed, some of his objections to Freud's ideas would appear decades later in Western critiques of psychoanalysis, stripped of the ideological framework which Luria was obliged to heed.

The Soviet involvement with Freud's theories continued throughout the 1930s, frequently on the borders of defying Stalinist orthodoxy. At a time when most observers abroad were convinced that all discussions on the subject had been closed down by Stalin's party psychologists, a conciliatory article on psychoanalysis appeared in the Soviet *Medical Encyclopedia* in 1933. The author of this article, V. Vnukov, centered his critique on "the fact that psychoanalysts are very militant in demanding their right to consider, in the light of their method, various phenomena which go beyond the limits of psychopathology and psychology." They study and make pronouncements, for example, on "problems of vast cultural and historical scope," which extended from matters concerning the customs of primitive tribes to the psychology of religious systems and the motives underlying the tensions of contemporary society. Vnukov criticized psychoanalytic theory for abolishing "all the barriers between a neurotic personality and a healthy one." This was done by applying the clinical findings from individual patients to the general society. While Vnukov mentioned that a vigorous psychoanalytic movement existed in Russia both before and after the 1917 revolution, he made it clear "that the only true evaluation is to consider [psychoanalysis] as a fragment of bourgeois democracy" and that its treatment method "stems from a basic theory which is faulty in its very conception." Nevertheless, Vnukov ended his article with the following passage:

> The entire theory of psychoanalysis must be critically examined, but on the other hand, one must not lose sight of the fact that through its application it was established that traumatic psychic experiences can be discovered and their pathogenic significance determined.
>
> For instance, for specialists on children, psychoanalysis supplied important material on the sexuality of childhood and on peculiarities of development. This type of material cannot be overlooked. Psychopathologists also cannot afford to disregard the importance of free association.
>
> Even though psychoanalysis as a theory is a direct product of a certain stage in the development of capitalist society, it still does not follow that all the material discovered by it must be regarded as defective. This material demands thorough consideration and examination and everything that is thus critically filtered out can become a part of our inventory.[26]

Shortly after this article appeared, another authoritative publication with full party sponsorship, the *Great Soviet Encyclopedia*, published a lengthy and thoughtful article on psychoanalysis. Although the authors unquestionably placed their discussion in the context of criticism, they did not conceal their obvious respect for certain aspects of Freud's work. They admitted that psychoanalysis had made a genuine scientific contribution and achieved "great significance" in expanding the understanding of the causes of certain mental disturbances, as well as explaining the motivation of human behavior in general. Much of this long article was devoted to a discussion of the basis of Freud's theory, which, as the authors stated, was rooted in the biological instinct of self-preservation and the sexual drives that motivated the human personality. Extensive quotations were included from the Russian translations by Wulff and Ermakov of Freud's *Totem and Taboo, The Ego and the Id*, and *Group Psychology*. In addition, the work of several of Freud's followers, including Wilhelm Reich and Otto Rank, was analyzed, though in a more disparaging tone.

The authors of this article also informed their readers of the lively debates during the previous decade when efforts were made by Soviet Freudians to find a theoretical accommodation with the work of Marx. The result, however, was that "Freudism has nothing in common with Marxism." The psychology of Freud was too "ultraindividualistic," too ignorant of "the social conditions of human behavior," and too dependent on "unconscious sexual drives" allegedly inherited from primitive tribal societies. Moreover, Freud's analysis of "the healthy person" was erroneously "derived from the behavior of the neurotically ill individual."[27]

AN ALTERNATIVE

The intent of these attacks on Freud and psychoanalysis were unambiguous, despite being modified in part by hidden respect and reluctant admissions of merit. Any psychological or psychiatric research which could be classified as idealist rather than materialist, subjective rather than objective, or introspective and individualistic rather than collective and class oriented was declared off-limits. Moreover, the convulsions associated with the attempt to formulate a Marxist-Stalinist psychology extended to a far wider field than Freudians. Prominent nonpsychoanalytic researchers of the 1920s such as Bekhterev and Kornilov were severely criticized, and journals dealing with research on psychology were discouraged. Institute directors and their staffs were removed and replaced with the intensity of a political party purge.

Indeed, the connection between scientific investigation and political orthodoxy was established beyond any doubt. In the words of a psychologist, writing in 1932, "one of the inescapable conclusions to be drawn from the Marxist-Leninist doctrine of the unity of theory and practice and of party vigilance in science is that every theoretical mistake, every error in the field of methodology is inescapably transformed into a political error." Furthermore, he wrote, "every such error not only weakens the front of socialist construction, but it arms our enemies."[28]

One of the younger psychologists whose work would provide an alternative to the discredited theories of the 1920s was Sergei Rubinstein (1889–1960). The oscillating contours of Rubinstein's career were determined by the shifting political currents at the party center, and their widespread ramifications in the professions. Rubinstein moved into the limelight, then suffered years of official condemnation, to be followed by a period as the leading theoretical psychologist in the Soviet Union.

Rubinstein was educated in his native Odessa prior to spending five years studying philosophy in Germany, where he wrote his doctoral dissertation. After returning to the Soviet Union, he was appointed the head of the department of psychology at the Institute for Public Education in 1921. During the 1930s he headed the psychology department at the Leningrad Institute of Pedagogy, where he established his reputation. In 1942, after he was awarded the Stalin Prize, he helped set up the psychology department at Moscow

University, which he directed in various capacities until 1950. His textbook, *Foundations of General Psychology* (1940), went through periods of being both celebrated and reviled.[29]

Rubinstein serves as a good example of the ways in which Freud and psychoanalysis were increasingly transformed into a shorthand way of branding individuals as undesirables while simultaneously heightening efforts to polarize Western and Soviet sciences. Although there was little direct mention of psychoanalysis in Rubinstein's writings, critics attacked him anyway. In his 1934 paper, "Problems of Psychology in the Works of Karl Marx," he made the "error" of mentioning that "Freud did recognize some social components to the 'I' [Ego] but found the driving forces in the Unconscious, which is seen as antagonistically and externally related to consciousness."[30] He also wrote that changes in people's consciousness are determined not by the "'depth psychology' perspective of Freudianism," but from changed conditions in society, especially those of social class relations and divisions of labor, as Marx had shown. Further, Rubinstein believed that Freud had narrowed the complexity of the causes and motives of behavior to the single source of sexuality, which negates "the ever-widening circle of motivations of human conduct."[31]

While these statements may appear to be typical examples of Soviet anti-Freudianism, they were later used against Rubinstein. He went on to do further research on the concept of consciousness and to write his influential textbook on the general principles of psychology. At the height of his career, however, he was suddenly and severely attacked by a new cadre of Stalinists. He was accused of "straying from Marxist philosophical materialism," of "bowing down before the altar of bourgeois science" and of a whole range of more specific charges regarding his textbook. In one particularly prominent attack, Rubinstein was criticized by E. T. Chernakov for what was regarded as his greatest error, namely, having participated in "the war against intellectualism in psychology . . . from a Freudian position."[32] Chernakov argued that although Rubinstein claimed to have analyzed critically the work of Freud and other Western psychological theories, he was in sympathy with them. Rubinstein's acceptance of the objective reality of emotions, feelings, drives, and instincts within the framework of his concept of consciousness, discussed at length in his books and articles, was nothing less than "a capitulation to bourgeois idealist theories of emotions." By admitting that "the starting point for the emergence of human will lies in drives," Rubinstein "demonstrates his departure from Marxism, and comes close to the theories of Schopenhauer and Freud." In a lengthy display of his manipulative, ideological skills, Chernakov counterposed quotes from Rubinstein and Freud to show that "Professor Rubinstein has actually not presented any conception of drives which could be regarded as different or opposed to Freud's formulation; it is essentially no different, but is merely a different way of saying what Freud had said."[33]

At the time of this attack on Rubinstein, the Stalinization of Soviet psychology and psychiatry was at its height. All research was now to be evaluated by adherence to the "historical-materialist interpretation" of the concept of consciousness. Having criticized the work of Vygotsky and Rubinstein, who were two of the major contributors to this theory, the new generation of "materialist psychologists" produced simpler variants of their original ideas, supposedly free of the contamination of bourgeois influences that tainted their earlier work. Doctrinaire notions were now propounded relentlessly and were continually couched in terms of battles. The need for the "imperialist policies of Western science to be conquered by conscious, purposeful action of Soviet cadres" was a frequent theme in the pages of scholarly journals and serious newspaper articles. For the ideologists now charged with responsibility for official pronouncements on theories about the mind, the enemy remained Freudian psychoanalysis, where there was a continual effort "to prove the dominance of the instinctual, the unconscious over the conscious; the irrational over the rational, the biological over the ideological, the individual over the social in the consciousness of men, in human activity, in social development."[34] The dangers posed by psychoanalytic theory were matters of concern not only to party-affiliated psychologists, but to the party leadership itself. Witness the following statement, published on behalf of the Central Committee:

> Soviet psychology and bourgeois psychology oppose each other in this respect: bourgeois psychology takes the "unconscious" as a point of departure, as though it were the basic determinant of human psychology, and as though it were the central core of man's personality. Soviet psychology has explicitly fostered the theory that consciousness is the highest, most specialized human level of development of the psyche and has indicated the dominant role which conscious influences play as compared with unconscious influences.[35]

All of this criticism of Freud, together with the polemics directed against Rubinstein, were stages in the larger process of formulating an ideologically acceptable Soviet science of the mind. Nevertheless, insecurity remained throughout the profession. Charges and countercharges continued to be hurled. A line from a publication years before could be unearthed and connected with an array of bourgeois enemies empowered with the authority to threaten socialist scholarship. The battle over theories during the 1930s drew its real power from its integration with a broader polemic on the need to externalize political difficulties facing the leadership, and to bring longstanding fears under control. Thus, the Soviet interpretation of Freud's ideas was blown up into a negative myth, full of threatening images of irrationalism and chaos. This imagery was implicitly nourished on ancient Russian fears of the spontaneous anarchic storm in nature (*buria*) and the violent, elemental, uncontrollable peasant uprising (*bunt*). The threat was also perceived in terms of a hostile Western capitalist world encircling the Soviet Union. Some party officials assumed that psychoanalysis was the nerve center of all of Western psychology, as the attack on Rubinstein made clear. In addition, this myth was used to justify greater control over society, greater obedience to a protective doctrine supposedly native to Soviet soil, and greater authority for the party leadership over professionals and intellectuals.

Lenin had built a political structure based on ordering this chaos, channeling the spontaneous passion of both nature and people in the service of defined aims. His followers constructed the myth of the new Bolshevik man who, armed with Marxist consciousness, would conquer the whirlwinds of history, resolve the contradictions of classes, and end the oppression of humanity. To do this, Soviet citizens had to plan, set goals, be vigilant, master the environment, and defeat all enemies. A new type of person was required for such mythic tasks, one who had transcended inner conflicts, who functioned in the external social world where the demons were visible. In such a world, there could be no tolerance for Freud's psychic demons who carried out their devastation deep within the unconscious.

Chapter 7 After Stalin

Men cannot remain children forever; they must in the end go out into "hostile life." We may call this "education to reality." Need I confess to you that the sole purpose of my book is to point out the necessity for this forward step?
—*Sigmund Freud,* Future of an Illusion *(1928)*

CRACKS IN THE WALL

After the abolition of the Soviet Union in 1991, historians were granted access to previously unavailable archival materials on the secretive years of the Stalin era. New research has appeared, and more will be forthcoming. There are now answers to some questions that were strongly suspected but could not be proven, such as the death of the poet Osip Mandelstam in a labor camp in 1938, and the killing of the psychoanalyst Sabina Spielrein in a Rostov synagogue in 1941 by invading German troops.[1] The emergence of this information from the government archives, and the ongoing debates over how many victims there really were in the Stalin years, does little to mollify our worst suspicions about the massive number of citizens who were arrested, subjected to the living death of labor camps, or sent directly to execution, including party officials, intellectuals, Jews, peasants, and all other declared "enemies of the state." The denunciations of the previous years led to severe punishments. In addition, while Stalin was attacking from within, the country was attacked from without by Hitler's army in 1941, which led to a period of savage warfare during which well over 20 million people lost their lives.

Freud died on September 23, 1939, in London, just as the war was beginning. He had remained in Vienna until it was almost too late. Feverish negotiations with German authorities after they took control of Austria in 1938 led to Freud's emigration and repatriation.[2] There was no mention of these events in the Soviet press.

There is little evidence of any clinical activity linked to psychoanalysis during the terrible years of the war. Even the public criticism of Freud ceased at this time. Yet, psychoanalysis continued to have a quiet presence. Evidence of this can be found in the reflections of a psychiatrist who worked during the Stalin years under one of the Soviet Union's leading child psychiatrists, G. E. Sukharova:

> Of course we were familiar with Freud. I had several of his books, which I unfor-
> tunately couldn't take with me [to America]. Formally we didn't mention his name in
> our papers or clinical analyses. It is impossible for me to write here my understanding
> of Freud's role, but certainly his theory helped us especially for neuroses. My mentor,
> Professor G. E. Sukharova, often told us in her explanation of some cases: "there we
> can't avoid Freud's theory."[3]

In the late summer of 1943, the Soviet literary journal *Oktiabr* (October) published an installment of a novel entitled *Before the Sunrise,* which was full of Freudian themes. Mikhail Zoshchenko, the author, was a popular writer, particularly known for his satirical and humorous short stories critical of Soviet life during the 1920s. Zoshchenko not only was very familiar with Freud's writings, but also carefully disguised his own positive feelings about psychoanalysis by feigning advocacy for the officially approved theories of Pavlov in order to publish the novel.

Before the Sunrise is an effort at self-analysis in which Zoshchenko sought to uncover the traumatic events of his infancy and childhood with the intention of reducing the painful symptoms of his depression. His purpose, as he put it, was to tear away "the dense fog which shrouded the first two years of my life," and thus to see the drama which had occurred "before the sunrise" of his conscious memories. Zoshchenko also made effective use of the war itself, comparing "the two warring halves of the brain," the conscious and unconscious dimensions, to the embattled Soviet and German armies, clearly identifying the Nazi invaders with the mind's "lower story" of violent instincts.[4] Publication of the novel was stopped and Zoshchenko was subjected to a bitter public attack, including the baseless but damning charge that he was not supporting the war campaign. He was reduced to silence, shame, and poverty.[5]

In Zoshchenko's novel, the narrator is depicted as making a reluctant choice favoring Pavlov over Freud. In real life, once the war was concluded, the Soviet authorities returned to their effort to ensure that any lingering sympathies for Freud would be eliminated. Thus, the Soviet authorities once again, as they had done in 1930, convened a conference to underline the boundaries of acceptable discourse. In 1950, the Soviet Academy of Sciences and the Academy of Medical Sciences jointly sponsored the "Pavlov conference," in honor of the centenary of the scientist's birth. In the year prior to the conference, a flood of newspaper and journal articles reviewed and celebrated Pavlov's achievements. Frequently the admiration of Pavlov was accompanied by criticism of Freud, whose work was portrayed as directly antagonistic to Pavlov's research.[6] At the conference itself, from June 28 to July 4, 1950, eighty-one speeches were delivered, each dealing with the application of Pavlov's work and "teachings" to a specific field of scientific investigation. The list of specialized areas was comprehensive, including not only subjects that had been of direct interest to Pavlov such as physiology, neurology, psychology, and medicine in general, but also less obviously related fields such as "rational dietetics," "physical culture," and "spa therapy."

The stated purpose of the conference was to encourage participants to engage in "a critical and self-critical examination of how matters stand with regard to the development of Pavlov's legacy in the Soviet Union." In one of the more surrealistic moments of this gathering, the keynote speaker stated that this examination was to take place in the spirit of free and open inquiry. To emphasize this point, S. I. Vavilov, the president of the Academy of Sciences, quoted Stalin in his address to the conference: "It is generally recognized that no science can develop and flourish without a battle of opinions, without freedom of criticism." Vavilov added that the conference should be the occasion for such a battle of opinions "without regard for established authorities, undeterred by long-standing traditions, and irrespective of persons."[7] In the aftermath of the purge trials and the war years during which Stalin enhanced his power as the successful military commander who defeated fascism—"Soviet freedom" required obeisant praise to his limitless power. In this spirit, the conference passed a resolution sending a letter to Stalin, who was cheered and gratefully acknowledged "as a preeminent scientist and genius" and as "the leader and teacher of the heroic Bolshevik Party." The letter concluded: "We promise you, dear Comrade Stalin, to bend all our efforts to eliminate as speedily as possible the shortcomings in the work of developing Pavlov's science, and to put it to the utmost use in furtherance of the building of communism in our country."[8]

In fact, the conference was devoted to demonstrating that "Pavlov's teachings must be made the foundation of the whole edifice of medicine . . . and all fields of science." The "battle of opinions" was reduced to "exposing" those of "Pavlov's pupils [who] have not fought hard enough and have not come forward in a united front to defend Pavlov's materialist teachings against the reactionary assaults" of Western "idealist" physiologists and psychologists. The purpose of this ideological criticism was to rectify these mistakes and direct all scientific work "along the correct road," to be established in a doctrinaire manner in the name of Pavlov's teachings.[9]

Freud and psychoanalysis were included among the "idealist" theories to be combatted. However, a new dimension was added to the critique of Freud. As a result of the emergence of the Cold War, psychoanalytic concepts were now associated with American capitalism and imperialism in a critique intended to discredit them all. According to K. M. Bykov: "Abroad, especially in America, where the expansionist tendencies of monopoly capital are manifested in their most brazen form, 'psychosomatic medicine' is forced to arm itself with the most reactionary theories in order to defend the interests of the ruling classes."[10]

Bykov argued further that psychosomatic medicine (which he did not define) was based on the Freudian notion that man is governed by aggressive instincts which were repressed in civilized society. This repression, in turn, intensified the hostile instincts. As a result, civilized society suffered from excessive "hypertension" which the psychiatrists of psychosomatic medicine sought to analyze and alleviate. Because of the widespread attention paid to this orientation, especially in the United States, where Freud's influence continued to grow, "it behooves us in our journals and monographs to concentrate the fire of criticism primarily on those postulates of the Freudian doctrine which are being refurbished and utilized by medicine abroad." Bykov also warned against the "attempts that have been made here in the Soviet Union to combine 'Freudism' with Pavlov's theory of the conditioned reflexes into a single system of 'reflexological Freudism.'" Although few attempts of this kind had been made, Bykov reminded his audience that "Pavlov disassociated himself from Freud on many occasions and sharply criticized his conceptions. . . . The Freudian conception is alien to Pavlov's disciples and followers, because of its unscientific character" and its foundation "in mystical conceptions, which reflect the decay of bourgeois society, its descent into fascism."[11]

These statements had little to do with what we know of Pavlov's own views on Freud. Some evidence shows that Pavlov, as a scientist, was curious enough to have taken Freud's theories seriously, and may have even reacted favorably to certain aspects of psychoanalysis. For example, one Western psychiatrist who visited Moscow in the early 1930s not only found substantial areas of agreement between Pavlov and Freud, but also reported a conversation in which Pavlov admitted that he set up several of his experiments as a result of his "reading some of Freud's work." Pavlov further said that he was "indebted to Freud for stimulating his thoughts and experiments" and added that he anticipated that "a deeper understanding of behavior would come from a fusion of the concepts of the conditioned reflex and of psychoanalysis." When told of this later, Freud commented: "It would have helped if Pavlov had stated that publicly a few decades ago."[12]

The point of the conference, however, was not to determine exactly what Pavlov thought of Freud, but rather to solidify an ideological edifice and to enforce conformity with the party's authoritarian pronouncements on scientific research. So long as Stalin lived, the instruments of terror were maintained and discipline was strictly enforced. There were very few instances of questionable views of Freud slipping past the watchful eyes of the censorship bureau, creating political embarrassment and requiring punitive action, as had been the case with Zoshchenko's novel.

Once this ideological edifice was constructed, however, it soon began to crack. In 1953 when Stalin died, a popular saying had it that the masses wept, the intelligentsia rejoiced, the party fled, and everyone was relieved. Nevertheless, after decades of rule based on fear, Stalinism could not be rolled back or obliterated either easily or quickly even in the absence of the leader. Throughout Soviet society in the years after Stalin's death, changes came gradually. Among the new currents were the return and rehabilitation of many of the "enemies of the people" from the Gulag, Nikita Khrushchev's secret speech to the Twentieth Party Congress in which he denounced Stalin's "crimes," and the publication of novels which departed sharply from the ethos of socialist realism, such as Ilya Ehrenburg's *The Thaw* (1954) and Alexander Solzhenitsyn's *One Day in the Life of Ivan Denisovich* (1962).

In the field of psychology, cautiously stated criticism of the Pavlovian mono-
lith, which had been promulgated at the 1950 scientific conference, began to
appear in newspaper and journal articles.[13] Scientists previously under attack
now published empirical as well as theoretical papers in professional publications. Rubinstein, who had been vilified in 1948 as a "cosmopolitan," as well as a
Freudian sympathizer, was reappointed to the position he had lost earlier,
chairing the psychology department at Moscow University. In 1955, Rubinstein
was commissioned to write the lead article in the premier issue of *Problems of
Psychology*, the first professional journal devoted exclusively to the field of
psychology since the early 1930s. In the article, called "Problems of Psychological Theory," Rubinstein criticized the doctrinaire nature of Pavlovian psychology while still supporting broadly a Pavlovian theory of stimulus-response
mechanisms.[14] This reevaluation in psychology continued throughout the
decade and led to the point where the pronouncements of the 1950 Pavlov
sessions could be criticized for *their* errors and excesses in the name of what was
now referred to as Stalin's "cult of personality."

In a similar reversal, "Freudism," which was supposedly both dead and
buried, turned out to be neither. Officially, the criticism of psychoanalysis
remained quite severe and uncompromising. Indeed, the campaign against
Rubinstein and the continued stridency of the criticism of Freud and his work
convinced the leading American expert on Soviet psychiatry at this time to state
that "psychoanalysis never gained a foothold in the Soviet Union." Moreover,
"the Freudian school will never be revived in the Soviet Union," he added, "and
all of the Freudian variants have gone with it: Adler, Reich and others. I could
not even find the works of Erich Fromm, Karen Horney, H. S. Sullivan and
other modern analysts mentioned in the Soviet literature."[15] As late as 1955, a
philosophical dictionary article on psychoanalysis, which was prepared for
publication before Stalin's death, reiterated the standard charges: "A reactionary
idealistic trend widespread in bourgeois psychological science," psychoanalysis
reduced the rational functions of consciousness to a status subordinate to the
commanding sexual urges of the unconscious. Scientific psychology, the article
asserted, rejected Freudian concepts of infantile conflicts, its "fatalistic pre-
determination of human destiny" and the concept of the libido as "the sole,
basic 'law' of the human psyche." These concepts merely justified "the basest
and most repellent instinctual tendencies" in humans.[16]

Nevertheless, despite this uncompromising and vitriolic posture, signs of a
countertrend were already appearing. Some were subtle and indirect. For instance, early in 1956, the main psychology journal published an article, "The

Twentieth Congress of the Communist Party and the Tasks of Psychological Science," which discussed early childhood. This subject had been neglected for many years because of its association with Freud. As a result, "a significant and extremely important period in the life of the child has altogether vanished from the horizon of psychologists and educators." The author of the article argued for the need to focus attention on childhood development, particularly in the years up to the age of three. If this need was not addressed by psychologists, the author warned, it would remain "quite impossible to direct [the child's] upbringing in a rational manner."[17]

FREUD WITHOUT FREUD: MIASISHCHEV
AND UZNADZE

More significantly, the work of two experienced and respected researchers in psychology who were familiar with Freud and psychoanalysis gained increasing influence. V. N. Miasishchev (1893–1973) had been conducting studies in his specialty of psychoneurology since the 1920s, but it was not until after Stalin's death that he was appointed the director of the Bekhterev Psychoneurological Institute in Leningrad and awarded a chair in the psychology department at Leningrad University. Also at this time, he began to devote more attention to the subject of neurotic disorders. Similarly, the Tbilisi psychologist Dmitry Uznadze (1886–1950) had earlier published numerous papers in his native Georgian language, but his work now spread to a far wider Soviet audience during the 1950s. One of the first discussions of his experiments and findings in a Russian journal appeared in 1956 in the newly founded *Problems of Psychology*, where an extensive treatment of the concept of the unconscious was found.[18] These topics—neuroses and the unconscious—had been virtually abandoned since the late 1920s when psychoanalytic investigations of these themes became unacceptable.

Miasishchev completed the program at the Psychoneurological Institute in 1919, having been trained by the Institute's founder, V. M. Bekhterev. In the course of his long and productive career, Miasishchev published more than 250 books and research papers, of which his large collection of essays, *Personality and Neurosis* (1960), was clearly his most influential single work. He also received many state awards, including the Order of Lenin, and chaired numerous commissions and scientific societies.[19] However, one honor was withheld from him. Although he was appointed corresponding member of the Academy of Educational Sciences, he was rejected from a similar position in the more prestigious

Academy of Medical Sciences. This has been attributed to the unyielding opposition of the orthodox Pavlovians who dominated the Academy of Medical Sciences. They refused to accept Miasishchev's work in neuroses and psychotherapy as scientifically valid and, in spite of Miasishchev's public homage to Pavlov's theories, considered him outside the scientific mainstream of Soviet medicine and psychiatry.[20]

In Miasishchev's work, there seems to be a contradiction between his acceptance of Pavlovian theory and his interest in psychoanalysis. Miasishchev often tried to state his closeness to Pavlovian neurophysiology, though their differences were indeed real. The problem was reversed in the case of Freud in that Miasishchev frequently expressed his opposition to psychoanalytic theory, though in fact he was quite influenced by not only Freud but also Alfred Adler and, among the post-Freudians, Harry Stack Sullivan. Officially, Miasishchev was celebrated in the Soviet Union for having "created a clinical psychological theory of neurosis and a system of psychotherapy for these disorders which are fundamentally distinct from psychoanalysis."[21] Nevertheless, considering how intensely interested he was in the psychopathology and psychotherapeutic treatment modes at the center of the Freudian canon, it is surprising that Miasishchev was able to accomplish so much without being ideologically condemned. He escaped this fate not only because of the more relaxed conditions that existed following Stalin's demise, but also because he successfully managed to incorporate into his work on the neurotic personality many of Freud's concerns without making explicit use of psychoanalytic content.

Miasishchev's contribution to clinical theory and practice are evident in his published case presentations, which were unusual for Soviet psychiatric journals at that time. Miasishchev generally assigned priority in his case studies to his patients' "internal" conflicts, which he believed had to be dealt with psychologically. "Neither sedatives nor cardiac drugs, neither baths nor sleep therapy" can help in certain cases. With neurotic patients, he stated, "there is a disturbance of the ability to regulate one's capacity to concentrate or to control one's emotions." In cases of obsessive neuroses, there is "a constant struggle with processes which are no longer under the control of the [individual's] personality. A sufferer from hysteria is completely overwhelmed by impulses; it is not he who controls them but they control him."[22]

In one of his more revealing case histories, Miasishchev described a patient who constantly feared she would be attacked by rabid dogs. She also frequently underwent episodes during which she acted like a dog, including emitting a fierce howling sound. During these episodes, she also felt a powerful compulsion to strike her small son, of whom she said she was very fond, with an axe. During psychotherapy the patient was able to recall an earlier trauma which appeared to be the buried stimulus behind her neurotic responses. Years before, the patient and her husband had lost their home due to the military campaigns of the Second World War. She was forced to live with her sister-in-law, with whom she had a competitive and hostile relationship. Feeling isolated, unloved, and powerless to make decisions affecting her life, she experienced uncontrollable, destructive urges. According to Miasishchev: "When she had the urge to destroy everything and everybody, she would go into the forest, unbutton her clothes, scratch her chest, throw herself to the ground and howl. It was then that she began to develop obsessive inclinations to kill her son. Afterwards, when irritated, she had taken to falling on the floor and howling while at home." This behavior was influenced by the patient's childhood experiences in her parents' home, where she was permitted to have her own way in almost all the instances she could recall. She brought the attitudes of her overly indulgent parents, who refused to set appropriate boundaries for her actions as a child, into her marriage. Soon after the marriage, which seems to have constituted her first deep emotional attachment outside of her relationship with her parents, she was forced to move into her sister-in-law's home. Unable to maintain the illusions of omnipotence, which her powerful sister-in-law refused to allow, she deteriorated into the condition of animal rage. Her desire for control was so strong that, thwarted, she turned her destructive urges upon her son. In a fantasy of bloody vengeance, she undoubtedly believed she would gain revenge by killing her son with her husband's axe, therefore depriving her husband and his despised sister of their dearest relative.[23]

This case was a psychoanalytically informed clinical study without a single reference to the psychoanalytic literature. Instead of speaking about traumatic and infantile sexual conflicts, Miasishchev described the "role of the past" and "the pathological situation." Moreover, though unstated, the role of the unconscious was a powerful motif in Miasishchev's description of his patient.

Nevertheless, the obligatory criticism of Freud was undeniably pronounced in Miasishchev's writings, at times even reaching the level of ideological labeling. In 1948, for example, he wrote that "the psychology of the personality and its relationships is the antithesis of the modern reactionary bourgeois psychology of the unconscious, typified by the psychology of Freud."[24] In another passage from this same discussion, Miasishchev stated: "Our Soviet psychotherapy relies for the achievement of its therapeutic purpose on the understanding of the pathogenesis of disease and of its control on the powerful resources of the conscious attitudes of the personality, and not on the 'biologized' mysticism of the instincts and the unconscious, as is the case with pseudoscientific or, more accurately, antiscientific psychotherapy of Western Europe and America."[25] In a 1956 essay on neurosis, Miasishchev wrote that "Freud distorted and greatly exaggerated, in his original theory, the importance of sex." Moreover, he wrote: "Freud subsequently attempted to subordinate the sexual inclination (as an inclination toward life) to another, more powerful and, in his new opinion, decisive inclination—that toward death. Although this did not alter the essentials of his system, this replacement of the optimistic inclination toward life and enjoyment by an inclination toward death was not fortuitous, for it expressed the pessimistic mood of the imperialistic bourgeoisie of the epoch of the 'twilight of Europe.'"[26]

Equally interesting was Miasishchev's discussion of the concept of the unconscious, which he claimed had suffered from "misuse" in Freud's work. This misuse has "introduced a significant handicap into our psychological and neurophysiological interpretations" of problems concerning the distinction between conscious and unconscious attitudes. However, it would be incorrect, Miasishchev said, to presume that "to speak about the unconscious is to lapse into Freudism." He went on to ask the central question directly: "Do unconscious attitudes and, consequently, inclinations and wants, exist in man?" Referring to a variety of experiments carried out with the cooperation of his colleagues, Miasishchev answered in the affirmative. Moreover, he stated that one of the main tasks of the psychotherapist was to help his patients "to understand, to grasp associations and the meaning of what determines their behavior, of which they were hitherto unaware." This process was essentially making the unconscious dimension a conscious one. What was formerly behavior motivated by unconscious attitudes and needs "may now reach the level of consciousness" in therapy.[27]

Freud's presence can be discerned throughout Miasishchev's papers, even when there was no explicit reference. For Miasishchev, the concept of the conscious, healthy, and socially functioning personality was strongly associated with its antithesis—the individual neurotic personality, ruled by powerful unconscious drives and crippled by the traumas caused by devastating and harmful relationships in the repressed past.

Near the end of his book *Personality and Neurosis,* Miasishchev discussed the "numerous and interesting experiments" conducted by a Soviet psychologist and his colleagues working at the Institute of Psychology of the Georgian Republic in Tbilisi.[28] Miasishchev was referring to the work of Dmitry

Uznadze, who was seeking to accomplish something that Freud had never done, namely, to establish empirical proof for the existence of the unconscious in the human personality.

Little is known of Uznadze's training beyond the fact that he received his doctorate in Germany in 1909. He obviously was familiar with the leading trends in European psychology, but he was influenced also by two important philosophers of this period—Vladimir Soloviev in Russia (the subject of Uznadze's dissertation) and Henri Bergson in France. Uznadze's interest in the phenomenon of the unconscious was quite likely stimulated by his reading of Soloviev and Bergson.[29] Comparisons have been drawn between the careers of Uznadze and Freud,[30] but the differences far outweigh any apparent similarities. To be sure, Uznadze's students attached themselves to his theoretical and experimental work with the kind of uncritical reverence that can be found among Freud's most devoted disciples. Moreover, Uznadze occupied an exalted role in Georgian psychology which can be compared to Pavlov's in Moscow. He was referred to often as the founding father of modern Georgian psychology as well as a figure of world historical significance, whose findings were of importance in a wide variety of areas.[31] However, all of this was conducted in a specific Soviet context which determined much of its character.

Uznadze's work was not well known among Soviet psychologists and psychiatrists until the 1950s. His audience remained limited for decades because virtually all of his significant research papers were published in Georgian.[32] Equally important in explaining Uznadze's obscurity is the nature of his work. He was investigating problems which were either neglected or criticized by his professional peers in Moscow. Indeed, Uznadze became most intensely interested in the phenomenon of the unconscious at the very moment when all traces of psychoanalysis either were being subjected to severe criticism or were being buried under the ideological doctrines of Pavlovianism. There is also the question of Stalin's role in this matter. On the one hand, Uznadze and his colleagues seem to have been permitted to conduct their research relatively undisturbed and were not involved in the savage Communist party struggles that prevailed in Moscow. Yet, on the other hand, Uznadze's influence remained contained and spread only after the death of his fellow Georgian in the Kremlin.

In his experimental studies, Uznadze outlined a theoretical explanation of what might best be called "the Soviet unconscious." It was very different from what Freud had described. Uznadze used the term "set" (*ustanovka*) to describe the phenomenon which he believed lay at the basis of all conscious mental activity. Set was a "fundamental reaction to a situation where there is a problem to be considered and solved." The preparation of mental activity in human consciousness actually takes place earlier, in a preconscious stage, which "determines the course and composition of mental activity in the problem-solving process at the conscious level." Uznadze was convinced that, through his experiments with perceptual illusions, he had "made the early, preconscious stage of mental development accessible to scientific analysis."[33]

Whether in normal or abnormal personalities, the early years, Uznadze believed, were crucial in the formation of sets. Based on the individual's training and education at home and later at school, a series of "unconscious sets" were constructed which would accompany that person throughout life. "Usually he is not aware of these sets, although this does not stop them from being active forces controlling his activity in a given direction," Uznadze wrote.[34]

Uznadze criticized Freud, but his understanding of certain psychoanalytic concepts appears limited. Uznadze argued not that Freud was wrong in seeking to fathom the nature of the unconscious, but that his theoretical explanation was "incorrect" because of his emphasis on the negative aspects of the unconscious. According to Uznadze, Freud defined as unconscious all processes which he could not explain as conscious. The basis of the unconscious thus is its function as "the negation of the conscious state."[35]

Despite this dismissive attitude, in the same discussion Uznadze makes one of the most supportive statements about Freud's clinical work to be found during the entire Stalin era: "[But] in practice, Freud has frequently achieved positive results in the treatment of psychoses. It would be facile to deny that such results have been obtained—they unquestionably have."[36] Although Uznadze believed that Freud's *theory* of the unconscious provided "no positive contribution to science," he was prepared to admit that clinical psychoanalysis was indeed valuable. Most important, however, was Uznadze's clear linkage of his own work with Freud's, and his presentation of his own work as a scientific advance over Freud's. "Hence we see that the unconscious actually exists in us, but that this unconscious is none other than the subject's set. Consequently, the concept of the unconscious from this moment ceases to be a purely negative concept, but acquires a fully positive significance and must be analyzed in science on the basis of ordinary methods of investigation."[37]

Uznadze did more than merely formulate another and more moderate variation on the theme of criticizing Freud. Intentionally or not, he was setting the stage for a full-scale renewal of the Soviet interest in Freud, which had been dormant since the 1920s. Above all, he introduced a new concept of the unconscious which would make possible not only a revised and informed critique of psychoanalysis, but also an alternative concept of the unconscious that was neither Freudian nor Pavlovian.

THE CRITICAL REVIVAL OF PSYCHOANALYSIS

No one could have foreseen the astonishing revival of interest in Freud's work that emerged in the 1960s. It came not only with great force but in a peculiarly Soviet style. The revival was not yet characterized by the return of practicing clinical psychoanalysts, but rather by another critical discourse. Freud was resurrected not to be celebrated but to be condemned anew. In addition, the critique was led by highly sophisticated specialists who were entirely familiar with Freud's writings. More intriguing is the fact that this revival involved individuals truly interested in psychoanalysis who learned that the way to gain access to the censored work of Freud was to become a critic of Freudian theory. They also learned that there were no guidelines as to how severe or mild the criticism had to be.

Timing was a crucial factor in shaping the scope, content, and significance of this renewed Soviet interest in Freud during the 1960s. On the one hand, the students of Uznadze in Tbilisi, for some time distanced from the political upheavals in Moscow, had assumed positions of national professional prominence as they continued their investigations into the problems of human motivation and unconscious behavior. On the other hand, the expansion of the Cold War competition with the United States in international affairs assumed new levels of confrontation. The "theater of operations" now extended deeply into the scientific professions. It was no longer possible merely to dismiss or to deny Western ideas which were perceived as antagonistic and threatening. For the new postwar generation of professionals, a comprehensive analysis was necessary. Instead of ideological polemics, a scientific critique was required. If Communist science was superior to bourgeois science, this had to be demonstrated, not merely asserted. Uznadze's followers appeared to be in the best position to mount the critique against psychoanalysis because they were the only group working on Freudianism with official approval.

The revival began with an ideological emphasis. In 1957, a politically well-placed Soviet psychiatrist responded to an invitation from the editors of an American socialist journal, *The Monthly Review*, to discuss the Soviet attitude toward Freud. The psychiatrist, D. D. Fedotov, was at the time director of the Institute of Psychiatry in the Ministry of Health. In his article he sought to explain to Americans why Soviet professionals viewed Freud's work so critically at the same time that psychoanalysis had achieved such widespread influence in the United States. After pointing out that Soviet psychiatrists read Western psychoanalytic papers "only for the purpose of keeping in touch with the scientific interests of our colleagues abroad," Fedotov went on to present some of the major objections to Freud. The theory and practice of psychoanalysis were "rejected as lacking in scientific substance." By way of contrast, Fedotov pointed to the "tremendous significance" of Pavlov's teachings in establishing a scientific means "for the objective exploration of the physiology of the brain" and its "psychic processes." Psychoanalysts believed, Fedotov continued, that these psychic processes were independent of the physiological functioning of the brain. The Soviet "materialist view renders such a dichotomy between the psyche and its material base quite unacceptable."

Fedotov also found problems in the conceptualization of the relationship between man and his environment. Soviet researchers started from the premise that "the psyche is a reflection in the brain of objectively existent reality." Human consciousness, therefore, was a reflection of man's external world. However, in Fedotov's view, psychoanalysis postulated that "the unconscious is a separate subdivision of the psyche, essentially independent of the external world," which "exerts a decisive influence on man's consciousness." This led psychoanalysts to embrace a theory in which man's "social essence" is denied. Rather than portraying man and his psyche as the products of the historical development of social forces, as Soviet science does, Fedotov argued that Freud and his followers had constructed a theory of infantile sexual instincts to account for man's behavior. Not only was this an inaccurate view in that it left man isolated from history and society, but in therapeutic practice it "pulls the patients away from the present, from the real conflicts in their immediate existence. . . . We hold that, while due consideration must be given to early, real, proved and not imagined psychological traumata, the doctor's main attention in the treatment of neurotics must be centered on their present life, on the perspectives of the immediate future; that in the process of psychotherapy the physician must keep closer to what presently disturbs the patient." Science has shown, Fedotov concluded, that the human personality was "shaped by history in a social setting," not by individualized elemental instincts operating irrationally and unconsciously.[38]

Although some of Fedotov's points were part of the traditional Stalinist critique, his mention of the clinical side of psychoanalysis was unusual. More important, his article was not simply the work of a concerned scientist acting on his own in response to a foreign invitation to discuss a topic within his professional domain. Fedotov's discussion of psychoanalysis, published in an American journal at the height of the Cold War, was directly connected to an overall reassessment of Freud which was taking place in the Soviet Union at this time. In October 1958, just ten months after the appearance of Fedotov's article, a special conference was held in Moscow under the auspices of the Presidium of the Soviet Academy of Medical Sciences to discuss "Problems of Ideological Struggle with Modern Freudism." To underscore the importance of the issue, scientists from such prestigious bodies as the Brain and Neurological Institutes of the Medical Academy, the Pavlov Physiological Institute, and the Ministry of Health, in addition to members of the Academy's Philosophical Faculty, were invited to this conference.

The stated purpose of the conference was the necessity for Soviet scientists to combat the growing influence of psychoanalysis in the West. According to the conference proceedings, Freud's teachings started as a theory "which sought to explain the causes and the nature of neuroses, but later began to lay claim to the role of a universal doctrine, extending its influence beyond the medical and biological sciences to the field of the social-economic and historical disciplines." In one of the most tendentious passages in the entire Soviet discourse on Freud, this "universal doctrine" was put into its proper context for the delegates to the conference: "Freudism, a typical product of bourgeois ideological reaction in the epoch of imperialism, was used by bourgeois ideologists to dupe the masses in the interests of imperialism and as an ideological weapon in the fight against Marxism."

This point was amplified by S. A. Sarkisov, a member of the Presidium of the Academy of Medical Sciences, who explained in his address how in the United States, "Freud's reactionary followers try to persuade the worker that all the difficulties of his existence have their root cause in himself and not in bourgeois society, that they are not the consequence of the relationships of production which exist in an exploiter society." These followers, moreover, were engaged in "plans for waging a psychological cold war" with the intention of reducing "the social role of the working class, to inculcate in it a passive attitude to the fight for the improvement of its own position." Sarkisov also criticized Soviet scientists for "not joining as actively as they should in the ideological fight against modern Freudism now in progress in the West."

He concluded his paper by reminding the delegates of the instructions from the Twentieth Party Congress, which stated that "peaceful co-existence of the two camps must not lead to the slightest relaxation of the ideological struggle against ideas and trends in bourgeois science and philosophy inimical to Marx-ism-Leninism."[39] Thus, the influence of psychoanalysis, thought to have been eliminated decades before, was once more a regenerated movement threatening Soviet society, not from within, as had been the case in the 1920s, but from without. Troops had to be remobilized for battle.

Another paper at the conference, "The Critical Analysis of Modern Freud-ism," presented by F. V. Bassin, took a more scholarly approach. Bassin, one of Uznadze's most successful followers, made a division between Freud's early and late work that was reminiscent of the distinction frequently drawn between the "early Marx," who was deeply engaged in the labyrinths of Hegelian philoso-phy, and the "later Marx," who was known for both his political analysis of contemporary events and his penetrating critique of capitalism. In this case, Bassin separated the "young Freud," of whom he spoke approvingly (partic-ularly with regard to Freud's empirically based neurophysiological work) from the "late Freud," of whom he was far more critical. Bassin reserved his greatest objections to Freud for the period when Freud did some of his most expansive theoretical and clinical work in psychoanalysis. Bassin considered Freud's the-ory of ego, id, and superego as "notorious." Worse, he believed that Freud took an unprovable hypothesis about the repression of aggressive instincts and ex-tended it into the realms of literature, sociology, and history, where it had further damaging influence. In spite of the criticism of psychoanalysis in many quarters which, Bassin believed, had demonstrated the futility of applying its methods in the treatment of mental illnesses, he admitted that "Freudism abroad is still a long way from final defeat."[40]

E. A. Popov and O. V. Kerbikov, both experienced psychiatrists, spoke to the conference delegates about the clinical dimension of psychoanalysis. They repeatedly criticized the application of Freudian theory to the treatment of mental illness, often anticipating later critiques raised in Europe and America. In particular, they found the Oedipal theory to be speculative and without any empirical basis in clinical treatment. They further argued that Freud's theory was entirely irrelevant to a wide range of circumstances, and went on to pose the following problems: "How can the Oedipus complex occur in children fed artificially and not from the mother's breast? What happened to the Oedipus complex in the matriarchal period when children did not know their fathers? What happens when children are brought up from infancy in orphanages?" The Soviet psychiatrists concluded that neither Freud nor his "modern Freud-ian" followers, such as Karen Horney, Harry Stack Sullivan, and Franz Alex-ander, had succeeded in answering these questions.

N. I. Grashchenkov and A. V. Snezhnevskii, both members of the Academy of Medical Sciences, also presented papers on Freud's philosophic views at the conference. Essentially, they disagreed with Bassin that Freud began his career as a materialist interested in physiology and neurology and later turned to idealism. They argued that "Freud was never a materialist," even though he had been trained by several of Europe's most eminent neurologists—Theodor Meynert and Ernst Bruecke in Vienna, and Jean-Martin Charcot in Paris. In fact, Freud was far more influenced from his earliest period of research by "idealists and mystics," including Nietzsche, Schopenhauer, and E. Hartmann. Grashchenkov and Snezhnevskii also argued that while Freud constructed "a psychological basis for Nietzsche's philosophy," they admitted that this took place primarily later in Freud's career, "after he began to extend his theory to the field of sociology."[41]

The paper most favorable to Freud at the conference was P. K. Anokhin's contribution, co-authored with V. N. Miasishchev. They emphasized the need for Soviet psychiatrists and psychologists to study psychoanalysis in greater depth in order to provide "a more profound and more concrete approach to the critique of Freudism." Without deeper study of Freud and the modern Freudians, Soviet specialists faced the danger of presenting an overly simplified criticism of psychoanalytic theory and practice. Only with a greater knowledge of the subject could "opposing scientific-materialistic data" be generated to "explain those complex intimate questions which Freudism has monopolized." Most important, the authors stated, "Freudism has not remained constant; it has changed and its arguments have changed also." Finally, it must be recognized that Soviet research on mental processes has "been preoccupied with the examination of the brain as a screen which reacts, forgetting that the brain retains a certain residue of impressions which is *outside the sphere of consciousness.*" In a thinly veiled criticism of the reigning Pavlovian doctrine, Anokhin and Miasishchev concluded that "the physiology of higher nervous activity does not seriously study the problem of the utilization of accumulated residual impressions in the brain and their influence on the sphere of consciousness and on behavior."[42]

Near the end of the conference, P. P. Bondarenko, head of the philosophy faculty in the Academy of Medical Sciences, presented a talk on Freud and sociology. His main point was that Freudians regard man "not as a social but as a biological creature whose whole life activity is governed by innate instincts and unconscious impulses." By stressing the unconscious, "they deny in effect the role of reason and social forms of consciousness in human behavior, and liken human society to a herd of animals." In addition to this "biologization" tendency in Freud's work, another serious sociological problem Bondarenko identified was the question of the social role of the father. According to Bondarenko, Freud's Oedipus complex theory explained "the rise to greatness of individuals in history" because "the vast majority of people have a consuming need to be under authority." This need was "an expression of that yearning for the father which dwells in human beings from infancy." Sociologically, Bondarenko concluded, this amounted to a denial of the "leading role of the masses in history, reducing them to the position of a passive crowd governed by great men who make history" by acting as "father substitutes."[43]

Bondarenko, whether intentionally or not, had wandered onto highly controversial turf with this discussion by bringing up the problem of Stalinism. In a manner typical of Soviet criticism, Freud was reproached in a way which permitted a far more serious issue to surface. The "great man of history" who "denied the leading role of the masses in history" was the ruler of the Soviet Union for almost three decades. It would be some time before this problem could be dealt with explicitly.

The conference, having "aroused much interest among the medical public," ended with a resolution that indicated the importance of Freud and psychoanalysis to the highest echelon of Soviet psychiatrists. First, it was resolved that "the struggle of Soviet scientists against the anti-scientific ideas of Freudism on the basis of dialectical materialism and the physiological doctrine of Pavlov" was to be intensified. Second, the resolution emphasized "the need for resolute criticism of improper attempts on the part of foreign authors to harmonize and reconcile the totally opposed teachings of Pavlov and Freud." Finally, the resolution drew special attention "to the efforts of the modern Freudians to extend Freud's theory to the field of social and political phenomena: "The psychoanalytical trend in the human sciences is one of the most hostile forms of bourgeois ideology, and it is the urgent task of Marxist sociology and philosophy to unmask it."[44]

This urgent approval for an intense critical study of Freud and the entire field of modern psychoanalysis was important. The image being presented was lucid. Freud's influence was already appearing in philosophy, literature, psychology, and psychiatry, and was gaining ground in other areas of knowledge. To combat this threat, an army of Soviet specialists in all these fields was needed.

Leading the vanguard was one of the participants in the 1958 conference, F. V. Bassin, a neurophysiologist and member of the Institute of Neurology in the

Soviet Academy of Medical Sciences. In a long two-part essay, "Freudism in the Light of Contemporary Scientific Discussion," which appeared in November 1958 in the leading Soviet psychology journal, Bassin presented the most detailed discussion of Freud's life and work to appear in the Soviet Union since the 1920s.[45] Bassin began with an admission that modern Freudianism's influence "has become widespread abroad," not only as a form of psychiatric treatment but also as "a philosophical system with a world outlook." This philosophy was described as "profoundly reactionary" and "hostile to dialectical materialist trends in the fields of neurological and humanist sciences." Although he was not clear about the reasons behind this "great revival of Freudian interpretations," Bassin mentioned recent advances in neurophysiology as well as the 1954 publication of Freud's previously unknown "Project for a Scientific Psychology," written in 1895. This document, a sketch of Freud's plans on the eve of his "psychoanalytic breakthrough," led Bassin into a discussion of the stages of Freud's development where he further advanced the theme of early and late Freud, a distinction he had mentioned in his presentation at the Academy of Medical Sciences conference.

In Freud's early phase, during his training years and the period of association with Josef Breuer, Bassin believed that he "was not as yet an adherent of antiphysiological idealism." On the contrary, his interests at that time "characterize him as a postivistically minded neuropathologist who concentrated on studying first aphasia and children's paralyses and later problems of the therapy of functional disorders." However, in the years leading up to the publication of *The Interpretation of Dreams* in 1900, and particularly in the ensuing decades, Freud shifted into the unscientific area of the psychological theory of suppressed sexual instincts. His methodology, Bassin continued, led him to develop his concepts "independent of physiology." By refusing to include physiological evidence in his psychological analysis, Freud moved further from empirical science, a pattern which climaxed in the speculative sociological and metapsychological work of his last years.

From the Soviet point of view, Bassin argued, the main objections to Freud's theory had to do with his psychoanalytic period, when he sought to prove that a direct relationship existed between the nature of a patient's suppressed impulses and the clinical symptoms manifested during treatment. Freud's thesis, according to Bassin, was that the clinical symptoms "were not only caused by the suppressed impulse but also symbolically expressed it in behavior." This relationship was never successfully demonstrated by Freud. It was, however, conceptualized by Pavlov independently of Freud, and moreover, worked on in an empirical manner by Uznadze and his students with a far greater claim to scientific validity than Freud was ever able to make. Although he did not elaborate on these experiments, Bassin was clearly seeking to reclaim for Soviet psychology the area of therapeutic exploration traditionally conceded to Freud.

Bassin also accepted the notion that, in some instances, pathological syndromes could be provoked by what he called "suppressed impulses," but he disagreed with Freud that there was "an obligatory symbolic transformation of them." Thus, he refused to accept the whole area of dream analysis as well as the concepts of sublimation and transference, some of Freud's most fundamental tenets. In addition, Bassin admitted that "there can be no doubt whatever that unconscious emotions do exist, that they can be expressed in behavior and leave a definite impression on the dynamics of the psychological, physiological, and clinical processes, and at the same time, can be connected with definite psychological content." Again he turned for support to Pavlov's work on "dis-inhibition" or the freeing of inhibited reactions, and the experimental work of the Uznadze school on post-hypnotic suggestion to support this point of view.

Bassin even went out of his way to point out why Freud could not resolve certain conceptual problems, such as finding a physiological foundation for the functioning of unconscious forces. Freud, he wrote, "can hardly be reproached for the absence of such an explanation at the time this concept was born, since it would have been an impossibility for physiology to provide it." Indeed, Bassin stated that Freud was on two occasions very close to recognizing the possibility of "the transformation of [unconscious] drives on the basis of their conscious connection with new psychological content." Here Bassin continued, Freud was on the verge of moving toward an understanding of how objective reality affects these drives and impulses at any point in one's life, but he reverted instead to the less scientific theory based on infantile sexuality and the mechanics of internal repression.

In his conclusion, rather than polemically dismissing the core of Freud's work, Bassin wrote: "Soviet psychoneurology and psychology should not ignore the problems posed by Freud. . . . It would be a mistake to assume that either the question of the psychological, physiological, or clinical manifestation of unconscious factors of behavior or those of the functional tension of these affects were born of the psychoanalytic concept, or that they can be developed only on its basis."

Having refuted Freud's theory, Bassin believed that it was now the task of Soviet scientists in this field to preserve the problems Freud had raised and "to develop them on the basis of concepts which have nothing in common with the categories of Freudianism."[46]

NEW AREAS OF INTERPRETATION

The literature on Freud which appeared throughout the 1960s revealed both the revival of Soviet interest in psychoanalytic ideas and a shift in attitudes toward the subject. Rather than relying on the innuendos and mythologies propounded by specialists in ideology, many of these writers had read Freud, as well as other European and American psychoanalysts. Also, the criticism of psychoanalytic concepts changed from political attacks to attempts at scholarly and scientific refutation, a reflection of the interests of the post-Stalin generation of students. Previously, Freud was criticized in order to be condemned. Now, however, the attack was more subtle and attracted genuine interest. To the outside world, this extensive criticism seemed as hostile to Freud as before, but young Soviet intellectuals, who were trained in the art of reading in codes and symbols, would arrive at a different interpretation.

The new criticism also permitted Soviet scholars to address themes which had been banned from public discourse during the Stalin years. For example, in 1961, the book *On the Threshold of Consciousness* by F. Mikhailov and G. Tsaregorodtsev explored the ways in which Freud's struggle to find answers to personal difficulties led him into a search for the causes of neurotic disturbances in the general population. In a chapter entitled "In the Depths of the Unconscious," the authors offered an extensive discussion of Freud's exposition of the mechanisms and dynamics of the unconscious. Despite the anti-Freudian context, this chapter was a statement about Soviet society itself. The authors described the underlying and often futile struggle of individuals to find an accord between their own needs and the demands of society, between "the pleasure principle" of satisfying one's own unconscious sexual and erotic needs in the presence of a punishing internal censor, and "the reality principle" of a restrictive system of laws and norms in the external world.

Convinced that Freud's work contained the evidence needed to understand this dilemma, they examined many of Freud's central texts and case histories, including the cases of Anna O. and Little Hans, and "The Ego and the Id," and "Mass Psychology and the Analysis of the Ego," which had not been discussed in print for decades. Further, this book explored Freud's interest in Sophocles' *Oedipus Rex*, spelling out the themes of the power of eros, the desire of the son to possess his mother and compete with his father, and the conflicts which resulted. Because *On the Threshold of Consciousness* was seen as part of the war against psychoanalytic influences as propounded at the official scientific congresses, it had a large print run. Its potentially subversive themes, therefore, reached a wide readership.[47]

Bassin, however, was the dominant figure in the critical revival. He brought the Soviet view of Freud to the attention of the international psychiatric community at the Third World Congress of Psychiatry in Montreal in 1961, where he gave a paper comparing Freud and Pavlov. The following year, the All-Union Conference on Philosophic Questions of Higher Nervous Activity and Psychology met in Moscow. It was an elaborate affair, sponsored by the Academy of Sciences and the Ministry of Higher Education, with more than a thousand delegates participating. The delegates represented the fields of physiology, psychology, psychiatry, and philosophy from all across the country.

The proceedings of this conference were published in a 771-page volume, which an American specialist has called "the best single source for an understanding of the philosophic issues in Soviet physiology and psychology since the passing of the Stalinist era."[48] At this gathering, Bassin presented a paper titled "Consciousness and the Unconscious" in which he reiterated his position that Soviet psychologists, clinicians, and psychiatrists needed to reassert control over areas to which "insufficient attention has been devoted in recent years and which have become quite incorrectly regarded abroad as monopolies of Freudianism."[49]

Other authors also were working on Freud. In 1965, I. T. Kurtsin, highly knowledgeable in Western language sources, published a study entitled *A Critique of Freudianism in Medicine and Physiology.* The book was actually an exhaustive and critical review of the research on psychosomatic medicine, which the author found to be a direct byproduct of the spread of psychoanalysis into the fields of physiology and, to a lesser extent, neurology.[50]

The same year, A. M. Khaletskii published an article in the authoritative *Journal of Neuropsychiatry and Psychiatry* (Moscow) on the relationship of psychoanalysis to existentialism, which took the Soviet critique of Freud into an entirely new realm. One of Khaletskii's most interesting points was his argument on the overlapping perspectives of the existentialist and the psychoanalyst, both of whom, in his view, believed that there existed no objective criteria against which to examine the concepts of good and evil. Freud's unconscious id "knows no moral standards, is asocial, anarchic and archaic," just as the mentality of existential man is portrayed as "senseless in an absurd world," devoid of ethics and the power of reason. Although this dilemma was supposed to have been a phenomenon of bourgeois society, Soviet readers could not have missed the message concerning the need to think critically about their own society in these terms.[51]

The critical studies of Freud went on unabated. *The Sociology of Personality* by I. S. Kon, a prominent sociologist at Leningrad University, was published in 1967. This book, the first major study of the problem of personality since Miasishchev's work, was an analysis of both Soviet and Western theory and research on personality. The book is noteworthy in that it devotes an entire section to a discussion of psychoanalytic personality theory from the standpoint of Soviet sociology.[52]

The climax of this stage in the evolution of the critical discourse on Freud was the appearance of Bassin's magnum opus, a huge study called *The Problem of the Unconscious*.[53] With this book, Bassin achieved recognition in the Soviet Union for what he had in effect already become—the country's leading specialist in a field which had been destroyed at least twice in his own lifetime. This was the first time that the term "Unconscious" was used in the title of a major scientific book in the Russian language since the 1920s. Moreover, although the concept of the unconscious had been studied in books and articles in the context of some larger problem, never before was it the central subject of an entire book. The publication of Bassin's book was further confirmation of the fact that Freudianism had become a legitimate and permanent field of knowledge, entitling researchers to pursue Freud in the original into any area necessary as long as it served the purposes of criticism.

Bassin's reputation as a specialist on the unconscious extended far beyond the borders of the Soviet Union. During the decade in which this book was in preparation, Bassin responded to numerous overtures from colleagues abroad, including many who were critical of his approach. He was not only able to thank them in his preface, but he also included the debates with some of these "valued opponents" in an appendix at the close of his book. To accord foreigners from the capitalist world such gratitude and even space to express their views was highly unusual in any Soviet work at this time, regardless of the area of specialization; in the Soviet literature on Freud, such acknowledgments were without precedent.

Bassin introduced his book with epigraphs from two thinkers rarely associated with one another in the Soviet era. One was a traditional Soviet quotation from Lenin: "The history of ideas is the history of change and, as a result, of the struggle of ideas"; the other was a passage from Spinoza's *Ethics:* "People regard themselves free in that they are conscious of their acts, but not aware of the causes which determine these acts." The quotations were chosen carefully, not as adornments, but as a signal to the reader that the ensuing explication was to be concerned as much with the larger problems of human motivation and conflict in society as with the more specifically psychological questions of consciousness and the unconscious. Bassin regarded the two areas as inseparable.

Bassin made it clear at the outset that he was interested in the unconscious but from a perspective entirely different from the psychoanalytic approach. His own method was to understand the unconscious as one of the many forms of "higher nervous activity" which were not subject to cognition and of which the subject might be entirely unaware. He even chose a specific Russian word, *neosoznavaemyi* (noncognizant), which he found to be more empirical and less abstract than the term *bessoznatel'noe* (without consciousness), which was used in Freud's sense. He also stated that he was interested in the unconscious in terms of its mechanisms and "material nature" as a physiological and neurological phenomenon, and as a system for the transmission of information and the regulation of behavior.[54]

In his book, Bassin traced the history of the concept of the unconscious from its philosophical origins before Freud to the post-Freudian present. He included a biographical portrait of Freud and a detailed examination of Freud's work as well as summaries of Adler's and Jung's criticisms of Freud. This criticism, however, did not prevent him from recognizing the "positive aspects of Freud's system."[55]

Bassin's main argument was that the problem of the unconscious was only one aspect of a general theory of consciousness.[56] Such a theory required an understanding of unconscious psychic activity as a product of work done by the brain to connect subjective needs and interests to the flow of information exchanged between the individual and his or her environment. In some cases, the subject was not aware or "cognizant" of the source of the stimuli, which could be a reflection either of a form of pathology or of normal adaptive behavior. He cited a number of Soviet experiments in which the clarity of perception and consciousness was impeded or distorted.[57]

Bassin included a lengthy investigation of Uznadze's theory of set. While in general agreement with Uznadze on the neurophysiological and psychological dimensions of his theory, Bassin cited his disagreement with Uznadze on two points. First, whereas Uznadze believed that set always operated unconsciously, Bassin argued that drives and attitudes could be conscious as well as unconscious. Second, Bassin found that set may function in a partial manner and affect behavior less than in the total way Uznadze had demonstrated in his experiments.[58]

In the final section of his book, Bassin reiterated his notion of the interdependent relationship between consciousness and the unconscious as varied forms of the regulation of brain activity. Consciousness essentially functioned on two levels, a higher level of objectification and rationalization and a lower one dominated by the activity of impulse, will, and emotion in which awareness and reason play little or no role. This permitted Bassin to explain slips of the tongue, dreams, and other phenomena dealt with by Freud as the unconscious processing of information.[59]

Ultimately, Bassin recognized psychoanalysis as an achievement for having devoted such attention to the role of unconscious psychic conflict in affecting behavior but he remained highly critical of Freud for the latter's decision to ignore the neurophysiological foundation of the unconscious in favor of purely psychological mechanisms. Bassin also wrote that the Soviet approach to the study of the unconscious was "action-oriented" and, as a theory of knowledge with direct therapeutic application, was capable of freeing man from pain and oppression. By contrast, Freud's concept of the unconscious, according to Bassin, was characterized by elements of passivity, victimization, and even of the hopelessness of change because of the human personality's subjugation by irrational and incomprehensible drives. Bassin never showed exactly how the Soviet approach could free human beings from these drives that Freud claimed were the basis of man's central dilemma in civilized society. Nevertheless, this book was a long way from Bassin's tendentious statements a decade earlier, when he had said Freudianism was "an incorrect scientific method" full of "deceitful conceptions" in the service of "reactionary ideological purposes."[60] His evolution in terms of attitudes toward Freud was far from over; the same could be said for Russian society as a whole.

Chapter 8 The Rehabilitation
of the Unconscious

Up to this time, we have unquestionably not paid enough attention to the processes of formation of what Freudianism calls the "subconscious." Carefully studying the reactions of the brain we forget that beyond the limits of the focus of the conscious, there remains an enormous fund of knowledge which we may call the memory of the brain; this fund of knowledge accumulates throughout a lifetime and proves to be, as shown in certain hypnotic experiments, remarkably stable. But have psychologists studied in sufficient depth how these traces survive and in what way they emerge into consciousness? It must be recognized that we have studied these questions very little. As a result, the business of combatting Freudianism has suffered.
—*P. K. Anokhin (1958)*

FROMM, LACAN, AND OTHER POST-FREUDIANS
THROUGH THE SOVIET PRISM

At the beginning of the 1970s, the political atmosphere in the Soviet Union was undergoing substantial change. The unpredictability of the Khrushchev years had left a deep imprint. On the one hand, Khrushchev orchestrated the pathbreaking official denunciation of

Stalin's "crimes" at the Twentieth Party Congress in 1956 and permitted the publication of Alexander Solzhenitsyn's exposé of life in the Gulag in his novel *One Day in the Life of Ivan Denisovich* in 1962. On the other hand, the Soviet leader was responsible for a number of erratic domestic and foreign policy initiatives, which included provoking and losing the nuclear confrontation with the United States during the Cuban Missile Crisis, breaking relations with the country's largest ally, China, and an unpopular agricultural reorganization that did not stimulate necessary levels of production.

Leonid Brezhnev's consolidation of power began slowly after Khrushchev's ouster in 1964 and reached its zenith during the 1970s. The Cold War continued to dominate world affairs as the public competition with the United States for global supremacy remained the controlling principle of Soviet foreign policy. Moreover, the government insisted on maintaining its authoritarian control over Soviet society, although unprecedented forms of resistance emerged at this time in reaction to the party's hegemony. Human rights activists and advocates of peaceful cooperation (not competition) with the West formed groups which the government refused to tolerate. The party leadership decided on a solution which engulfed part of the psychiatric profession more directly than at any time since the initial Bolshevik demands that physicians renounce private practice in the immediate aftermath of the 1917 revolution. Psychiatrists were asked to assume the role of a punitive judiciary. Dissidents were labeled with psychiatric disorders and then sent for "treatment" to the Serbskii Institute of Forensic and General Psychiatry in Moscow. As news of specific cases of psychiatric abuse surfaced in the West, the British delegation of the World Psychiatric Association (WPA) led a campaign against their Soviet colleagues to force them to end the internment of dissidents in psychiatric hospitals. These efforts reached a climax at the 1977 meeting of the WPA Congress in Honolulu, where resolutions were passed condemning Soviet psychiatric abuse. With pressure mounting from a number of psychiatric organizations abroad, the Soviets abruptly resigned from the WPA in January 1983 rather than face possible expulsion at the association's congress that summer.[1]

While attention in the Soviet medical establishment was focused on refuting the negative images of the psychiatric profession which appeared with great frequency in the Western media, specialists in psychoanalysis were moving in a somewhat different trajectory. By the beginning of the 1970s, "Freudianism" had become an officially sponsored field of criticism in the Soviet Union. It required specialists in many areas who were familiar not only with Freud's work, but also with the content of the post-Freudian psychoanalytic movement which had developed in the West largely since Freud's death in 1939. These Soviet specialists, in addition to well-known figures like Bassin, included graduate students who were launching their careers as Freud critics and sympathizers in a variety of disciplines, from traditional fields to newly developing areas of interest.

Soon after Bassin's book on the unconscious was published, other related works appeared. These books and articles were viewed as part of the continuing competition with the West. The goals were to combat psychoanalysis as a threatening force in the arsenal of bourgeois ideology and to claim areas of investigation traditionally dominated by psychoanalytic influence for a new communist-based science. Yet, because this Brezhnev-era criticism was still both in formation and also not under any specific government ministry or university department, there was no general agreement on how much prominence to give to Freud's work. Similarly, there were no clear guidelines on how critical one needed to be. Since most topics about the West were discussed under headings like "problems of bourgeois historiography" and "critiques of the capitalist world," it was crucial for Soviet researchers to know how to discuss and evaluate such themes from the appropriate critical perspective. The Freud literature published in the Soviet Union during the 1970s and early 1980s demonstrated the range of possibilities in the absence of ideological clarification. Although Pavlov's name was still invoked by scientists in a variety of fields, including psychiatry, the official interpretation of his work no longer carried the doctrinal authority that had at the 1950 Academy of Sciences conference.

The discourse on Freud and psychoanalysis published in the Soviet Union during the 1970s can be divided into three categories. One set of writings emerged from the beleaguered psychiatric community, bearing witness to Freud's continuing influence in that area. The revised and expanded edition of A. M. Sviadoshch's volume *Neuroses and Their Treatment* provides evidence of this influence. Originally published in 1959 in a smaller format, Sviadoshch published a second edition in 1971 with new material. The book was a good illustration of the confusion Soviet psychiatrists and psychologists experienced over how to evaluate Freud critically. Psychoanalysis and Freud were discussed only briefly in this rather large book of 443 pages. However, the entire book was pervaded by Freudian categories and interpretations. It was not that the book was covertly favorable to Freud, but rather that it clearly revealed the author's extensive knowledge of Freud's work. Sviadoshch criticized Freud for what he believed was an unproven theory of the role played by infantile sexual conflicts in the etiology of neurotic disorders. As proof of the "mistaken" nature of the theory, Sviadoshch argued that one of Freud's own disciples, Adler, had rejected it in favor of an alternative theory of neurosis. This theory was, in Sviadoshch's view, rooted in the more realistic and acceptable notion of a conflict in the human personality between the individual's striving toward power (potency) and feelings of inferiority (impotence). The book also discussed psychotherapy as a treatment mode, dwelling specifically on the work done by such psychoanalytically oriented therapists as Edith Jacobson.[2]

Other publications revealed an increasing interest in Freud which was being expressed in less critical terms than had been the case before. A. E. Lichko, a psychoneurological researcher at the Bekhterev Institute in Leningrad, published an article in 1977 called "The Psychology of Relations as a Theoretical Concept in Medical Psychology and Psychotherapy." While the thrust of the article was devoted to the ongoing usefulness of Miasishchev's concept of the psychology of relations, Lichko also discussed the Miasishchev school's "adherence to the primacy of consciousness over unconsciousness" in their analyses of the functions of the human personality. He mentioned the importance of devoting attention to the impact of the earliest period of psychological relationships on the development of the individual's personality, including "the dynamics of the first months of life observed by Freud as 'unconscious.'" According to Lichko, it was during this period that the "first systems of relationships" were established between the child and his or her immediate surroundings, particularly with the mother and father. The child has a direct relationship with each parent, but the relationships are interactive, as Lichko put it, in this "unconscious childhood." Few conscious memories of this period tend to survive, Lichko continued, although "clear fragments remain in one's memory" to be retrieved in later life. These early systems of relationships have a dominating presence even though they appear to be inoperative in later years due to the difficulty of recalling them, and in spite of the fact that they "give way to alterations" and changes which make them difficult to identify later in life. Lichko recognized that his colleagues had neglected this important area of study. "Unfortunately," he wrote, "until recently, the psychology of relations has devoted almost no attention to early childhood. A serious analysis of the development of this fundamental system of relations, which is shaped in early childhood, will strengthen our position in discussions with representatives of the various schools of psychoanalysis."[3]

A second category of writings on psychoanalysis in this period came out of the Uznadze school, led by Bassin, who carried on the paradoxical work of rehabilitating Freud's concept of the unconscious in order to discredit it in favor of Uznadze's theories. The problem of the Freud critique undoubtedly was discussed by the party leadership in 1971, since permission was granted to publish an article on the subject in *Kommunist*, the official ideological journal of the Communist party. This was the first time since the 1920s that any article discussing psychoanalysis and Freud had appeared in a ranking party organ specializing in politics and ideology. The article listed three authors, including Bassin and V. E. Rozhnov, chief of the All-Union Psychotherapeutic Center. While Bassin, the country's leading Freud critic, was an obvious choice to write this article, Rozhnov's participation was important both professionally and politically. His credentials, from the perspective of the Brezhnev authorities, were impeccable, and he was, in addition, a longtime specialist on psychotherapy and hypnosis.[4]

Despite this display of official scientific status, the *Kommunist* article provided little more than a restatement of previous work done by Soviet anti-Freudians. Entitled "Freudism: A Pseudoscientific Interpretation of Psychic Phenomena," the article first reviewed the basic details of Freud's theory with a mixture of accuracy, exaggeration, and error. The disagreements remained the same. Bassin and his colleagues objected to what they perceived to be Freud's reduction of the psyche to mere biological instincts and drives, the exaggerated emphasis on sexual instincts as the motive force behind human behavior, and the fact that Freud's theory was rooted, ultimately, in myth and not science.

What seemed most intolerable to Bassin and his co-authors was the challenge posed to the determining role of social relations (as elaborated in the philosophy of dialectical materialism) by Freud's notions of the power of the individual's "interior world." This inner world was conceptualized as the sphere of unconscious conflicts in which irrational desires were constantly in battle with rational norms. Bassin saw this as a conflict "between the spheres of 'desire' and 'necessity.'" The notion of the unconscious "standing over consciousness," creating the "reign of instincts over reason," fueled the search for a competitive explanatory theory of human motivation to replace the Freudian concepts which remained intolerable and therefore unacceptable. Bending with the ever shifting winds of Soviet politics, Bassin and his colleagues chose this occasion to recommend as a Marxist antidote to Freud the work not only of Uznadze, but also of Vygotsky, Rubinstein, and Luria, each of whom, the authors failed to mention, had been subject in the past to severe criticism because of their alleged sympathies for Freud.[5]

Another Freud study appeared in Kiev, indicating the further spreading of Soviet specialization on the unconscious to include Ukrainians as well as Georgians and Russians. This book, *The Problem of the Unconscious in Philosophy and the Concrete Sciences* by A. N. Boiko, was based heavily on Bassin's recent research and Uznadze's earlier experiments. Boiko's book was a further illustration of both the complexity and the ambivalence in Soviet attitudes toward Freud. In the book, Freud was criticized methodologically for his idealism, his exclusive focus on sexuality as the primary motive in human relationships, and his refusal to appreciate the significance of the social environment for both individuals and groups. Nevertheless, after tracing interpretations of the unconscious from Descartes to the present, Boiko concluded that the main function of the unconscious was to facilitate the "adaptation of the human organism to the surrounding world." By providing mechanics for coping with the necessary adjustments essential to growth and development, the unconscious "liberates consciousness for constructive and creative activity in the conditions of the ever-changing environment."[6]

The third group of writings on psychoanalysis published during the 1970s was the most innovative. Until this point, the Soviet critical literature had focused on Freud's own works, with only scant attention being paid to the rest of the psychoanalytic spectrum. This changed in the early 1970s as a new generation of social scientists in the Soviet Union became interested in contemporary Western psychoanalysis, especially the work of Erich Fromm and Jacques Lacan.

The first Soviet studies on Fromm were published in 1972. The choice of Fromm as a subject of separate study was not a totally random one. Fromm presented Soviet specialists on psychoanalysis with a challenging professional background. He was a psychoanalyst who was in disagreement with orthodox Freudians on a number of technical issues, he had been affiliated with the Frankfurt Institute for Social Research in Germany prior to his emigration to the United States, and he was a Marxist associated with various social movements and American circles of intellectual criticism which the Soviets characterized with more than mild approval as "progressive."

This new trend emerged rather quietly in a review article which used one of Fromm's books, *The Crisis of Psychoanalysis,* as a launching point for a wider discussion about the field of psychoanalysis. The article appeared in the country's leading philosophical journal. The author, V. M. Leibin, an academic researcher in philosophy in Moscow, titled his article "Conformism and the Respectability of Psychoanalysis." Since he knew that Fromm's ideas were unfamiliar to his Soviet colleagues, he not only reviewed the recent *Crisis* book (which was published in 1970 in the United States), but also Fromm's earlier books. None of the works by Fromm mentioned in Leibin's article were as yet available in bookstores in Russian translation or in any other language.

Most of Leibin's article focused on Fromm's thesis that psychoanalysis had been transformed from social critique to conformist theory. According to Leibin, Fromm argued that Freud had formulated his theory of the power of the unconscious with implications that boldly challenged some of the assumptions governing bourgeois society. However, psychoanalysis had evolved in the hands of Freud's successors into "a theory of respectability, accommodating itself to the demands of the new 'technical' society."

Leibin's article broke new ground in the post-Stalin era in at least two ways. He was the first commentator on psychoanalysis during this period to maintain that the part of Freud's work usually referred to most negatively—his "meta-psychology"—was compatible with Soviet values. Leibin reproduced, without polemical flourishes, Fromm's argument that the nonclinical elaboration of Freud's theory contained radical social implications before it was transformed by his followers into a "theory of conformism." This was precisely the dimension of Freud's theory which Bassin, Fedotov, and other Soviet psychiatrists and psychologists had so severely criticized. In addition, Leibin introduced to Soviet readers the work of other prominent psychoanalysts, such as Karen Horney, Harry Stack Sullivan, and Erik Erikson, as well as the essence of Herbert Marcuse's criticism of Fromm's writings on Freud.[7]

A fuller account of Fromm's work appeared a few months later in 1972 in a long essay published as a pamphlet, *A Critique of the Neo-Freudian Conceptions of Erich Fromm,* by a young Moscow sociologist, V. N. Dobren'kov. After a brief obligatory introductory statement in which the author placed Fromm in the camp of "liberal bourgeois theorists" who remained a threat to Communism, Dobren'kov presented a summary of both Freud's and Fromm's psychoanalytic work. He analyzed Fromm's most influential books, all of which were cited in English editions unavailable legally in the Soviet Union. In spite of the author's critique, supported by decorative quotations from both Marx and Lenin, the exposition of Fromm's work was both sensitive and insightful, and was the most extensive published discussion of Fromm in the Soviet Union. Two years later, Dobren'kov published an even fuller analysis of Fromm's work in the context of the neo-Freudian movement in the West.[8] With this work, Dobren'kov achieved a very Soviet distinction—in a very public manner, he became the country's leading expert on a Western intellectual whose work was officially not yet available to read.

Meanwhile, attention shifted to the French psychoanalyst Jacques Lacan.

Near the end of 1973, N. S. Avtonomova published a broad-ranging article entitled "The Psychoanalytic Conceptions of Jacques Lacan" which both described and assessed his work in depth. However, unlike most Soviet work on psychoanalytic theory, this article did not interpret Lacan as a bourgeois antagonist of socialism. Moreover, there was not a single quotation from the "classics of Marxism-Leninism" in her discussion of Lacan's complex thought.[9]

Other works on Lacan and psychoanalysis continued to appear during the mid-1970s,[10] but they were somewhat overshadowed by V. M. Leibin's *Psychoanalysis and the Philosophy of Neo-Freudianism,* unquestionably the most authoritative and objective work on the international psychoanalytic movement to be published in the Soviet Union. Leibin discussed the vast influence of psychoanalysis in Europe and America in the fields of psychiatry, philosophy, sociology, history, anthropology, and art, as well as the evolution of "classical psychoanalysis." Leibin also included a penetrating analysis of Freud's antagonists from within the growing psychoanalytic movement, Jung and Adler, and an account of Wilhelm Reich's theories of "sexual revolution," the psychology of fascism, and the fusion of Marxism and psychoanalysis. Moreover, he devoted a lengthy section to the "neo-Freudians," particularly Horney, Sullivan, and Fromm. Leibin's evidence was taken directly from the writings of these theoreticians of psychoanalysis, as well as from an array of Western thinkers from Sören Kierkegaard and Henri Bergson to Jean-Paul Sartre and Marshall McLuhan, materials rarely cited in Soviet publications during the Brezhnev era with such scholarly neutrality.[11] By clearly eschewing ideology in his discussion of the "neo-Freudian movement," Leibin had succeeded in further undermining the official critical attitude toward psychoanalysis in the Soviet Union.

THE SOVIET INTERNATIONAL CONGRESS ON THE UNCONSCIOUS

The contradictory state of affairs on psychoanalysis in the Soviet Union could not be sustained. By the end of the 1970s, psychoanalytic works could be read but not published, discussed but not approved, presented in a paper at a scientific meeting but not practiced in a hospital or psychiatrist's office. A substantial number of specialists in the philosophy, history, and sociology of psychoanalysis were at work, but the subject could not be taught in university or medical school courses. Further, the emphasis on the concept of the unconscious, though a central part of Freud's psychological theory of human motivation, was to be used mainly to advance a more physiologically based Soviet alternative.

For some years, several of Uznadze's followers had been working to establish contacts both in the Soviet Union and abroad with the intention of holding an international and interdisciplinary meeting on the concept of the unconscious. One of the initiators was Sergei Tsuladze, a Georgian psychologist who had been trained in psychoanalysis in Paris. Though he died before the realization of his idea, his work was carried on by Bassin and several of his colleagues. In addition to Bassin, the main Soviet organizers of the planned conference were A. S. Prangishvili, a research psychologist in the Academy of Sciences of the Soviet Georgian Republic, and A. E. Sheroziia, a psychologist at Tbilisi State University.

There were, in addition, clear signals of professional support from the outside world. One of the participants in the conference, Nancy Rollins, was an American psychiatrist who had spent four months in Moscow studying Soviet child psychiatry in the winter of 1968–69 and helped to organize the meetings. In the book she wrote based on her Moscow research, she made a specific recommendation that an international symposium be arranged which would make possible a professional interchange of Soviet and American research on psychoanalysis.[12] Another important source of support was Leon Chertok, a French psychiatrist with psychoanalytic training at the Centre de Médecine Psychosomatique in Paris, who for many years had been at the forefront of efforts to forge alliances between Soviet and Western psychiatrists. According to Chertok, invitations to present papers were sent out to experts in the Soviet Union, Europe, and America "from every branch of science, including all the different schools of psychoanalysis."[13]

The response to the call for papers was overwhelming. The organizers received more than one hundred and fifty papers, about two-thirds of which were from the Soviet Union, and included submissions from specialists not only in medicine and science but also in literature, art, music, theater, sociology, history, and philosophy. Over 1,400 people convened in Tbilisi during the week of October 1–6, 1979, for the meetings of the First International Symposium on the Unconscious. Among them was the world-renowned linguist Roman Jakobson, who dazzled his audience by delivering his paper in the Georgian language. Jacques Lacan was invited and expected, but did not attend.

Judging from most of the published accounts of the meetings, the organizers achieved more than they had expected. Chertok considered it "a major event," particularly "when viewed in the light of the history of Soviet psychology." By this he meant that the conference on the unconscious was a triumph for those professionals in the Soviet Union, particularly among psychologists, who had fought for the demythologizing of Pavlovian doctrine and for the rehabilitation of the study of psychoanalytic theory.[14] George Pollack, director of the Chicago Institute for Psychoanalysis, returned from the Tbilisi meetings with a positive assessment: "The Symposium was exciting and my memory is filled with many personal impressions. . . . Throughout the meeting we were treated kindly, generously, and as colleagues with whom dialogue was sought."[15] Nancy Rollins noted that the papers that Western psychoanalytic researchers sent to the conference organizers had a direct impact: "Our Soviet colleagues not only organized participants' contributions into coherent themes; they also read Western psychoanalytic literature, evaluated internal dilemmas in the psychoanalytic movement, and expanded their own position regarding the unconscious." Rollins also mentioned some of the problems she and her colleagues from Western Europe encountered.

> In considering how to convey what has been going on in Tbilisi, there were formidable difficulties. At the linguistic level, we experienced the Tower of Babel, the confusion of many tongues, as papers were published and presented at the meetings in Russian, English, French, and German. The simultaneous translation provided turned out for me to be a mind-jamming experience. Some knowledge of a foreign language created conflicting sets, interfering with understanding both the original and the translation.
>
> At the semantic level, there were definitional problems. For example, was consciousness to be taken as a quality of mental experience or as a system of psychic activity? Was [the Uznadzean term] "set" identical with the unconscious, or did the term unconscious imply many additional kinds of psychic activity?
>
> At the conceptual level, I was reminded of a group of scientists studying an elephant with blindfolds over their eyes. I imagined one researcher floating in the air close to the beast's back, palpitating its long spine, another investigating the trunk, one holding a large ear, etc. The Uznadze school had studied the unconscious through laboratory experiments on perceptual sets, while the psychoanalysts had studied the unconscious through the method of free association, largely in neurotic patients.[16]

There were also less enthusiastic reactions which were described in other accounts of the meetings. The French delegation, which was divided by its own factional struggles, was unhappy with what some of its members perceived to be the suppression of certain topics by the Soviets. A few even boycotted the conference, believing that their attendance would contribute to legitimizing

the Soviet psychiatric profession, which had only recently been forced to with-
draw from the World Psychiatric Association as a result of charges regarding the
clinical abuse of dissidents. The French delegation in Tbilisi also complained
about the lack of clarity concerning which kinds of psychoanalytic materials,
whether clinical cases or theoretical explorations, were deemed acceptable by
the Soviet conference organizers for presentation.[17]

The vast scope of the Tbilisi conference is most evident from the 248 papers
which were presented and later published by the Georgian Academy of Sciences
in four thick volumes totalling 2,710 pages.[18] In their introduction, the editors
stated that this "collective monograph" was a reflection of "the major approaches to the problem of the unconscious in world science" as evidenced by
the broad spectrum of authors whose diverse work appeared in its pages. The
editors were quite aware of the differing Soviet and Western perspectives on the
unconscious. In the language of the conference organizers, they acknowledged
the existence of "deeper, fundamental differences of a methodological order
that exist between the initial theoretical lines of approach, the directions of
analysis and the ways of interpretation characteristic of different authors." To
emphasize their efforts at fairness, the editors mentioned that earlier research
on the unconscious bore the imprint of either "idealistic philosophy" or of
"simplified mechanistic constructions," a critical statement meant to encom-
pass both Western and Soviet work prior to the congress.

In spite of their recognition of the conflicting interpretations at the conference, the editors made clear their own "theoretical propositions." These included: the belief in the reality of the unconscious as a psychological phenomenon; the conviction that "it is impossible to gain a deep insight into the
psychological structure of any act of human behavior" without a consideration
of the unconscious; a proper understanding of the unconscious requires the
application of dialectical materialist concepts; and a scientific theory of the
unconscious can be constructed on the basis of the research on the concept of
set as developed by Uznadze and as elaborated by his followers.[19]

These carefully worded "propositions" revealed the dissension underlying
the entire conference. Most psychoanalysts in the West would have agreed with
the first two, but not with the third and fourth, which were the product of the
controlled rehabilitation of the unconscious in the Soviet Union. The question
that a few delegates raised, however, was to what degree was this different from
an "orthodox" Freudian meeting in reverse?

The tension between Uznadzean and Western orientations was evident in
the organization of the initial volume of papers, called "The Development of

the Idea." The book was divided into three sections. The first dealt with the problem of evaluating the psychological reality of the unconscious, the second with the evolution of the concept of the unconscious before, during, and particularly after Freud, and the third with the neurophysiological mechanisms of unconscious behavior. While the papers in the first section were largely contributed by the Soviet Georgian researchers of the Uznadze school, the second part contained an array of conflicting points of view. This section included papers by the French philosopher Louis Althusser on Freud's "rapport" with Marxist theory, Chertok on the concept of the unconscious in France before Freud, Leibin's comparative analysis of Freud's and Jung's views on the unconscious, Rollins's critique of Uznadze, as well as other papers on Alfred Adler, Pierre Janet, and Jacques Lacan by Soviet and Western authors. The third section showed the parallel areas of interest in the neurophysiological bases of unconscious mental activity in the work done in the Soviet Union and abroad, particularly during the previous thirty years.

The second volume was more oriented toward clinical applications and experimental studies. Awkwardly titled "Sleep, Clinic, Creativity," it was also divided into three sections. The papers were classified according to their pertinence to the following areas: the activity of the unconscious in conditions of sleep hypnosis and other altered states of consciousness; manifestations of the unconscious in clinical syndromes; and the role of the unconscious in artistic creativity. The editors of the volume found a degree of thematic unity in these three areas on the basis of the importance of "the language of the unconscious." By this they meant that dreams, clinical symptoms, and works of art all allowed for the expression of unconscious conflict in various forms. They referred directly to Lacan's work on the structure of the language of the unconscious, which they saw both as an advance over Freud's study of symbolic communication in dreams, and as a way of linking Western concepts of the unconscious to the emphasis on language which had been developed by Uznadze empirically and by Vygotsky more theoretically.[20]

This volume included not only many more American contributors than had the first volume, but also submissions from a number of prominent Moscow and Leningrad psychiatrists who in the past had been vocal adherents of the anti-Freudian critique. Represented among the latter were A. M. Sviadoshch, D. D. Fedotov, and A. E. Lichko, most of whom discussed the topic of psychotherapy at the conference as a way of treating the symptoms of unconscious conflict. Although the criticism of Freud remained in these papers, it was now frequently mixed with admiring praise for his achievements or punctuated by substantive discussions which were more clearly psychoanalytic in basic orien-tation.[21]

The third volume was entitled "Cognition, Communication, and Person-ality," and also included papers on "Methods of the Study of the Unconscious," in addition to those which addressed the themes in the title. In this volume, an attempt was made to integrate the works of Vygotsky and Uznadze,[22] and the contributions of Silvano Arieti on cognition and Roman Jakobson on lin-guistics appear here as well.[23]

The fourth and final volume in the series appeared in 1985 and was dedicated to the memory of Sheroziia, who died after the conclusion of the symposium. This volume, "Results of the Discussion," was largely the work of the Georgian researchers involved in the symposium, with hardly any participation from abroad.[24] The Soviet analysis of the proceedings made clear in the minds of the organizers that the symposium "should be characterized as an extensive con-frontation of the two basic approaches to the problem of the unconscious," namely, the Freudian and post-Freudian psychoanalytic orientations "domi-nant in the West," and the research methodology of the followers of Uznadze. The Soviet editors presented Uznadze's theory of set, particularly as modified by Sheroziia, as the most scientific and advanced method of studying the functions of unconscious mental activity. Nevertheless, Freud's accomplish-ment was openly recognized as fundamental to this enterprise.[25]

Although there were further discussions about this complicated effort to counterpose Freud and Uznadze in terms of similarities as well as differences,[26] the work accomplished at the Tbilisi symposium was a turning point in the history of psychoanalysis in the Soviet Union. For the first time since the 1917 revolution, a genuine effort was made to bring together psychoanalytic research on the unconscious conducted in the West with parallel developments in the Soviet Union. The convening of the conference certainly entailed some risk since it was not clear how the authorities would respond to it. Indeed, a public attack on the symposium surfaced early in 1980, soon after its conclusion, branding Prangishvili, Sheroziia, and their colleagues as Freudians for devoting so much attention to the alleged scientific legitimacy of the unconscious.[27] The organizers of the symposium, however, maintained their position and rejected calls that they retract their earlier published statements. They stated at the symposium that they were fully aware of the arguments and differences "be-tween our ideological opponents and ourselves" and that they "remained un-compromising" about their commitment to a Marxist methodological ap-proach to the problems of the unconscious.

However, they went on to say that "it would be wrong to interpret this stand as a refusal to try to understand the point of view of our opponents and to cooperate with them in areas in which the differences are rather formal than radical—where these differences tend to reflect the distinctive developmental history of investigations and established traditions rather than an adherence to definite philosophical systems and methodological premises. Such refusal would imply intolerance and would manifestly inhibit the further growth of our knowledge." They concluded ominously, with an implicit reference back to the rigidities of the Pavlovian period, that such intolerance "could have even broader negative implications."[28] At the same time, they announced their intention of keeping the dialogue with the West open and active, to the point of publishing a supplementary volume to the symposium proceedings if the response justified it.[29] Viewed in the context of the larger world of Cold War political competition with the West, Sheroziia and his colleagues were taking a stand with the moderate side on the spectrum of Soviet political attitudes. They were, from the party leadership's perspective, clearly supporting the view of peaceful cooperation with the capitalist enemy.

For some of the Western participants who attended the Tbilisi conference, hopes remained high. Chertok wrote, following a return to the Soviet Union after the meetings, "that the symposium had, despite [a] few incidental reactions, brought about an indisputable opening, the consequences of which will certainly be fruitful."[30] Another Western commentator, writing in the *Bulletin* of the Sigmund Freud House in Vienna, went even further: "It is possible that the Georgian school of psychology will turn out to be the first to accomplish the integration of a theory of the unconscious into the larger field of general psychology. If this is true, we might see how the abyss which traditionally has separated psychoanalysis from the mainstream of classic psychology may be crossed."[31]

By contrast, according to a French participant, "it is improbable that the symposium, however broad and open, allowed the slightest reimplantation of Freudianism in the Soviet Union. For in order for such a penetration to occur, it would have been necessary for the practice of psychoanalysis not to be forbidden, nor its works to be banned."[32] This was precisely what was about to happen.

Chapter 9 Psychoanalysis
and Soviet History

The nature of man himself is hidden in the deepest and darkest recesses
of the unconscious, the elemental and the submerged. Is it not self-
evident that the greatest efforts of inquiring thought and of creative
initiative will move in that direction?
—L. D. Trotsky

PSYCHOANALYSIS AND ITS USES DURING
THE PERESTROIKA REGIME

In 1987, two years after the start of Soviet leader Mikhail Gorbachev's
ambitious program of political restructuring (perestroika) and cultural openness (glasnost), a feature article concerning psychoanalysis
appeared in the government's main newspaper, *Izvestiia*. The author
was Andrei Voznesensky, one of the Soviet Union's most respected
poets. Voznesensky's essay was both a somber declaration of recognition about the deceitful manner in which the past had been officially
conceptualized and an explicit call for Soviet society to move toward a
more truthful understanding of that past. The poet had in mind the

necessity of confronting the political immorality of the previous decades, and of realizing what he called "the conscience of thought." He mentioned "those who had been arrested by the arbitrariness of the Stalin system" and "the falsified textbooks of history" where "the portraits of the undesirables" were removed. "How shameful it is to me now," he wrote, "to realize that in my childhood I believed the slander about the purest of people." He also discussed the great writers who were not permitted to be included in the books he read as a student, like Akhmatova, Bulgakov, Mandelstam, and Pasternak. Freud, he recalled, was one of the many European intellectuals whose work he was not able to read. "Why," he asked in the article, "have Freud's works not been published?" Inquiring further, he wanted to know "why has psychoanalysis been excluded from clinical practice" in the Soviet Union? For Voznesensky, the ability to choose what to read was an integral part of the creation of "a science united with humanism, one that is free, open and limitless, like thought itself."[1]

Questions similar to Voznesensky's were being asked in public across the Soviet Union as demands for change accelerated. The process of change started before Gorbachev's call for "new thinking," and was noticed by at least some observers who were interested in the fate of psychoanalysis in this transitional political climate. According to one report in the late 1970s, based on first hand experience, "there is a rather flexible attitude to various forms of psychotherapy. Some wild psychoanalysis seems to be going on unofficially. There is considerable interest in Freud among the intellectuals and also in the younger generation of physicians and medical students. The spokesmen of psychiatry, who have done away with Freudism again and again, are still trapped in the same repetitive situation, but the rejection of psychoanalysis is neither total nor unanimous today. Recently, the signs of renewed interest and fascination have accumulated."[2]

Debate remains as to whether it was the party's relaxation of controls under Gorbachev that inspired the outpouring of books and articles on previously disapproved themes, or whether the intelligentsia itself pressed for the right to think and act in ways that earlier would have brought repressive forces to the front door, thereby forcing the party to lessen its grip on society. There is no disagreement, however, about the nature of the changes themselves. Writers whose works had been condemned under Stalinism appeared in bookstores and kiosks, often under the imprint of one of the divisions of the monopolistic State Publishing House. Similarly, banished and executed political figures like Trotsky and Bukharin, whose very names had been erased from the official record, became the focal points of heated public roundtables and debates about the hideous and, according to some commentators, irrevocable damage done to the country by the terror of the 1930s.

The major thrust of this intellectual reawakening was, as Voznesensky had said, the search for a means of understanding the past, and the commitment to conduct the search in public space, which until now had been defined by the ruling authorities. As the accumulated weight of those joining this effort grew, the need to reclaim that past seemed to intensify. Not surprisingly, individuals interested in psychoanalysis played an important role among those who were either producing or consuming the flow of the new and often revealing information. An open discussion of psychoanalytic concepts returned to the journals and newspapers, free of the ideological constraints imposed since the early 1930s. Moreover, these concepts were used to reinterpret the troubled Soviet past in a variety of ways. For some, the effort was part of a realization that comprehending the past was a means of escaping from it. For others, the dissolving boundaries of what was politically acceptable presented opportunities to reestablish new public identities in accordance with the fresh winds of glasnost. Regardless of motive, many people were willing to take full advantage of the altered political atmosphere to write about the totalitarian controls that rigidly ruled, sternly judged, and severely punished Soviet party members and ordinary citizens over the decades.

Discussions of Freud returned to the medical profession even before the Gorbachev years, but more quietly and less critically than in the writing that appeared in the popular media. Freudian terminology in psychiatric textbooks and monographs continued to appear, almost always without attribution. This was especially true in the material that dealt with neurotic disorders and techniques of psychotherapy, much of which was presented in terms of the need to develop a more sophisticated, socialist-based personality theory.[3] Even the much repressed subject of sexual pathology was revived in a medical textbook that remained in demand well after its publication in 1977, especially among readers who were not medical specialists.[4]

At the same time, the more scholarly Freudian criticism extended its influence. Applications of psychoanalysis to the study of problems like the motivations behind artistic creativity were published, and doctoral dissertations built on the earlier work of Dobren'kov, Avtonomova, and Leibin.[5] Also, the work of Bassin and the Uznadze school continued to have an impact not only in Moscow, but also in the Caucasus, as evidenced by a book on the unconscious published by the Academy of Sciences in Baku, capital of Azerbaizhan.[6]

Some of the published material on psychoanalysis during the Gorbachev regime was either rather tame or fixed in scholarly paradigms established in the period before perestroika.[7] Much of it, however, moved into untraveled pathways. There were even public disagreements about interpretations of Freud in which the arguments focused on how to *defend* his legacy.[8] Some scholars who had already published books about psychoanalysis continued to expand their work. Valery Leibin wrote an erudite book in 1990 in which he investigated the relationship of psychoanalysis to "philosophical anthropology," existentialism, phenomenology, hermeneutics, structuralism, neopositivism, and the Frankfurt School.[9]

Beyond the written word, Freud and psychoanalysis appeared for the first time in the cinema. Although psychoanalytic themes had been detected in earlier films, Andrei Zagdansky's *Interpretation of Dreams* was the first Soviet movie to show extensive documentary footage of Freud. The filmmaker's attitudes toward psychoanalysis were hardly subtle: he juxtaposed graphic footage from the savage history of imperialism, warfare, and revolution during the first half of the twentieth century against quotations read from Freud's works which, uncannily, seemed to interpret the events. As seen through Zagdansky's eyes, the era of mass violence and the obedience to fascist and communist leaders were bound together in the framework of unchecked, relentless, and aggressive instincts of murderous gratification, controlled by the symbols of modern politics—flags, party logos, gigantic public rallies—all displayed in the public space created by the architects of totalitarianism. To underscore the connection between repression, whether individual or societal, and the long-standing intolerance of psychoanalysis in the Soviet Union, the film closed with these words alone on the screen: "From 1929 to 1989, Freud was not published in the USSR."[10]

The real change in attitudes about psychoanalysis, however, and the degree to which this shift reflected the mood of much of Soviet society at this time, was most noticeable in the interpretations of Freud which appeared in newspaper and journal articles. Many of the country's most widely read publications, such as the government newspaper *Izvestiia* and the popular magazine *Ogonek,* began to carry stories in which Freud and psychoanalysis were mentioned or discussed.[11] One of the first publications to give prominent space to psychoanalysis, and to break with the anti-Freud critique of the past, was the widely read weekly, *Literaturnaia gazeta,* which devoted an entire page to a Freud tribute in early June 1988. Freud's photograph was included, together with a laudatory essay by Aaron Belkin and a long excerpt from Jean-Paul Sartre's screenplay on Freud's life. The editors introduced this material by mentioning that "Sartre had succeeded in creating an expressive image of Freud, as an honest scientist, a noble person and a courageous seeker of the truth."

Belkin, the director of the National Psychoendocrinology Center at the Ministry of Public Health in Moscow, stated that after a period of widespread popularity in the 1920s, Freud had come under severe attack by Soviet authorities "followed by the total persecution of psychoanalysis. Attempts to use psychoanalytic methods to treat patients were punished by repressive measures." The consequences of this repression for the Soviet Union were immense, Belkin wrote. By eliminating psychoanalysis, "we not only denied medical care to hundreds and thousands of people; we also reduced the ability of whole generations of creative people to work in their fields." Belkin summed up the main problem in his conclusion:

> It is always more difficult to recover than it is to get sick. However, the recovery of a society as a whole, like that of an individual, requires the overcoming of internal resistance, the mastery of fear, the acknowledgement of one's mistakes and an understanding of their origins. It requires that they be raised to the level of consciousness and, moreover, that their genesis be understood as well.
>
> That is why it seems to me that Sigmund Freud's teachings are in need of new approaches today, from the standpoint of recent advances in biology, the natural sciences, and the humanities.[12]

Many others who had been working on Freud now took full advantage of the policies of glasnost by reinterpreting psychoanalysis. In the Soviet Union's leading journal of psychology L. A. Radzikhovskii published an article entitled "The Theory of Freud: A Change of Purpose," in which the contrast was sharply drawn between the official criticism of Freud in the past and the current revival. With intended exaggeration, Radzikhovskii wrote, "Since the 1930s, Freud was 'criminal number 1' from the point of view of official psychology." In censuring and condemning Freud and his theories, the Soviet Union had deprived itself of the work of the man "who defined the face of world psychology" in this century more than any other single person, including the once-deified Pavlov. Moreover, without psychoanalysis, Soviet society was prevented from developing "the nucleus of a humane culture," with its representative expression in literature, the cinema, painting, and philosophy. In the West, Freud and his work became "a universal symbol of the culture of the twentieth century," providing a discourse of criticism and explanations for human behavior and motivation. Freud, the author continued, created a cultural paradigm and a portrait of the unconscious functions of the psyche which were comparable to Newton's map of the physical world. He successfully translated the symbols of this unconscious realm of private and individual experience into a language accessible to all. Because Stalin, "the great dictator," banished this entire field of knowledge in the Soviet Union, Radzikhovskii concluded, "authoritarian conditions have survived in our consciousness until now, and have made our consciousness neurotic."[13]

Radzikhovskii's effort to draw a link between the mutual repression of psychoanalysis and human freedom in the Soviet Union was bold. He was, nevertheless, quite aware of the danger of shifting from an ideologically informed discourse of stringent criticism of Freud to one dominated by excessive valorization. The desire to construct a new explanatory narrative, and to empower it with inordinate authority, was palpable beneath the surface of Radzikhovskii's text.

Personal conversations and unpublished materials held for decades either in previously inaccessible state archives or secretly in private hands were now discussed in print.[14] M. G. Yaroshevky, a prominent psychologist (and formerly a hard-line communist scholar) involved in the Freud renaissance, made public a discussion he had years before with the late Alexander Luria in which Luria had told him that one of the children in the psychoanalytic school run by Vera Schmidt in the early 1920s was Stalin's son, Vasily. Although this story had been suspected privately for some time, it had lacked valid evidence.[15]

Also at this time, unpublished materials appeared on the career of Ivan Ermakov, one of the most important figures in the psychoanalytic community during the 1920s. Much of this material was taken directly from Ermakov's private papers, including the recovery of a chapter from Ermakov's psychoanalytic study of Dostoevsky's life and work.[16] In a related development, in January 1989, Belkin published a feature article in the country's national medical newspaper urging his colleagues to make clinical use of Freud's work, which he said was "necessary for physicians in a variety of specialties."[17]

There was another level of inquiry as well, which had to do with the question about the Stalinist terror asked on behalf of many by Nadezhda Mandelstam in her poignant memoir, *Hope Against Hope*—"Why did we let it happen?" The notion of the citizen as victim, which had become a frequent answer to this question, was now being challenged by the notion of societal complicity in the terror.

This interpretation, using psychoanalytic terminology, was demonstrated in a lengthy essay written in 1989 by two psychologists and published in the Leningrad literary-intellectual journal *Neva*. The thesis of the article was that conditions of freedom could not be realized in the Soviet Union until it evolved from a society that was historically subordinated to "the cult of power" to one that placed power in the hands of the people. To appreciate the nature of the problem, the authors, Leonid Gozman and Alexander Etkind, stated as a proven proposition that the Stalin regime was "the most barbaric" dictatorship in a century in which millions also died at the hands of murderous rulers like Adolf Hitler and Pol Pot. What, they asked, was the meaning of this grotesque and unequal war of the state against its citizens? Their answer was that it had to be found in the complicit depths of the society where the totalitarian state found its base of acceptance and support. "To understand authority," the authors wrote, "and not to merely accuse it, it is necessary to comprehend how our needs were satisfied by such pathological forms."

Toward this end, Gozman and Etkind conducted a psychological dissection of Soviet history since the 1917 revolution. Simultaneously promising a glorious future while destroying the existing basis of human relationships, the Stalin regime created a vast network of controls over every aspect of ordinary life. "Mystification" was used so effectively that citizens gradually renounced political responsibility and abandoned it to the "genius of the leader." Monopolizing the available means of communicating information, the regime created an imagined world of simplicity and order within, and one of mistrustful enemies in the universe of hostile nations beyond its borders. It was also portrayed as an unchanging and benign power, established by Stalin to resolve all problems for all time. Ultimately, the authors argued, Stalin established a tyranny based on the "love of power," while communicating to society a "dictatorship of love." To oppose the regime, even in thought, was tantamount to betrayal, automatic guilt, and denial of the right to live. To break through this structure, a new political psychology and a fundamental shift in the society's values would have to take root. Soviet citizens would have to realize the consequences of their previous subordination to authority, in all its forms, and be willing to foster new institutions and new social relationships based on the rule of law. Instead of the former vertical structure of power, Gozman and Etkind argued for a horizontal reorganization of institutions in society with full citizen participation.[18]

At this juncture, the Freud critique had turned completely around. From an object of scorn and attack as ordered *by* the governing authorities, psychoanalytic theory was converted into a critical weapon *against* the government. This trend was expanded further by Belkin's effort to see psychoanalysis as a barometer of liberty in the context of Soviet history. In Belkin's introductory essay to his 1989 edition of Freud's collected works (one of the first Freud anthologies to appear since the 1920s), he wrote that the very appearance of Freud's ideas suggested "a new approach to our social existence." One of the major achievements of psychoanalysis was to permit members of society to examine their inner selves, the determining factor behind many daily activities and relationships. There, beneath the conscious level lie "the awesome echoes of past times: furious rage, violence, fanaticism, stagnant stereotypes, crazy wars, numerous acts of aggression and even signs of personality disintegration." Examining these sources of unconscious conflict through the microscope of psychoanalytic inquiry, Freud demonstrated, in Belkin's words, that it was possible for an individual "to cease to be a slave to his desires as unconscious impulses, to gain control over them, and to become an authentic [*podlinnyi*] personality."[19]

Moreover, Belkin wrote, the condemnation of Freud's work in the early Stalin years was a symptom of Soviet communism as a system, which "decreased the effectiveness of creative work for whole generations of people," and obliterated the nation's collective past. He experienced some of this first hand, as he explained in describing his "first steps toward psychoanalysis." Belkin learned about Freud in the early 1950s from two of his mentors in Irkutsk, the capital of Eastern Siberia. There, far from Moscow, Belkin read volumes of Freud's work which a resident psychotherapist, Igor Sumbaev, preserved in his personal library. Belkin also was able to gain clinical knowledge from Sumbaev's assistant, Nikolai Ivanov, who secretly used psychotherapy to treat patients suffering from neurotic disorders. Ivanov was well aware that this was a precarious endeavor, and told Belkin not to talk to anyone about it. With a touch of black humor, Ivanov said that the worst that could happen if they were discovered would be that Belkin might lose his job and have his degree nullified. "But don't be anxious . . . they can't send you any farther than Siberia."[20]

In his article, Belkin also discussed the destructive consequences of Soviet ideology and its totalitarian institutions on both psychoanalysis and the country as a whole. Belkin reminded his readers that efforts had been made to find an accommodation with psychoanalysis during the 1920s. The real threat came not from the open debates, but from the institutionalization of totalitarianism of the 1930s both in Nazi Germany and the Soviet Union that took place without substantial protest by members of society.

Belkin believed he had found an explanation for this situation in what he called "the social Oedipus," a process permitting societal complicity in the totalitarian experience. In this "social Oedipal" situation, the sons join with the father to kill themselves. In understanding the dynamics of this situation,

Belkin argued that the ego was filled with totalitarian values of the regime, and the judgmental role of the superego was reversed to accept what, in normal conditions, would be considered as morally unacceptable. The process, Belkin concluded, tended to tear apart the relationship of the ego and the id, "destroying the psychological integrity of the individual personality." As a result, "the superego did not suffer from the sins of the ego." Citizens were thus able to inform on colleagues, friends and family, and to commit crimes on behalf of the state, free of both punishment from the external world and of guilt from within. Conscience itself was eroded, and people lived in a world of illusions and "areality" while participating in the "destruction of the cultural heritage of the past."[21] The dangers facing Soviet citizens in the aftermath of this Stalinist experience were serious, because the unrealized promises of the regime produced extreme forms of behavior. To rebel against the system was to act in a criminal manner as defined by the values of the state; to behave loyally meant to act as a criminal by carrying out the demands of the totalitarian regime. The only other choice, which was taken by many, was to be apathetic and indifferent. Writing in 1990, in the twilight of the Soviet era, Belkin stated that regardless of the choice one took, there was a marked disrespect for norms and laws. This situation had to be reversed if Russian society were to transcend its totalitarian past. Belkin believed that the renewed interest in Freud could only contribute to this process.

CONCLUSION: THE PAST AS FUTURE?

Belkin's efforts to bring psychoanalysis back into the public domain in the Soviet Union did not go unnoticed abroad. The interpretations and assumptions of motive, however, suggested far more about the deep suspicions of communism harbored by observers in the West than about the context of the Freud revival in the Soviet Union. The *New York Times* gave prominent space to Belkin's 1988 full-page article in *Literaturnaia gazeta*, but explained it as follows: "Dr. Belkin did not say so, but by giving intellectual responsibility back to Freud, Soviet psychiatry would be earning back a measure of international responsibility for itself. Its image has been badly marred by persistent reports of the wide use of psychiatric confinement as a method of repressing dissidents."[22]

Belkin's article was part of a larger public conversation about Freud, psychoanalysis, and Soviet history. In terms of historical perspective, the most striking aspect of this discourse was the *volte face* that had taken place since the original Soviet debate about psychoanalysis during the 1920s. At that time, followers of

Freud had sought to fuse psychoanalytic theory with Marxist ideology. Given the conditions in which they had to work, Soviet Freudians had little choice; without the approval of the authorities, their enterprise would not have survived. In the changed circumstances of the late 1980s under Gorbachev's regime, psychoanalysis was not only returned to respectability but was utilized to demonstrate what was now seen as its utter incompatibility with Marxism.

Looking back on the history of Russian psychoanalysis, it is clear that some aspects of the evolution reflect developments which have occurred in other countries where Freud's ideas attracted followers, while others appear to be the result of the special conditions facing practitioners and theorists in Russia. Nowhere else, for instance, was psychoanalysis established institutionally three times. The original Russian Psychoanalytic Society was rendered inoperative by the exigencies of the First World War and the revolutions of 1917. It was reconstituted in 1921 as the Soviet Psychoanalytic Institute, in conformity with certain Bolshevik strictures. The condemnation of psychoanalysis ended that chapter in 1930, and an entirely new situation arose in 1989 when several competing psychoanalytic societies and institutes emerged.

Furthermore, in no other country was there a state-supported and government-funded psychoanalytic institute. Psychoanalysts in the West have generally functioned within capitalist economies where profit-making private practice and doctor-patient confidentiality have been, if not guaranteed, at least the assumed modes of professional activity. Governments have had no discernible influence. This was generally the case in prerevolutionary Russia for the early Freudians, though even there, the state's role was more significant than was the case in most pre–World War I Western European countries. However, following the Bolshevik seizure of power in 1917, this relationship was fundamentally altered. Psychoanalysts soon found that they could not operate private practices in a communist society, and initially succeeded in attracting government support for their work. They were aided by the fact that high-level party members, including Trotsky and Lunacharsky, were willing to accommodate, or at least tolerate, the therapeutic and theoretical work of psychoanalysis.

State support, however, meant dependence on the state. Indeed, in the document that established the Soviet Psychoanalytic Institute in 1921 the government retained the right to order the organization to cease its activities, which is exactly what it did in the late 1920s. There is no other case of a government literally closing down the entire structure of psychoanalytic work, from therapy in the office to research in the journals. The closest one comes is the case of Nazi Germany, but even there the Psychoanalytic Institute in Berlin continued to operate, albeit in a severely distorted form of existence under Hitlerian authority and with a completely revamped and coerced personnel.[23]

Forced to function in a centralized state legitimized by a revolutionary ideology, the members of the psychoanalytic community in the Soviet Union had to justify their very existence in that doctrinal context. For over thirty years, a far longer period of time than the number of years in which psychoanalytic practice was actually permitted, Soviet politicians and scholars carried on an unrelenting "ideological struggle" against Freudian ideas and influences. This campaign, in which careers were both made and lost, went on while Soviet psychoanalysis was supposedly extinct. Party officials obviously felt that psychoanalysis represented a challenge to the postrevolutionary state. No other government in this century devoted as much attention, critical or otherwise, to Freud's ideas as did the Soviet regime. Because the discourse on psychoanalysis went on without interruption throughout the entire Soviet era, responsibility was shared by every party leader, including, of course, Stalin, under whose regime the attack on Freudians was most severe.

What threat did psychoanalysis pose to the Soviet Union to merit such attention, even after its institutional structure was crushed? Many contrasting reasons were given by the Soviet scholars who composed the attacks on psychoanalysis. A number of the critiques were products of the regime's ideological commitments; others were not dissimilar to the criticism leveled against psychoanalysis in the West—at times even anticipating various aspects of that criticism. Freud's work was seen, on the one hand, as too "idealistic," meaning that it was rooted in concepts which were antithetical to scientific empiricism as well as to the ideological doctrines of Marxist historical materialism. On the other hand, psychoanalysis was charged with being dominated by "physiological reductionism." According to this charge, Freud was "biologizing" psychology by explaining human behavior in terms of instinctual drives. Yet another reason given for the intolerance of psychoanalysis was that Freud and his followers were "opposed to neurophysiology and psychiatric science."[24] Still others objected to the pessimism and sexuality in Freud's writings. "The Freud problem," as one Russian psychologist observed, centered on the fact that psychoanalysis "locked man in the circle of hopeless psychical causality, in which the blind forces of sexuality and aggressiveness determine the things the subject sees on the screen of consciousness."[25]

There was, in addition, concern that Freud's dangerous influence could be found in other fields, extending from psychology and psychiatry to philosophy, aesthetics, art, sociology, literature, and history. This trend, according to one critic, was "one of the most harmful forms of bourgeois ideology," against which Soviet science had to defend itself.[26] To these were added the charges that psychoanalysis "has the arbitrary characteristics of dogma" and that it actually brought "harm to public health by diverting attention from the real possibilities of medical intervention." Perhaps the most damaging indictment was that psychoanalysis had "a demoralizing influence" wherever it has been practiced in that it "raises the forces of sexual attraction to the level of a leading social factor, thereby encouraging unhealthy trends among youth, decadent literature and art, etc."[27] Freud, in other words, was held responsible for the ancient canard of corrupting the young, much as Socrates had been long before him.

If psychoanalysis required continued attack even after it was shown to be unscientific and erroneous as a theory of personality motivation, and useless and ineffective as a therapeutic treatment, the real enemy must have been neither Freud nor his ideas, regardless of who was interpreting them. In fact, psychoanalysis became a powerful symbol of a deep problem endemic to the Soviet system itself. To view the entire communist experiment in the Soviet Union from the vantage point of the Stalinist terror is to oversimplify the historical situation. The Bolsheviks first won and then maintained power not only through coercion but also through the voluntary participation of many people who believed in the ideology of revolution and who were inspired by the possibilities of a postimperial and postbourgeois socialist society. To be sure, few of those people knew very clearly what this new order would look like. Nevertheless, many were willing to trust in the party leadership and to make contributions themselves toward that future, even at the price of personal sacrifice. The place to witness this phenomenon is not in the minutes of the party meetings, but in the trenches of the new culture itself—the innovative posters, films, public spectacles, literacy schools, and factory drama clubs set up all over the country by the party and its enthusiasts.[28]

In the process, a battle raged between competing value systems. Subscribing to the ideological appeals of the party leadership meant accepting the priority of collectivist values over individualist concerns. Power could then be marshalled, at various levels of the political hierarchy, in the service of an organized force designed to protect the proclaimed values of the newly emerging socialist society against the enemy. The enemy was identified as the perceived chaos of extreme individualism, which was branded "bourgeois" and threatening to the success of the revolution. The Russian psychoanalysts who survived the pre-

revolutionary period were forced to confront this situation and to face a narrowing spectrum of difficult choices.

In the years prior to the revolution, however, when reports on, and translations of, Freud's work initially appeared in Russia, the overall situation was
different. The first generation of analysts was engaged primarily in the task of
establishing a psychotherapeutic clinical milieu in Russia along the lines developed by Freud and his original followers in Europe. Whether treating patients
or publishing research articles in psychiatric journals, they were not exclusively
oriented toward Freud's theories. Osipov, Wulff, Spielrein, Ermakov, and their
colleagues also sought training and treatment from Jung, Adler, and Stekel, as
well as from nonpsychoanalytic practitioners like Dubois.

They may have received training and a measure of inspiration from their
colleagues in the West, but they did not adopt the tendency to create a founding
father with reverential, if not uncritical, loyalty expected of the followers. It is
ironic that while psychoanalytic institutes and societies in the democratic West
invested their leaders with near charismatic authority, psychoanalysts in authoritarian Russia both before and after the 1917 revolution never invented or
subscribed to such a leadership principle as one finds with Freud in Vienna,
Carl Jung in Zurich, Karl Abraham in Berlin, Sandor Ferenczi in Budapest,
Jacques Lacan in Paris, and Anna Freud or Melanie Klein in London.

At the same time, the early Russian psychoanalysts had to face their own
problems. On the one hand, they sought to demonstrate to their psychiatric
colleagues that psychoanalysis was a legitimate medical therapy and that its
diagnostic classifications were acceptable in a medical context. Osipov's early
publications hammered away at these themes, explicitly and implicitly. On the
other hand, the Russian psychoanalysts had concerns about encroachment of
the tsarist government into their professional world, though it was largely
limited to criticisms of the state's insensitivity to psychotherapy in psychiatry
and lack of appropriate financial support to expand and improve hospitals and
clinics for the mentally ill.

After the revolution, the psychoanalytic community faced a far more serious
problem of state power which manifested itself in terms of the primacy of
ideological demands and a vast societal mobilization undertaken on behalf of
the largely undefined revolutionary order to be established at the Bolshevik
party's insistence. To accomplish this, the ruling authorities draped a "cultural
curtain" over the whole society. Although this effort was relaxed sufficiently for
a few years during the New Economic Policy period, it was expanded and

solidified during the 1930s with a combination of attacks on "bourgeois" structures identified with either the West or the tsarist past, and with the creation of
new Soviet and proletarian values. The Soviet leadership's assertion was that the
brutality of the class conflicts that had dominated history under capitalism
could not be alleviated without putting necessary controls in place over history
and politics. The essence of what has been conceptualized as totalitarianism
resides in the ability of a governing elite to amass intimidating power, with the
complicity (intentional or involuntary) of the society, to institute these controls. In this way, the party called for painful sacrifices across the spectrum of
the society to build the new order, thereby mythologizing the very process of
control and obliterating competing versions of politics and history. The West
was ideologized not only as the capitalist antagonist to communism, but also as
an intolerable alternative that threatened to sabotage the path to communism
and the imposition of its collectivist values. Psychoanalysis, labeled as a Western
import, was easily placed in this category.

It was not fortuitous that the two historical moments in the entire Soviet era
when psychoanalysis was permitted to function as a psychological theory and as
a mode of therapeutic practice came when the cultural barrier to the West was
lifted. The first time was during the New Economic Policy in the early 1920s
when Western influences were allowed to flow into the country in a variety of
forms. The second occurred during Gorbachev's perestroika policies when
Westernization was encouraged on an even greater scale. In both instances,
there was a relaxation of the hegemony of the values of Soviet collectivism over
the desire for individualist activity and private space in society that functioned
apart from state control. Psychoanalysis has traditionally flourished in precisely
these historical situations not because of any valid claims to scientific truth
about the nature of the human personality, but because its interpretation of
reality could be tolerated, and because it seemed to offer answers to the needs,
whether therapeutic or epistemological, of some sectors of society.

Another problem facing psychoanalysis in the Soviet Union was the conflict
over how to interpret the past. One of the central characteristics of Soviet
communism was the recasting of history. The authorities created an epic national narrative which was determined by a specific interpretation of class
relations in history. With the coming to power of the Bolsheviks in 1917, a new
stage of history had allegedly begun, in which the underclass of society, as
represented by the victorious political party, would assume the mantle of power
from its historic masters and abolish exploitation and injustice. To ensure the
believability of this mythic narrative of the transition from capitalism to social-

ism long before it could possibly be realized, the history of Russia and the entire world was recast in this framework in which collectivist values received the highest priority.

This interpretation presented the practitioners of psychoanalysis with a difficult challenge. They had their own narratives to construct, but of a very different kind. Instead of the Marxist vision of a Manichean class struggle of heroic proletarians guided by a beneficent party against their capitalist antagonists, both domestic and foreign, Freudians believed in the primacy of conflicting personal relationships, whether against the self or the other. The psychoanalyst's stated purpose was to uncover a patient's layers of repression in order better to understand and to mitigate, for example, masochistic or sadistic patterns of behavior. The process was made more complicated because of the individual's complicity in receiving a measure of satisfaction from the destructive behavior. These conflicts were understood not only in individual terms but in the context of private space. They thus stood in direct contradiction to the ideology of Marxism-Leninism, which posited a social context for the resolution of the class struggle under the party's control. The competing visions were not reconcilable, despite the great efforts by Soviet Freudians in the 1920s to find an accommodation.

The return of psychoanalysis and the widespread republication of Freud's works in the late 1980s were parts of the larger attempt at permitting alternatives to the ruling ethos of collectivist values that had been upheld by the state authorities and accepted, for the most part, by Soviet society for decades. Russians at all levels began the painful process of examining their past, collectively as a nation and individually as citizens, during the Gorbachev years. For many, it involved a confrontation with the sinister and ruinous forces of Stalinism, and the difficult task of sorting out one's role in that process. Hardly a day went by in Gorbachev's last years in power without new revelations of "crimes of the Stalin era," and the stagnation, corruption and duplicity of the Soviet regime. Instead of the state denouncing the society, as was the case before, the reverse was true, and with a manifest vengeance motivating much of the effort. It was as though the collective unconscious of the country's repressed past was being unlocked now that the Soviet Union itself was being banished to history. Indeed, the regime ultimately collapsed in 1991 in part because it could no longer control the attacks against it, and it could not exist without that control. Psychoanalysis played a role of some significance in this last phase of the Soviet Union as a methodology to interpret the past, and as part of the reassertion of the values of individualism in the larger society.

With the demise of the Soviet Union in 1991, an entirely new chapter in the evolution of psychoanalysis in Russia began, one that, however, goes beyond the parameters of this study. In the new political conditions established after the fall of communism, psychoanalysis was able to function as a clinical discipline without the restrictions imposed upon it by the Soviet authorities, but also without the support it received from that same government for a brief time during the early 1920s. Time will tell whether the newly trained Russian psychoanalysts follow more closely Western standards, as did the original Russian followers of Freud in the prerevolutionary years, or, as an earlier generation did during the postrevolutionary era, create entirely new pathways that will be distinctively Russian contributions.

Appendix Freud's Letters
to Osipov

In 1920, Dr. Nikolai Osipov (1877–1934), one of the founders of Russian psychoanalysis, emigrated from Russia and settled in Prague the following year. He had been in touch with Freud since their first meeting in Vienna in 1910, and Freud helped make the arrangements for his arrival. Osipov was later appointed Dozent at Charles University in Prague, where he established a psychoanalytic group which introduced Freud's method to physicians in training.

The six letters which follow were purchased many years ago by the Psychiatric Institute at Columbia University but apparently were left unexamined for some time. Largely through the efforts of the late Dr. John Weber, who formerly headed the Institute's Clinic at Columbia, efforts were made to learn more about Osipov. Weber contacted Dr. Theodor Dosuzkov, a former student of both Osipov and Otto Fenichel, whose own analyst, Annie Reich, was instrumental in having the letters brought to the attention of the Psychiatric Institute. Dosuzkov supplied enough biographical information to Weber to make it possible for an exhibition of the letters to take place in 1979. I was then studying in the Psychiatric Epidemiology program at the Columbia

University Medical Center and was introduced to Weber. I am enormously grateful to him for his cooperation in facilitating the publication of these documents. I also thank Sigmund Freud Copyrights (Wivenhoe) for permission to publish these letters for the first time. The letters were translated from the German originals by Weber and his colleague, Dr. Andre Ballard, with only minor, mostly grammatical revisions added on my part. A substantial file of Osipov's letters to Freud from this same period are deposited in the Freud Archive at the Library of Congress in Washington, D.C., where they can be read but not quoted in full or published due to restrictions on the collection.

I have benefited from the help of several colleagues in identifying obscure references in these letters: Peter Gay (Yale University), Daniel Rancour-Laferriere (University of California at Davis), James Rice (University of Oregon), and Nellie Thompson (New York Psychoanalytic Institute).

February 18, 1921
Vienna IX, Bergasse, 19
My dear colleague:

What a surprise! Fortunately not an unpleasant one. You are indeed in safety with good friends and again eager to work. Your wishes that your great fatherland may soon awaken again, and come out of its crisis, find in us the strongest sympathetic response. I, too, miss your fellow countrymen, the enthusiastic, incredibly richly gifted women and the passionate, naively serious men, with whom, as a rule, we parted as the best of friends. How much would I have liked—protected by powerful connections—to see your magnificent Moscow. All gone! There will be no change during my lifetime.

I answer you briefly, even though your letter contains an infinite number of stimulations for an exchange of thoughts (and ideas), since I don't have to give up hope of seeing you here with us. For I have connections to a very influential man who, himself a Russian, will obtain for you immediately the residence permit or the visa of immigration, should you choose to address yourself to him (via my address) while submitting all your data. Do not procrastinate, and let me know, should you like to do it.

A Miss Frieda Teller (Plasskat), a Germanist, is living in Prague. She is a member of our Society, who already has contributed several papers (essays) to the *Imago*.[1] I do not doubt that you will receive a friendly welcome from her, should you come to see her and want to bring her regards from our Association. She ought to have a number of analytical books; even better, her father owns a bookshop in Prague, from which you can obtain whatever you may need. We shall open a credit account for you in his place, since we ourselves are now being called a publishing house, namely the "International Psychoanalytic Publishing House," and we are providing books plentifully which find a good market. Make use of our name unhesitatingly. I will be very happy if we can make the exile more bearable for you.

Looking forward to news from you,

With cordial greetings,

Your,

Freud

19 May 1921

My dear colleague:

Please send us in any case whatever you have written. I shall read it with utmost interest and I suspect that it will bring enjoyment to other readers also.

Do not be aggravated for not being able to read all of the new publications. You know, not 5% of all that is printed is altogether worth reading. Had I read everything, I wouldn't have written even one line. I had the good fortune to enter a field in which there was as yet no literature. So I could live.

Warm thanks for your charming children's story. With your consent, it shall not get lost to posterity.

I too have heard of Dr. R.'s death and I also don't know any details about it.[2]

I understand your mood in view of the present conditions. I hardly had a fatherland of my own and yet I feel uprooted. If it were not for the interest in psychoanalysis, one would have to envy R.

With cordial greetings,

Your,

Freud

23 June 1921

Vienna IX, Bergasse 19

Dear Doctor:

Your letter arrived one day after I had finally read your paper and it made my task of critical evaluation much easier. The manuscript is now with Rank, who should arrive at his own judgment on what we could do with it, since we surely value highly everything that is coming from you. Your announced paper on Tolstoy we shall put into the *Imago* sight unseen except for some corrections of style, which I hope to make with your permission.[3]

Your "Organic Philosophy" sounds very engaging, but I do not dare to commit myself to a widely comprehensive theory and I have always intentionally limited myself to the already difficult [psycho]analytical experience.

That the Russian nation could perish, you surely don't believe yourself, even during your gloomiest days.

Expecting to hear from you again soon.

Your cordially devoted,

Freud

Seefeld i T.

Kurheim, 17 August 1921

Dear Doctor:

I am very glad about your readiness to take on the Russian translation of my lectures. I hope you looked at it carefully and saw how extensive and also time-consuming the job would be. If, however, you wish to do it, then the question is settled. If I can have Osipov as my translator, then I do not need anyone else.

Of course, I do not know whether we shall be able to come to a final agreement with the Russian publishing house in Berlin. Sooner or later, however, it will come to publishing such a translation, and at that time it would be good for you to be ready.

Your faint remarks concerning the analysis of Tolstoy have made me very eager to read the full, detailed presentation. Let us hope that you will soon get around to completing it.

I wish you a nice time in Teplitz. I know the place. Seefeld, where I may stay perhaps until the middle of September, is a beautiful high plateau (1,800 meters) with forest and mountain vistas.

With cordial greeting,

Your

Freud

20 January 1922

Vienna IX, Bergasse 19

Dear Doctor:

Your Tolstoy has been in the hands of Dr. Rank for quite some time. I only wanted to wait for his decision before writing to you about it. He wants to take advantage of your permission to make some cuts, and then he wants to publish this beautiful piece of work as the first volume of an *Imago* book series.[4] We are expecting great interest in it. May I ask you to move forward with your future work plans as soon as possible. Fables have not found any consideration as yet, except for a few remarks by Rank on fairy tales.

What you write about the Futurists, etc., will not make you popular with the moderns, but it seems quite convincing to me. There is in existence a not very profound study on the subject by Pfister.[5]

I am sorry that you obtained the joke from somebody else. But I have really offered to send you whatever material you might want to read. Prof. Pötzel now occupies the chair of psychiatry in Prague. He is a member of our Society and he will, together with Dr. Pollak, transform the "Psychological Association" into a psychoanalytic one.[6] This means, indeed, an end to your and Miss Teller's isolation. Wulff reported once from Moscow in the name of Ermakov,[7] holding out the prospect of more extensive contact. My reply has not as yet produced an answer.

With cordial greeting,

Your

Freud

23 March 1923

Vienna IX, Bergasse 19

My dear doctor:

How it is churning in you, how rich you are in thoughts and plans to work. This time you hit upon something which seizes you from more than one side, something which establishes a synthesis between your strongest scientific interests and your deepest personal experience. I think you should not miss out on it again. Think it through thoroughly and condense it into a beautiful paper for the *Imago*. The main difficulty you have recognized yourself: it lies in not confusing superficial analogies with essential identities, and also to show the deeper substantiation for more similarities.

I, too, am glad that your isolation will soon end. Prof. Pötzel has definitely promised to establish the psychoanalytic group in Prague in collaboration with Dr. Pollak.[8] A number of Hindu scholars in Calcutta have already anticipated you and have established a local chapter there.

With cordial greetings and best wishes,

Your

Freud

Notes

CHAPTER 1. PSYCHIATRY IN RUSSIA AND ITS DISCONTENTS

1. See the interesting evidence used in N. A. Bogoiavlenskii, "O dushevnykh i nervnykh bolezniakh na Rusi epokhi feodalizma (XI–XVII vek)," *Zhurnal nevropatalogii i psikhiatrii,* 66 (1966): 1706–1713. For a different approach to the early period, see T. I. Iudin, *Ocherki istorii otechestvennoi psikhiatrii* (Moscow: Medgiz, 1951), pp. 7–22.

2. Naomi Raskin, "Development of Russian Psychiatry before the First World War," *American Journal of Psychiatry,* 120, 9 (March 1964): 851.

3. See the discussion in Iudin, *Ocherki istorii,* pp. 23–26. Also see Kenneth S. Dix, "Madness in Russia, 1775–1864: Official Attitudes and Institutions for Its Care" (Ph.D. diss., UCLA, 1977), pp. 24–31. For the language of the actual legislation, see Charles Vallon and Armand Marie, *Les Aliénés en Russie* (Montrevain: Imprimerie typographique de l'école d'Alembert, 1899), pp. 7–8.

4. Iu. Kannabikh, *Istoriia psikhiatrii* (Leningrad: Gosmedizdat, [1929]), p. 283.

5. The report written by G. F. Müller was titled *On the Founding of Homes for Lunatics.* See the discussion in Iudin, *Ocherki istorii,* p. 33, and the fuller account in N. N. Bazhenov, *Istoriia moskovskogo dolgauza* (Moscow, 1909).

6. A. M. Shereshevskii, "Sozdanie v Rossii pervykh spetsial'nykh uchrezhdenii dlia dushevnobol'nykh," *Zhurnal nevropatalogii i psikhiatrii,* 78 (1978): 1:131–134.

7. On Riul', see Dix, "Madness in Russia," p. 118, note 26 and p. 119, note 44. See also Iudin, *Ocherki istorii*, pp. 60–63.

8. Kibal'chich's work, *Notes sur la mode de traîtement employé à l'hôpital des alienes de Moscou* was published originally in Paris in 1813. See D. D. Fedotov, *Ocherki po istorii otechestven-noi psikhiatrii* (Moscow: Ministerstvo zdravoohkraneniia SSSR, 1957), I:104–105, 276–278.

9. Iudin, *Ocherki istorii*, pp. 67–68. Sabler published in European journals and was one of the first Russian specialists in psychiatry to achieve a reputation abroad. There is a large literature on the practice of moral therapy. See, e.g., Andrew Scull, "John Conolly: A Victorian Psychiatric Career," *Social Order/Mental Disorder: Anglo-American Psychiatry in Historical Perspective* (Berkeley: University of California Press, 1989), pp. 164–212.

10. Ibid., pp. 98–99, 108–114, 164–168. Balinskii once commented that conditions at the psychiatric section of one of the major institutions in St. Petersburg were so poor that it might better be called "an affiliated department of Dante's Hell." See Kannabikh, *Istoriia psikhiatrii*, p. 379. Balinskii has been compared to Jean-Etienne Esquirol and Philippe Pinel, two of France's major psychiatric reformers in the first half of the nineteenth century. See A. G. Roitel'man, "Psikhiatricheskie aspekty deiatel'nosti vrachei v medit-sinskikh obshchestvakh nezemskikh mestnostei Rossii," *Zhurnal nevropatalogii i psikhiatrii*, 86 (1986): 1238.

11. T. B. Belgrave, "The Asylums for the Insane in St. Petersburg and Copenhagen," *Journal of Mental Science*, 13 (1867): 11, 13–14. On the origins of "zemstvo psychiatry," see Iudin, *Ocherki istorii*, pp. 86–101.

12. Quoted from the 1879 decree, in Julie V. Brown, "The Professionalization of Russian Psychiatry: 1857–1911" (Ph.D. diss., University of Pennsylvania, 1981), p. 85. According to the statistics of the Ministry of Interior, for this period Russia had 40,000 registered insane people, of whom 75 percent were regarded as "dangerous to public security." Only 18,000 of these people were in hospitals. Rates of admissions rose rapidly during the 1860s, reaching as high as thirteenfold in some provinces, creating unresolvable diffi-culties given the budget constraints. See Vallon, *Les Aliénés*, especially pp. 15, 43–45, 185–188, 211–212, 261–268.

13. See the discussion in Kannabikh, *Istoriia psikhiatrii*, pp. 381–397, on this period. Also see G. Zilboorg, "Russian Psychiatry: Its Historical and Ideological Background," *Bulletin of the New York Academy of Medicine*, 9 (October 1943), especially, pp. 718–726. A recent general discussion of the work of Pinel and Kirkbride in the context of the history of psychiatry can be found in Gerald Grob, *The Mad Among Us: A History of the Care of America's Mentally Ill* (Cambridge, Mass.: Harvard University Press, 1994). A truly objec-tive and balanced portrait of Korsakov's career remains to be written.

14. See the discussion in Fedotov, *Ocherki*, passim.

15. Quoted in Joseph Wortis, *Soviet Psychiatry* (Baltimore: Williams and Wilkins, 1990), p. 18. For an overview of Sechenov's career, see *I. M. Sechenov i materialisticheskaia psikhologiia* (Moscow: Akademiia nauk, 1957); A. A. Smirnov, "Vklad I. M. Sechenova v razvitie nauchnoi psikhologii v Rossii," *Razvitie i sovremennoe sostoianie psikhologicheskoi nauki v SSSR* (Moscow: Pedagogika, 1975), pp. 51–65; and M. G. Yaroshevskii, "I. M. Sechenov: The Founder of Objective Psychology," B. Wolman (ed.), *Historical Roots of Contemporary*

Psychology (New York: Harper and Row, 1968), pp. 77–110. For a discussion of the controversy generated in the government over Sechenov's book, see Daniel P. Todes, "Biological Psychology and the Tsarist Censor: The Dilemma of Scientific Developments," *Bulletin of the History of Medicine*, 4 (1984): 529–544. For a more recent and interesting reassessment of Sechenov and his work, see David Joravsky, *Russian Psychology* (Oxford: Blackwell, 1989), pp. 57–63, 96–101. An attempt to show the influence of Turgenev's fictional character Bazarov on Sechenov can be found in Michael Holquist, "Bazarov and Sechenov: The Role of Scientific Metaphor in *Fathers and Sons*," *Russian Literature*, 15 (1984): 359–374.

16. Kavelin's articles originally appeared in *Vestnik evropy* in 1868 and 1872. They were republished in Konstantin Kavelin, *Sobranie sochinenii* (St. Petersburg: Stasiulevich, 1899), II:365–802. See also Joravsky, *Russian Psychology*, pp. 96–104.

17. Quoted in E. Babayan, *Structure of Psychiatry in the USSR*, p. 47.

18. S. Korsakov, "Etude medico-psychologique sur une forme des maladies de la mémoire," *Revue philosophique de la France et de l'étranger* 28, 2 (1889): 521, 529; A. A. Portnov, D. D. Fedotov, *Psychiatry* (Moscow: Mir, 1969), pp. 21, 255.

19. On this environmental etiological model in nineteenth-century America and Jarvis's views, see David Rothman, *Discovery of the Asylum* (Boston: Little, Brown, 1971), pp. 112, 115–118, 120–121. On the issue of mental illness among slaves in the American South, see Gerald Grob, "Class, Ethnicity and Race in American Mental Hospitals, 1830–75," *Journal of the History of Medicine*, 28 (July 1973): 207–229, and Todd Savitt, "Insanity," *Medicine and Slavery* (Urbana: University of Illinois Press, 1978), pp. 247–279.

20. For Merezheevskii's speech, see *Trudy pervogo s"ezda otechestvennykh psikhiatrov* (St. Petersburg: Stasiulevich, 1887), pp. 15–37.

21. "Vstupitel'naia rech' P. I. Kovalevskogo," Ibid., p. 13. See also S. A. Gurevich, "P. I. Kovalevskii: Osnovatel' pervogo Russkogo zhurnala psikhiatrii," *Zhurnal nevropatologii i psikhiatrii*, 79 (1979): 350–352.

22. Quoted in Julie Brown, "Professionalization," p. 265. See also the discussion of Iakobii's work in Iudin, *Ocherki istorii*, pp. 196–200. Iakobii's book was entitled *The Principles of Administrative Psychiatry [Printsipy administrativnoi psikhiatrii]* (Orel: Tip. gub. pravleniia, 1900). The innocuous, textbook-sounding title, its enormous size of over 700 pages, and the fact that it was published by an obscure provincial press contributed to its escaping the censor's critical gaze. It should be pointed out that in spite of Iakobii's critique, many psychiatrists were at work in the provinces of Russia with a far less radical perspective on their situation. See the archival evidence in A. G. Roitel'man, "Psikhiatricheskie aspekty," pp. 1237–1242. For an example of another form of criticism, see the discussion of Bekhterev's opposition to tsarism on the eve of World War I in Joravsky, *Russian Psychology*, pp. 83–91.

23. See D. D. Fedotov and V. M. Lupandin, "O deiatel'nosti vrachei-psikhiatrov v revoliutsionnom dvizhenii Rossii," D. D. Fedotov (ed.), *Voprosy psikhopatologii i psikhoterapii* (Moscow, 1963), 40:310–320. Also see Julie Brown, "Revolution and Psychosis: The Mixing of Science and Politics in Russian Psychiatric Medicine, 1905–13," *Russian Review*, 46 (1987): 283–302. According to one scholar, out of a total of 2,639 zemstvo physicians, 1,300 were sentenced to administrative exile between 1905 and 1907 as a direct result of the revolutionary upheaval. Many psychiatrists were included in these arrests. In

addition, psychiatrists in provincial asylums were occasionally attacked, sometimes with fatal results, by people who sought to blame them for the country's crisis. Nevertheless, the number of psychiatrists and neuropathologists rose dramatically between the 1905 revolution and the outbreak of the First World War. See Iudin, *Ocherki istorii*, pp. 315–317, 321. In another part of this arena of combat, the national medical society's journal began listing "martyrologies" in the aftermath of the 1905 revolution. According to one estimate, the number of "repressed physicians" between 1905 and 1907 sentenced to prison, exile or "physical punishment" was 1,324. See N. Frieden, *Russian Physicians in an Era of Reform and Revolution* (Princeton: Princeton University Press, 1981), p. 320.

24. For discussions of this transformation and some of its consequences, see James H. Bater, *St. Petersburg: Industrialization and Change* (Montreal: McGill-Queen's University Press, 1976); Daniel Brower, *The Russian City between Tradition and Change* (Berkeley: University of California Press, 1990); and Reginald Zelnik (ed. and trans.), *A Radical Worker in Tsarist Russia: The Autobiography of Semen Ivanovich Kanatchikov* (Stanford: Stanford University Press, 1986).

25. Anton Chekhov, "A Nervous Breakdown," *The Oxford Chekhov* (Oxford: Oxford University Press, 1980), edited and translated by Ronald Hingley, IV:157–179. The psychiatrist in the story was based on V. M. Garshin, according to Chekhov, who "shared the protagonist's concern for the suffering of others" and the futility of his efforts (p. 265). This portrait of a psychiatrist is one of the earliest in the history of Russian literature.

26. For a discussion of these unpublished letters and other private responses to the Tolstoy story, see Peter U. Møller, *Postlude to the Kreutzer Sonata* (Leiden: Brill, 1988), pp. 115–127. There are numerous editions of "The Kreutzer Sonata" in Tolstoy anthologies.

27. Valerii Briusov, "Now When I Have Awakened (Notes of a Psychopath)," *The Silver Age of Russian Culture,* edited by Carl Proffer and Elendea Proffer (Ann Arbor: Ardis, 1975), pp. 303–308.

28. Pavel Nilus, "Summer Heat," ibid., 321–324.

29. See the discussion in Michel Niqueux, "La critique marxiste face à l'érotisme dans la littérature russe (1908–1928)," Leonid Heller (ed.), *Amour et érotisme dans la littérature russe du XXe siècle* (Bern: Peter Lang, 1992), pp. 83–90; Richard Stites, *The Women's Liberation Movement in Russia* (Princeton: Princeton University Press, 1978); and Laura Engelstein, *The Keys to Happiness* (Ithaca: Cornell University Press, 1992), pp. 375–376. Mikhail Petrovich Artsybashev's novel has been translated in *Sanin* (New York: Huebsch, 1915). For an example of contemporary concern over the immoral influence of the novel and the dangers of "Saninism," see the observations by Semen Frank and A. S. Izgoev in *Vekhi. Landmarks,* translated and edited by Marshall Shatz and Judith Zimmerman (Armonk, N.Y.: M. E. Sharpe, 1994), pp. 76, 132. See also the discussion in Engelstein, who used the title of Verbitskaia's novel for her own book, especially pp. 404–414. In addition, see Bernice Rosenthal (ed.), *Nietzsche in Russia* (Princeton: Princeton University Press, 1986), p. 28.

30. See especially V. V. Rozanov, *Solitaria* (London: Wishart, 1927). On Rozanov's life and thought, consult Spencer E. Roberts (ed. and trans.), *Four Faces of Rozanov: Christianity, Sex, Jews and the Russian Revolution* (New York: Philosophical Library, 1978), which includes the text of "People of the Moonlight," pp. 39–194. The best study of Rozanov in

English remains *Rozanov* by Renato Poggioli (New York: Hillary House, 1962). See also Poggioli's *The Phoenix and the Spider: A Book of Essays on Some Russian Writers and their View of the Self* (Cambridge, Mass.: Harvard University Press, 1957), pp. 185–207. On Rozanov's connection with Nietzsche, see Anna Lisa Crome, "Nietzschean, All Too Nietzschean? Rozanov's Anti-Christian Critique," Bernice Rosenthal (ed.), *Nietzsche in Russia*, pp. 95–112. Readers interested in Rozanov's influence should read D. V. Filosofov, "V. V. Rozanov," *Slovo i zhizn'* (St. Petersburg, 1909), pp. 139–161, and Engelstein, *Keys*, pp. 318–333. For an excellent scholarly edition of Rozanov's major writings, see V. V. Rozanov, *O sebe i zhizni svoei* (Moscow: Moskovskii rabochii, 1990). For a comprehensive bibliography, see O. S. Ostroi, "Pervyi bibliograf V. V. Rozanova," *Sovetskaia bibliografiia*, 5 (September–October 1989): 82–91.

31. Most of the data cited by Izgoev came from a research project directed by a young lecturer at the university, M. A. Chlenov, which was titled "A Sexual Poll of Moscow's Students" (1909), and another study, "A Page from the Sexual Confessions of Muscovite Students." See Alexander Izgoev, "On Educated Youth: Notes on Its Life and Sentiments," Boris Shragin and Albert Todd (eds.), *Landmarks* (New York: Karz Howard, 1977), pp. 88–111, especially pp. 90–92. The original Russian volume, edited by Mikhail Gerzhenson, sold out five editions in the first year of its existence.

32. See Engelstein, *Keys*, especially pp. 215–253 and also Gerald Surh, "A Matter of Life or Death: Politics, Profession and Public Health in St. Petersburg before 1914," *Russian History*, 20, nos. 1–4 (1993): 125–146. On the general problem of the motivations behind the increasing interest in sexual matters in educated society during this time period, see Lawrence Birken, *Consuming Desire: Sexual Science and the Emergence of a Culture of Abundance, 1871–1914* (Ithaca: Cornell University Press, 1988).

33. Iwan Bloch, *The Sexual Life of Our Time in Its Relations to Modern Civilization* (New York: Allied Book Co., 1925), pp. vi–xii. It is noteworthy to point out that in the preface to the English-language edition, the following statement appears: "The publishers have, after very serious and careful consideration, come to the conclusion that the sale of the English translation of the book shall be limited to members of the legal and medical professions" (p. v). No such restriction was included in either the German original or in the 1910 Russian translation.

34. Iwan Bloch, M.D., "Appendix: A Contribution to the Psychology of the Russian Revolution (History of the Development of an Algolagnistic Revolutionist," *The Sexual Life of Our Time*, pp. 587–607.

35. See Engelstein, *Keys*, pp. 255–264, for a discussion of the correlation between revolution and insanity as drawn by the psychiatrists in their articles and speeches during and immediately after 1905. Also see Julie Brown, "Revolution and Psychosis." One of the earliest examples of diagnosing revolution as an external cause of mental disturbances can be found in the work of the French psychiatric reformer Philippe Pinel; see his book, *A Treatise on Insanity* (London: Cadell and Davies, 1806).

36. Walter Reich, "Serbsky and Czarist Dissidents," *Archives of General Psychiatry*, 40 (June 1983): 697–698, quoting from the 1912 edition of Serbskii's *Psikhiatriia*.

CHAPTER 2. THE BEGINNINGS OF RUSSIAN PSYCHOANALYSIS

1. See Marc Micale, *Approaching Hysteria* (Princeton: Princeton University Press, 1995).
2. See the comprehensive discussion in Henri Ellenberger, *The Discovery of the Unconscious* (New York: Basic Books, 1970), especially pp. 254–321.
3. A. I. Smirnov, *O soznanii i bezsoznatel'nykh dukhovnykh iavleniiakh* (Kazan, 1875).
4. Leonid Rutkovskii, "Gipoteza bezsoznatel'nykh dushevnykh iiavleniiakh," *Zhurnal ministerstva narodnago prosveshcheniia* (1895): 323–371.
5. N. N. Bazhenov, *Psikhiatricheskiia besedy na literaturnyia i obshchestvennyia temy* (Moscow, 1903), p. 88.
6. A. Pokrovskii, "Sushchestvuiut-li bezsoznatel'nye psikhicheskie protsessy, i esli sushchestvuiut, to kakova ikh deistvitel'naia priroda?" *Vera i razum* (Kharkov), 11 (1912): 640–655.
7. Orshanskii's major works and ideas are discussed in V. F. Kruglianskii, *Psikhiatriia: Istoriia, Problemy, Perspektivy* (Minsk: Vysheishaia shkola, 1979), pp. 122–142, especially pp. 135–140. For discussions of the concept of the unconscious before Freud in its European context (Russia is not mentioned), see the following: Edward L. Margetts, "The Concept of the Unconscious in the History of Medical Psychology," *Psychiatric Quarterly* 27 (1953): 116–138; Lancelot Law White, *The Unconscious Before Freud* (New York: Basic Books, 1960); Henri Ellenberger, *The Discovery of the Unconscious* (New York: Basic Books, 1970), especially pp. 311–321; and Leon Chertok and Raymond de Saussure, *The Therapeutic Revolution* (New York: Brunner-Mazel, 1979), pp. 153–184.
8. V. Kh. Kandinskii, *O psevdogalliutsinatsiiakh* originally appeared in 1890. It was reissued in 1952 by Gosizdatmedlit in Moscow, with a biographical sketch by A. V. Snezhnevskii. See also L. L. Rokhlin, "Filosofskie i psikhologicheskie vozzreniia V. Kh. Kandinskogo," *Zhurnal nevropatologii i psikhiatrii* 69, 5 (1969): 755–761, and Rokhlin, "Les conceptions psychopathologiques de Kandinsky," *L'évolution psychiatrique* 36, 3 (July–September 1971): 475–488.
9. S. Korsakov, "Etude medico-psychologique sur une forme des maladies de la mémoire," *Revue philosophique de la France et de l'étranger* 28, 2 (1889): 501–530, especially p. 530.
10. The biographical and related literature is too vast to cite, but two good recent guides are the bibliographies in *Beyond the Unconscious: Essays of Henri F. Ellenberger in the History of Psychiatry* (Princeton: Princeton University Press, 1993), pp. 379–413, and John Kerr, *A Most Dangerous Method: Jung, Freud and Spielrein* (New York: Knopf, 1993), pp. 571–592.
11. See Hannah Decker, *Freud in Germany: Revolution and Reaction in Science, 1893–1907* (New York: International Universities Press, 1977), and Nathan Hale, *The Beginnings of Psychoanalysis in America* (New York: Oxford University Press, 1971). See also the special issue of *Social Research* (Winter 1991) devoted to the reception of psychoanalysis internationally.
12. See Herman Nunberg and Ernst Federn (eds.), *Minutes of the Vienna Psychoanalytic Society,* 4 vols. (New York: International Universities Press, 1962–1975). For an interesting and critical discussion of the "movement," see Ernest Gellner, *The Psychoanalytic Movement, or The Coming of Unreason* (London: Paladin-Granada Publishing, 1985).
13. The translation was published in the supplement to issue 5, 1904, of *Vestnik psikhologii, kriminal'noi antropologii i gipnotizma* (St. Petersburg: Brokhaus-Efron). For this refer-

ence, I am indebted to Igor Maximov (Paris). See his "La psychanalyse russe," *L'Ane,* 10 (1983): 3.

14. N. E. Osipov, "Psikhologicheskie i psikhopatologicheskie vzgliady Sigm. Freud'a v nemetskoi literature 1907 goda," *Zhurnal nevropatologii i psikhiatrii im. S. S. Korsakova,* nos. 1–2 (1908): 564–584. Osipov's references in the article reflect his wide reading of the German literature on Freud's work, both pro and con, as well as the leading researchers in the related areas of neurosis, hysteria, dementia praecox, psychotraumatic symptoms, and manic-depressive psychosis. Notice of Osipov's article was taken in Freud's own journal. See J. Neiditsch, "Über den gegenwärtigen Stand der Freudschen Psychologie in Russland," *Jahrbuch für Psychoanalyse* 2 (1910): 347–348. Osipov may not have been aware that this "cathartic method" was practiced as well by Dr. N. Krestnikov, who had no known connection to Freud. See A. Atanasov, "Problema katarsisa v nauchnom nasledii N. Krestnikova," *Zhurnal nevropatologii i psikhiatrii,* 86 (1986): 758–760.

15. For information on E. A. Osipov's career, see Peter F. Krug, "Russian Public Physicians and Revolution: The Pirogov Society, 1917–1920" (Ph.D. diss., University of Wisconsin, 1979), pp. 19–23, 35–36; and Nancy M. Frieden, *Russian Physicians in an Era of Reform and Revolution, 1865–1905* (Princeton: Princeton University Press, 1981), pp. 92–96.

16. M. P. Polosin, "Dr. Med. N. E. Osipov," A. L. Bem, F. N. Dosuzhkov, and N. O. Losskii (eds.), *Zhizn' i smert': Sbornik pamiati D-ra N. E. Osipova* (Prague, 1935), p. 10. I am grateful to Dr. Alex Kozulin for alerting me to this valuable collection of materials on Osipov.

17. Hans Lobner and Vladimir Levitin, "Short Account of Freudism: Notes on the History of Psychoanalysis in the USSR," *Sigmund Freud House Bulletin,* 2, 1 (1978): 7. Dubois's most influential work was *Les psychoneuroses et leur traitement moral* (1905), which was translated into English in 1907 and into Russian in 1912.

18. F. N. Dosuzhkov, "Nikolai Evgrafovich Osipov kak psikhiatr," A. L. Bem, F. N. Dosuzhkov, and N. O. Losskii (eds.), *Zhizn' i smert'. Sbornik pamiati D-ra N. E. Osipova,* p. 33. See also Rene and Eugenie Fischer, "Psychoanalyse in Russland," *Die Psychologie des 20 Jahrhunderts,* 3 (1977): 122. The "Friday Group" was Osipov's homage to Freud's Psychological Wednesday Society. In addition, he sought to differentiate his meetings from the "big Friday" meetings of the Psychiatric Society.

19. Dosuzhkov, "Nikolai Evgrafovich Osipov," p. 34.

20. *The Freud-Jung Letters:* pp. 282–283. In this letter to Jung, dated January 2, 1910, Freud also asked Jung to invite Osipov to the second international psychoanalytic congress, which met in Nuremberg, March 30–31, 1910.

21. N. E. Osipov, "Psikhologiia kompleksov i assotsiativnyi eksperiment po rabotam tsiurikhskoi kliniki," *Zhurnal nevropatologii i psikhiatrii im. S. S. Korsakova,* 8, 1 (1908): 1044.

22. Ibid., p. 1073.

23. "Posledniia raboty Freud'ovskoi shkoly," *Zhurnal nevropatologii i psikhiatrii im. S. S. Korsakova,* 9 (1909): 526–586.

24. Ibid., p. 534.

25. N. E. Osipov, "O nevroze boiazni (*Angstneurose*)," *Zhurnal nevropatologii i psikhiatrii im. S. S. Korsakova,* 9, 1–2 (1909): 783–805. There is some difference of opinion regarding

the first clinical publication in the history of Russian psychoanalysis. According to Dr. M. Wulff, "the first original psychoanalytic publication" in Russia was a paper on "Compulsion States treated according to the psychoanalytic method of Breuer and Freud," which appeared in *Obozrenie psikhiatrii,* 4, 1909. The author, A. A. Pevnitskii, military physician in Odessa whose paper was originally delivered as a lecture in 1908 in St. Petersburg, discussed the successful treatment of several cases of infantile trauma through hypnosis and suggestion in psychotherapy based on the Breuer-Freud method. Levitin, the pseudonym of the author of the history of Russian psychoanalysis cited earlier, claims that the history of psychoanalysis in Russia began with this lecture by Pevnitskii. See M. Wulff, "Die russische psychoanalytische Literatur bis zum Jahre 1911," *Zentralblatt für Psychoanlyse,* 7–8 (April–May 1911): 365, and Lobner and Levitin, "Short Account of Freudism," p. 7. I have not been able to locate this article since the citation given by Wulff and repeated by Levitin is inaccurate. Therefore it is not possible to verify whether these were Pevnitskii's own patients, how long they were treated, and other matters of clinical importance. More significant, although Pevnitskii published at least one further article on clinical psychoanalysis ("Neskol'ko sluchaev psikhoanaliza," *Psikhoterapiia,* 2 [1910] 51–62), it is not clear that he ever had psychoanalytic training. Furthermore, whatever influence he may have had was vastly overshadowed by Osipov's work at this time. Therefore, my claim for Osipov's article is made subject to future revision regarding the Pevnitskii article if warranted.

26. Osipov, "O nevroze boiazni," pp. 783–785. Osipov cited not only Freud's 1895 paper on "Angstneurosis" in the *Neurologische Zentralblatt,* 2 (and republished in 1906 in *Samml. Kleiner Schriften zur Neurosenlehre*), but also Wilhelm Stekel's more recent book, *Nervöse Angstzustände und ihre Behandlung* (Berlin: Urban und Schwarzenberg, 1908), in this discussion.

27. This section of the case analysis resumes in Osipov, "O nevrose boiazni," p. 794 after a brief interruption in which Osipov discusses Freud's theory of sexuality in connection with *Angstneurosis* on pp. 791–794.

CHAPTER 3. THE CONSOLIDATION OF A MOVEMENT

1. "Concluding Remarks on Lay Analysis," *International Journal of Psychoanalysis,* 8 (1927): 394.

2. For citations to these articles and a discussion of them, see Wulff, "Die russische psychoanalytische Literatur bis zum Jahre 1911," *Zentralblatt für Psychoanlyse,* 7–8 (April–May 1911): 365, 366–367.

3. Ibid., p. 365.

4. Ruth Jaffe, "Moshe Woolf: Pioneering in Russia and Israel," in F. Alexander (ed.), *Psychoanalytic Pioneers* (New York: Basic Books, 1966), p. 200. I am grateful to Dr. Jaffe for permitting me to interview her in June 1985 at her home in Tel Aviv about her reminiscences of Wulff.

5. Hilda C. Abraham and Ernst L. Freud (eds.), *A Psychoanalytic Dialogue: The Letters of Sigmund Freud and Karl Abraham,* 1907–1926 (New York: Basic Books, 1965), p. 82. The letter is dated October 11, 1909. Jones suggests that once back in Odessa, Wulff corre-

sponded with both Freud and Ferenczi (Ernest Jones, *Life and Work of Sigmund Freud,* 2:76), but neither Dr. Jaffe, his biographer and former colleague, nor the Israel Psychoanalytic Association have any evidence of these letters. According to Lobner and Levitin, "Short History of Freudism," p. 8, Wulff completed his analytic training with Abraham and thus became "the first fully trained and competent Russian analyst."

6. O. B. Fel'tsman, "K voprosu o psikhoanalize i psikhoterapii," *Sovremennaia psikhiatriia,* 3 (1909): 215–216.

7. Ibid., pp. 260–262. See also M. Wulff, "Die russische psychoanalytische Literatur," pp. 369–371, for a critical summary of Fel'tsman's paper. Wulff felt that Fel'tsman's objections were not to be taken seriously since he lacked a firm and accurate understanding of Freud's work. Nevertheless, Fel'tsman's article is a thoughtful and broad-ranging critique, which ends up favoring the Dubois school quite explicitly.

8. Wulff, "Die russische psychoanalytische Literatur," p. 368. Berg's report was published in *Sovremennaia psikhiatriia,* January 1909.

9. Lobner and Levitin, "Short Account of Freudism," p. 8. There is, however, a difference of opinion among two authorities as to the date of this competition. Maximov claims it occurred in October 1908 while Lobner and Levitin place it at "the end of 1909." See Maximov, "La psychanalyse russe," *L'Ane,* 10 (1983): 3, and Lobner and Levitin, p. 8.

10. In 1910, 5 of the journal's 12 articles (42 percent) were concerned with psychoanalysis. The following year, 8 out of 13 published articles (62 percent) were psychoanalytic. In 1912, 71 percent and in 1913, 87 percent of the journal's articles were on psychoanalytic themes. See Igor Maximov, "La psychanalyse Russe," *L'Ane,* 10 (1983): 4.

11. S. Spielrein, "Russische Literatur," *Bericht über die Fortschritte der Psychoanalyse in den Jahren* 1914–1919 (Leipzig: Internationaler Psychoanalytischer Verlag, 1921), p. 357.

12. J. Neiditsch, "Über den gegenwärtigen Stand der Freudschen Psychologie in Russland," *Jahrbuch für psychoanalytische und psychopathologische Forschungen* 2 (1910): 347–348.

13. Wulff, "Die russische psychoanalytische Literature," pp. 364–371. For mention of additional Russians whom Freud either met or knew about at this time, see James Rice, "Russian Stereotypes in the Freud-Jung Correspondence," *Slavic Review,* 41, 1 (Spring 1982): 19–21, 25; Igor Maximov, "La psychanalyse russe," p. 4; Rene and Eugenie Fischer, "Psychoanalyse in Russland," *Die Psychologie des 20 Jahrhunderts,* 3 (1977): 122; and Lobner and Levitin, "Short Account of Freudism," pp. 9–10.

14. *Freud-Jung Letters,* p. 283.

15. *Letters of Sigmund Freud and Karl Abraham,* p. 89. Freud's letter is dated May 6, 1910. Freud's "Worcester lectures" were presented at Clark University in 1909 during his visit to America, and were translated and published in Russian by Osipov in 1911 as the initial volume in the Psychotherapeutic Library series referred to earlier. Freud also wrote to Ferenczi at this time that Osipov was "a magnificent chap, clear head, an adherent of honest conviction; he will be a good acquisition." See *The Correspondence of Sigmund Freud and Sandor Ferenczi,* vol. 1, 1908–1914, edited by Eva Brabant, Ernst Falzeder, and Parizia Giampieri-Deutsch (Cambridge, Mass.: Belknap Press of Harvard University Press, 1993), p. 177 (letter dated June 5, 1910). Freud's respect for Osipov continued to grow with time. Freud personally arranged for Osipov's arrival in Prague in 1921 when the latter decided to emigrate from Russia. This episode will be discussed in the next chapter.

16. F. N. Dosuzhkov, "Osipov kak psikhiatr," Bem and Dosuzhkov, *Zhizn' i Smert'*, p. 33. On occasion, Serbskii's support for this new psychoanalytic research was explicitly acknowledged. See, e.g., M. M. Asatiani, "Psikhoanaliz odnago sluchaia istericheskogo psikhoza," *Psikhoterapiia*, 1 (1910): 172; and Asatiani, "Sovremennoe sostoianie voprosa teorii i praktiki psikhoanaliza po vzgliadam Jung'a," *Psikhoterapiia*, 1910, p. 117. For another side of Serbskii at this time, see Julie Brown, "Heroes and Non-Heroes: Recurring Themes in the Historiography of Russian-Soviet Psychiatry," Mark S. Micale and Roy Porter (eds.), *Discovering the History of Psychiatry* (New York: Oxford University Press, 1994), pp. 304–315.

17. N. E. Osipov, "O psikhoanalize," *Psikhoterapiia*, 1 (1910): 11–28, 106–116.

18. N. E. Osipov, "Eshche o psikhoanalize," *Psikhoterapiia*, 1 (1910): 153–172. The quoted passages are on pp. 170–171.

19. N. E. Osipov, "Idealisticheskiia nastroeniia i psikhoterapiia," *Psikhoterapiia*, 1 (1910): 248, 249.

20. Ibid., p. 252.

21. N. E. Osipov, "Psikhoterapiia v literaturnykh proizvedeniiakh L. N. Tolstogo," *Psikhoterapiia*, 2 (1910): 5. This paper was part of a larger study which Osipov called "Tolstoy and Medicine." An earlier version of it was presented to Serbskii's seminar on psychoanalysis in January 1911.

22. Ibid., p. 6.

23. Ibid., pp. 9–11. Osipov quotes a passage from the novel which shows without doubt that Natasha's illness was severe. See p. 11.

24. N. E. Osipov, "O naviazchivoi ulybke," *Zhurnal nevropatologii i psikhiatrii* 12 (1912): 570–578. The Russian word *naviazchivaia* can mean either compulsive or obtrusive here. The literature on V. M. Bekhterev (1857–1926) is vast. See, e.g., the recent discussion of his work in David Joravsky, *Russian Psychology* (Oxford: Blackwell, 1989), especially pp. 83–88, 271–281. It is worth pointing out that Adler presented a case to Freud's group on February 3, 1909, in Vienna titled "A Case of Compulsive Blushing." See Herman Nunberg and Ernst Federn (eds.), *Minutes of the Vienna Psychoanalytic Society* (New York: International Universities Press, 1962–75), 4 vols., II:125–144. It is not known whether Osipov read this case before he wrote up his own case study with the similar title.

25. Osipov, "O naviazchivoi ulybke," p. 578.

26. See *Correspondence of Sigmund Freud and Sandor Ferenczi*, 1:272. The names of Vyrubov, Drosnes, and Osipov are mentioned in the letter as the founders of the Moscow Society.

27. N. A. Vyrubov, "K voprosu o geneze i lechenii nevroza trevogi kombinirovannym gipno-analiticheskim metodom," *Psikhoterapiia*, 1910, pp. 29–41.

28. *Minutes of the Vienna Psychoanalytic Society*, vol. 2, meetings of January 24 and 31 and February 14, 1912.

29. Tatiana Rosenthal (Rozental), "'Opasnyi vozrast' Karin Mikhaelis v svete psikhoanaliza," *Psikhoterapiia*, 1911, pp. 189–194, 273–289. The novel deserves to be reissued for its compelling portrayal of a woman seeking an independent life. See Karen Michaelis, *The Dangerous Age* (New York: John Lane Co., 1911).

30. A. A. Pevnitskii, "Neskol'ko sluchaev psikhoanaliza," *Psikhoterapiia*, 1910, pp. 51–62.

31. See, e.g., V. N. Likhnitskii, "Osnovnyia napravleniia sovremennoi ratsionalisticheskoi psikhoterapii," *Psikhoterapiia*, 1912, pp. 1–11, 103–120. This paper concludes with an informative bibliography in the original languages of the psychotherapists under discussion.

32. N. E. Osipov, "Mysli i somneniia po povodu odnogo sluchaia 'degenerativnoi psikhopatii,'" *Psikhoterapiia*, 1912, pp. 189–215, 299–306.

33. N. E. Osipov, "O bol'noi dushe," *Zhurnal nevropatologii i psikhiatrii*, 13 (1913): 657–673.

34. M. Wulff, "Beiträge zur infantilen Sexualität," *Zentralblatt für psychoanalyse*, 1912, 2, pp. 6–17. See also, in addition to Wulff's 1911 review essay on the Russian psychoanalytic literature cited earlier (ibid. 1911, 7–8, pp. 364–371), the following papers: "Kleine Beiträge aus der psychoanalytischen Praxis," ibid. 1911, 1, pp. 337–341, and "Eine interessanter Zusammenhang von Traum Symbolhandlung und Krankheitssymptom," *Internationale Zeitschrift für ärztlich psychoanalyse*, 1 (1913): 559–560. Max Eitingon was another Russian who played a role abroad in the formative years of psychoanalysis, but who had no discernible impact on psychoanalysis in Russia before or after the 1917 revolution.

35. *Freud-Jung Letters*, p. 7. The date of Spielrein's arrival in Zurich for treatment at the Burghölzli hospital has been established by Aldo Carotenuto, *A Secret Symmetry: Sabina Spielrein between Jung and Freud* (New York: Pantheon, 1982), p. 140. Freud's letter on Spielrein, dated October 27, 1906, is in the *Freud-Jung Letters*, pp. 8–9. For Jung's description of Spielrein's hysterical symptoms, see *The Collected Works of C. G. Jung*, ed. Sir Herbert Read et al. (Princeton: Princeton University Press, 1953–80), IV:20–21.

36. See Jung's 1907 paper, "The Freudian Theory of Hysteria," *Collected Works*, 4, pars. 53–58. For Jung's "confession" to Freud, and further details on this matter, see Carotenuto, *A Secret Symmetry*, pp. 159–160 et seq. The most detailed study of the Spielrein-Jung relationship is recounted in John Kerr, *A Most Dangerous Method: The Story of Jung, Freud and Sabina Spielrein* (New York: Knopf, 1993).

37. "Über den psychologischen Inhalt eines Falles von Schizophrenie," *Jahrbuch*, 3 (1911): 329–400. See Carotenuto's discussion, *A Secret Symmetry*, p. 141.

38. "Die Destruktion als Ursache des Werdens," *Jahrbuch*, 4 (1912): 465–503. For the response, see Carotenuto, *A Secret Symmetry*, pp. 141–152. For another important paper by Spielrein at this time, see "Beiträge zur Kenntnis der kindliche Seele," *Zentralblatt für psychoanalyse*, 3 (1912): 57–72. This paper shows the definite influence of Jung. A more recent assessment confirms this initial appreciation of Spielrein's talent. Bruno Bettelheim wrote that Spielrein was "one of the great pioneers of psychoanalysis." He also said she "was not only brilliant and extremely sensitive, but had extraordinary psychological intuition." He considered her work on the destructive impulse to be a "seminal paper" in the annals of psychoanalysis. See Bruno Bettelheim, "Scandal in the Family," *New York Review of Books*, June 30, 1983, p. 44. On the revision of Spielrein's theory, see John Kerr, *A Most Dangerous Method*, pp. 500–502. For a list of Spielrein's publications, consult Carotenuto, pp. 238–239.

39. Carotenuto, *A Secret Symmetry*, pp. 74–75, 127. For additional information on Spielrein at this time, see Rice, "Russian Stereotypes in the Freud-Jung Correspondence"; Adeline Van Waning, "The Works of Pioneering Psychoanalyst, Sabina Spielrein," *International Review of Psychoanalysis*, 19 (1992): 399–414. On Piaget's reflections of his analysis with

Spielrein, see Howard Gruber and J. Jacques Voneche (eds.), *The Essential Piaget* (Northvale, N.J., and London: Jason Aronson, 1995), p. 864.

40. A. A. Ioffe, "Po povodu 'bezsoznatel'nogo' v zhizni individuuma," *Psikhoterapiia,* 1914, pp. 234–238. At this time, Ioffe was a close political comrade of Trotsky, whose connection to the psychoanalytic movement after the revolution is discussed in the next chapter.

41. The editorial board at the end of 1913 consisted of the following names, which are listed here as they appear on the journal's title page: A. Adler (Vienna), M. M. Asatiani (Moscow), F. Asnaurow (Geneva), R. Assagioli (Florence), A. N. Bernshtein (Moscow), I. A. Birshtein (Odessa), E. Wexberg (Vienna), Vera Eppelbaum (Zurich), Iu. V. Kannabikh (Moscow), O. Kaus (Vienna), V. N. Likhnitskii (Odessa), N. E. Osipov (Moscow), Stein (Budapest), W. Stekel (Vienna), Ch. Strasser (Zurich), O. B. Fel'tsman (Moscow), Frischauf (Vienna), N. A. Vyrubov (Moscow, editor).

42. On the conflicts among Freud's disciples at this time, see Ellenberger, chapters 8 and 9.

43. Lobner and Levitin, "Short Account of Freudism," p. 10. Earlier, Osipov had published a paper on this topic on which the lecture was undoubtedly based. See "O 'panseksualizme' Freud'a," *Zhurnal nevropatologii i psikhiatrii,* 11, 1 (1911): 749–760.

44. S. Freud, *On the History of the Psychoanalytic Movement* (New York: Norton, 1967), p. 33. This essay was first published in 1914.

45. Freud to Jung, August 9, 1909, *Freud-Jung Letters,* pp. 244–245. Nikolai Bazhenov was chief of the Preobrazhenskii psychiatric hospital in Moscow at that time. The identity of the patient is not specified.

46. Quoted in Magnus Ljunggren, "The Psychoanalytic Breakthrough in Russia on the Eve of the First World War," Daniel Rancour-Laferriere (ed.), *Russian Literature and Psychoanalysis* (Amsterdam: John Benjamins, 1989), p. 180.

47. *The Wolf Man,* by the Wolf Man, edited by Muriel Gardiner (New York: Basic Books, 1971), p. 153, note.

48. Ibid., p. vii. More recently, Freud's analysis of the Wolf Man has been called an "immortal case history" with a "legendary patient" that provided evidence of "a primal scene read round the world." For these exaggerated claims, see Patrick Mahony, *Cries of the Wolf Man* (New York: International Universities Press, 1984), pp. xi, 4.

49. The Wolf Man in his memoir referred to this psychiatrist as "Dr. D." but his identity has been known for many years in the professional literature. See, e.g., Ernest Jones, *Life and Work of Sigmund Freud,* II:96, 273, and also William McGuire (ed.), *The Freud-Jung Letters,* p. 495, note 2. Two of Drosnes's early psychoanalytic papers are discussed in S. Spielrein, "Russische Literatur," *Bericht über die Fortschritte der Psychoanalyse in den Jahren* 1914–1919 (Leipzig: Internationaler Psychoanalytischer Verlag, 1921), p. 362. See also James Rice, *Freud's Russia: National Identity in the Evolution of Psychoanalysis* (New Brunswick, N.J.: Transaction, 1993), pp. 93–121.

50. *The Wolf Man,* p. 83.

51. *The Correspondence of Sigmund Freud and Sandor Ferenczi,* I:133.

52. Ibid. The Wolf Man is the only patient of Freud's known to have written about his analysis. In addition to the memoir in *The Wolf Man* volume, edited by Gardiner, see also Karin Obholzer, *The Wolf Man Sixty Years Later* (New York: Continuum, 1982), for a

critical reassessment by the former patient during an interview conducted when he was an aged and embittered man. One of Pankeev's letters to Freud (dated 1926), together with a 1959 letter to the Freud Archives about his analysis, were published in "Letters Pertaining to Freud's 'History of an Infantile Neurosis,'" *The Psychoanalytic Quarterly* (October 1957): 449–460.

53. For a summary of selected abstracts of this wartime Russian psychiatric research, see Mabel W. Brown and Frankwood E. Williams (eds.), *Neuropsychiatry and the War: A Bibliography with Abstracts* (New York: National Committee for Mental Hygiene, 1918), pp. 189–208.

54. Ibid., p. 189.

CHAPTER 4. FREUD IN THE HOUSE OF LENIN

1. Sara Neiditsch, N. Osipov, and M. Pappenheim, "Psychoanalysis in Russia," *International Journal of Psychoanalysis* (December 1922): 513–514. This is a slightly abridged translation of the original report, which was published in German as "Die Psychoanalyse in Russland während der letzten Jahre," *International Zeitschrift für ärztliche psychoanalyse*, 7 (1921): 381–388. The German original makes clearer the separate contributions by Neiditsch about developments in Petrograd and Osipov and Pappenheim on Moscow. The actual date that *Psychotherapy* ceased publication was 1914.

2. See Tatiana Rosenthal, "Stradanie i tvorchestvo Dostoevskogo: Psikhologicheskoe issledovanie," *Voprosy izucheniia i vospitaniia lichnosti*, 1 (1919): 88–107. According to Neiditsch, Rosenthal's article actually appeared in the February 1920 issue of the journal (see Neiditsch, p. 382 of the German version). Most of what we know of Rosenthal's life comes from Neiditsch's obituary ("Die psychoanalyse," pp. 384–385). In addition to her activities mentioned here, Rosenthal was politically active (she was part of the welcoming committee for Lenin when he returned to Russia in April 1917 and had been a Marxist at least since the 1905 revolution), had published poetry in a 1917 miscellany in Petrograd, and had begun a study of neuroses associated with war, which was left unfinished at her death. Rosenthal's work was not the first time that psychiatrists had been fascinated with the psychological dimensions in Dostoevsky's fiction. Both V. F. Chizh (see James Rice, *Dostoevsky and the Healing Art* [Ann Arbor: Ardis, 1985], pp. 200–210; and N. N. Bazhenov, *Psikhiatricheskie besedy na literaturnyia i obshchestevennyia temy* [Moscow: Tipografiia A. I. Mamontova, 1903], chapters 2 and 3), published earlier than she did on the general theme. However, hers appears to be the first psychoanalytic interpretation. Freud, as is well known, was himself fascinated by Dostoevsky's characters. His essay, "Dostoevsky and Parricide," was published in 1927, seven years after Rosenthal's essay had appeared. See James Rice, *Freud's Russia*, on Freud's interest in Dostoevsky.

3. Neiditsch, Osipov, and Pappenheim, "Die Psychoanalyse in Russland," pp. 387–388, in the more complete German version, and pp. 519–520 in the abridged English translation, "Psychoanalysis in Russia." The training of the children's caretakers by requiring them to examine their own emotions in this context remains a fundamental part of psychoanalytic training, called countertransference, though the Russians did not use the term at this point.

4. A. R. Luria, *The Making of Mind: A Personal Account of Soviet Psychology*, edited by Michael and Sheila Cole (Cambridge, Mass.: Harvard University Press, 1979), pp. 23, 24.

5. For the list of the Kazan Psychoanalytic Society's members and a summary of its activities, see the report by Luria in the *International Journal of Psychoanalysis* 4 (1923): 397–399.

6. See Rene Van der Veer and Jaan Valsiner (eds.), *Understanding Vygotsky* (Birghton, Eng.: Harvester Press, (1988), pp. 85–86.

7. Sabina Spielrein, "Russische Literatur," pp. 356–365. Her essay covers the years 1909 to 1914.

8. S. Freud to S. Spielrein, February 9, 1923, in Aldo Carotenuto, *A Secret Symmetry*, p. 127. Spielrein was already a member of the Vienna and Swiss Psychoanalytic Societies at this time when she was admitted to the new Russian Psychoanalytic Institute. The phrase "difficult times" probably is a reference to Freud's recent diagnosis of cancer in his jaw and palate, which necessitated the first of a lifetime of operations to contain the malignancy.

9. The information on the Institute can be found in the *International Journal for Psychoanalysis* 5 (1924): 258–260.

10. *Int. Zeitschrift für Psychoanalysis* 8 (1923): 504.

11. Jean Marti, "La psychanalyse en Russie et en Union soviétique de 1909 à 1930," *Critique* 32, no. 346 (March 1976): 219–220; Roudinesco, *Jacques Lacan and Co.: A History of Psychoanalysis in France, 1925–1985* (Chicago: University of Chicago Press, 1990), p. 40.

12. Marti, "La psychanalyse," p. 221.

13. Lobner and Levitin, "Short Account of Freudism," pp. 13–14; Joravsky, *Russian Psychology*, p. 236. Adolf A. Ioffe (1883–1927) had been analyzed by Alfred Adler in Vienna before the revolution and had known Trotsky since that time. After 1917, Ioffe was an important Soviet diplomat until he became ill in the period before his suicide. Though Ioffe may have been Trotsky's initial informant about psychoanalysis before the revolution, there is little direct evidence of his support for psychoanalysis in the 1920s. See Alexander Etkind, *Eros nevozmozhnogo* (St. Petersburg: Meduza, 1993), pp. 276–282.

14. Tsentral'nyi gosudarstvennyi arkhiv soveta ministrov RSFSR, *fond* 2307, *opis* 2, *delo* 412, *listy* 1–3. Apart from Ermakov and Wulff, the following signatures are listed: "I. I. Grivenko, Professor of Literature; G. P. Weisberg (Veisberg), Head, Main Soviet of Enlightenment (Glavsopros); O. Iu. Schmidt, Professor of Mathematics; Iu. P. Kannabikh, Professor of Psychology; P. P. Blonskii, Professor Psychology; A. A. Sidorov, Professor Aesthetics; A. G. Gabrichevskii, Professor Aesthetics; V. A. Nevskii, Head, Central House of Enlightenment; N. E. Uspenskii, Professor of Physics; S. Lapkii, Pedagogue; A. Voronskii, Literary Critic; V. A. Belousov, Physician." Accompanying notes from Shatskii and Voronskii are dated September 16 and 18, 1922, respectively.

15. Tsen. gosudar. arkhiv, RSFSR, *fond* 2307, *opis* 8, *delo* 294, *listy* 4–7. The document is dated September 29, 1922.

16. Vera Schmidt, "Education psychanalytique en Russie soviétique," *Les Temps Modernes,* 273 (March 1969): 1631. This version is a translation of the original report, *Psychoanalytische Erziehung in Sowjetrussland: Bericht über das Kinderheim-Laboratorium in Moskau* (Leipzig, Vienna, Zurich: Internationaler Psychoanalytischer Verlag, 1924). This

report was never published in Russian, nor has it ever been translated into English, though it appears to be the first report ever done on a psychoanalytic preschool.

17. Schmidt, "Education psychanalytique," pp. 1634, 1640, 1641.

18. Tsen. gosudar. arkhiv RSFSR, *fond* 298, *opis* 1, *delo* 1, *list* 54. Reference to the committee's opinion is mentioned in Vera Schmidt's report, "Education psychanalytique," p. 1629.

19. Tsen. gosudar. arkhiv RSFSR, *fond* 298, *opis* 1, *delo* 45, *list* 49.

20. Ibid., *fond* 298, *opis* 1, *delo* 58, *list* 109.

21. Ibid., *fond* 298, *opis* 1, *delo* 58, *list* 110. Meeting of September 17, 1923. The members of this commission were O. L. Bem, F. N. Petrov, O. Iu. Schmidt, K. N. Kornilov, and E. B. Zombe.

22. Ibid., *fond* 2306, *opis* 1, *delo* 2168, *list* 75, for the Lunacharsky committee, and *fond* 2306, *opis* 1, *delo* 2208, *list* 3, for the central committee of the Communist party's verification.

23. Alexander Luria, "Report of Meetings for the Fourth Quarter, 1923," *International Journal of Psychoanalysis*, 5 (1924): 260. The exact date given for the meeting of the Schmidts with Freud, Abraham, and Rank was October 18, 1923.

24. The most recent and complete list of this series, divided into those volumes that actually appeared and those which did not, can be found in *Sovetskaia bibliografiia*, 3 (1989): 64. See also the bibliography of Freud's works in Russian in I. T. Kurtsin, *Kritika Freidizma v meditsine i fiziologii* (Moscow: Nauka, 1965), pp. 279–280. Ermakov published two of his own books in the series, one on Pushkin and the other on Gogol, which were interesting applications of psychoanalysis to literature. On this, see Donald Young, "Ermakov and Psychoanalytic Criticism in Russia," *Slavic and East European Journal*, 23, 1 (Spring 1979): 72–86. Material on Ermakov has been published by his daughter, some of which is based on Ermakov's unpublished papers. See M. I. Davydova, "Ivan Dmitrievich Ermakov (1875–1942)," *Psikhologicheskii Zhurnal*, 10, 2 (1989): 156–159, and "Nezavershennyi zamysel: K istorii izdaniia trudov Z. Freida v SSSR," *Sovetskaia bibliografiia*, 3 (1989): 61–64. Ermakov was arrested in 1941 on political charges and died a year later in the Butyrsk prison.

25. See M. Wulff, "Zur Stellung der Psychoanalyse in der Sowjetunion," *Die Psychoanalytische Bewegung*, 2 (1929): 70–75. Evidence for the diffusion of Freud's ideas and the interest in them at this time outside of Moscow and Petrograd can be found in Nadezhda Mandelstam's memoir. Speaking of her life in Kharkov during the 1920s, she wrote: "News of the theory of relativity and of Freud, delayed because of the war, had only now reached Russia. Everybody was talking about them, but actual information was vague and amorphous." See *Hope Abandoned* (New York: Atheneum, 1974), p. 74.

CHAPTER 5. THE DECLINE AND FALL OF SOVIET PSYCHOANALYSIS

1. Pavlov's research was conducted at the Institute for Experimental Medicine, and Bekhterev headed the Institute for Brain Research in Petrograd, where Tatiana Rosenthal had done her psychoanalytic work.

2. The psychologists and psychologically oriented philosophers who were removed included Nicholas Berdiaev, Sergei Bulgakov, Nicholas Losskii, and Semen Frank. G. V.

Chelpanov was forced to resign as director of the Institute of Psychology. His successor was Konstantin Kornilov, who invited Luria to come to Moscow from Kazan at the moment when Luria was an active proponent of psychoanalysis. See A. Kozulin, *Psychology in Utopia* (Cambridge: MIT Press, 1984), pp. 11–13. The warfare among the psychologists as a whole in this period is an important part of the formative period of the Communist party's consolidation of authority over Soviet society. See also the discussion in Joravsky, *Russian Psychology,* especially pp. 220–231; and Rene Van der Veer and Jaan Valsiner, "Konstantin Kornilov and His Reactology," *Understanding Vygotsky: A Quest for Synthesis* (Oxford: Blackwell, 1991), pp. 112–140.

3. The presentations by Luria are listed in the report on the Kazan Psychoanalytic Society which appeared in the *International Journal of Psychoanalysis,* 4 (1923): 397–399. Levitin pointed out that Luria's lectures "opened the discussion of the ideological implications of experimental psychology" with respect to psychoanalysis. See Lobner and Levitin, "Short Account of Freudism," p. 13.

4. Bernard E. Bykhovskii, "O metodologicheskikh osnovaniiakh psikhoanaliticheskogo ucheniia Freida," *Pod znamenem marksizma,* 11–12 (November–December 1923): 158–177.

5. Lobner and Levitin, "A Short History of Freudism," p. 13. Also see Jean Marti, "La psychanalyse en Russie et en Union soviétique de 1909 à 1930," *Critique,* 32, 346 (March 1976): 216–217. Reisner was, in addition, an associate of the Russian Psychoanalytic Society and one of the founding members of the Communist Academy, both in Moscow. His best-known work at this time was *Gosudarstvo burzhuazii i RSFSR* (Moscow, 1923).

6. *Totem and Taboo*'s first edition was 1922. Reisner's psychoanalytic sources were the original German texts, whereas Bykhovskii had used the Russian translations of Freud's earlier writings. Reik's book was published in Vienna in 1919. James's book was published in Russian translation as *Mnogoobrazie religioznogo opyta* in Moscow in 1910. Reisner considered James "an apologist for religion" but found his analysis of religious motivation useful as a starting point for understanding Freud's critique.

7. M. A. Reisner, "Freid i ego shkola o religii," *Pechat' i revoliutsiia,* book 1 (January–February 1924): 40–60; book 3 (May–June 1924): 81–106.

8. G. Daian, "Vtoroi psikhonevrologicheskii s"ezd," *Krasnaia nov',* 2, 19 (1924): 155. Of the 906 delegates, 429 were from the medical profession (p. 163). Nechaev's speech may have been given with some reluctance since he was in opposition to both Chelpanov and Kornilov, the former and present directors of the influential Institute of Psychology, at various points during the 1920s.

9. Ibid., 3, 20 (1924): 227–228.

10. Ibid., 2, 19: 161–163. See also A. S. Griboedov's speech on Freud's importance from a clinical standpoint in 3, 20: 232.

11. A. [B.] Zalkind, "Freidizm i Marksizm," *Krasnaia nov',* 4, 21 (1924): 163–164. The references are to Trotsky's book *Literature and Revolution* (1923), which we shall discuss further in the section on Trotsky below, and to "a leading article in *Pravda,* 1923" written by Radek, whom Zalkind considered one of Freud's "most passionate Marxist defenders." I have been unable to locate this article.

12. Ibid., pp. 166–167, and 183–184.

13. Ibid., pp. 177, 179, 185. Zalkind also published a book in 1924, *Essays on Revolutionary Culture,* parts of which are referred to in this article. See the discussion in Kozulin, *Psychology in Utopia,* pp. 16–17.

14. V. Iurinets, "Freidizm i Marksizm," *Pod znamenem marksizma,* 8–9 (1924): 51–93.

15. Ibid., pp. 51–52.

16. Ibid., pp. 91–93. Iurinets also published a critical attack on a book by G. Malis, *Psikhoanaliz kommunizma* (Kharkov, 1924), a rather utopian application of Freud's ideas to a communist society of the future. See. V. Iurinets, "Psikhoanaliz i Marksizm," *Pod znamenem marksizma,* 1 (1925): 90–133.

17. M. A. Reisner, "Sotsial'naia psikhologiia i uchenie Freida," *Pechat' i revoliutsiia,* book 3 (May 1925): 54–69; book 4 (June 1925): 88–100; book 5–6 (July–September 1925): 133–150, On the Frankfurt School's efforts in this regard, see Martin Jay, *The Dialectical Imagination* (Boston: Little, Brown, 1973), pp. 86–111, and also, on related matters, Paul Robinson, *The Freudian Left* (New York: Harper and Row, 1969). Neither of these scholars seems to have been aware of the earlier work done in Russia by Reisner, Luria, Vygotsky, and others who sought to establish what Jay has referred to as "the unnatural marriage of Freud and Marx" (p. 86). One striking illustration of the groundbreaking work done in this theoretical field by the Russians can be seen by comparing Erich Fromm's 1932 essay, "Notes on Psychoanalysis and Historical Materialism," with the published essays of the Russians discussed in the present chapter. For Fromm's article, see Andrew Arato and Eike Gebhardt (eds.), *The Essential Frankfurt School Reader* (New York: Urizen Books, 1978), pp. 477–496.

18. This was indeed evident, and was mentioned even by those who were skeptical, ambivalent, or antagonistic to "Freudianism." See, e.g., A. Voronskii, "Freidizm i iskusstvo," *Krasnaia nov',* 7 (1925): 241, where Voronskii wrote in the very opening line: "The theories of Freud's psychoanalysis are enjoying greater and greater attention from our scholars and publicists in recent years."

19. "Psychoanalysis as a System of Monistic Psychology," in Michael Cole, ed., *The Selected Writings of A. R. Luria* (White Plains, N.Y.: Sharpe, 1978), pp. 4–5. Translated from K. N. Kornilov, ed., *Psikhologiia i marksizm* (Leningrad: Gosizdat, 1925), pp. 47–80. The Russian original contains 120 footnotes of interest to specialists, which were reduced to 62 in the English translation. Luria stated that this article was the initial chapter of a book in preparation called *Printsipy psikhoanalizma i sovremennyi materializm* which, to my knowledge, has never been published. He also referred to his earlier essay *Psikhoanaliz v svete osnovnykh tendentsii sovremennoi psikhologii* (Kazan, 1923).

20. "Psychoanalysis as a System," p. 11.

21. Ibid., p. 16.

22. Ibid., pp. 16, 17.

23. Ibid., pp. 30, 31.

24. Luria, *Making of Mind,* 38–39. For a discussion of Vygotsky's early years, see Alex Kozulin, "Vygotsky in Context," in Lev Vygotsky, *Thought and Language* (Cambridge, Mass.: MIT Press, 1986), especially pp. xi–xvi. On Vygotsky's lecture, see Daian, "Vtoroi psikhonevrologicheskii s"ezd," pp. 164–166, 234–237. The lecture has been translated; see

"The Methods of Reflexological and Psychological Investigation," Rene van der Veer and Jaan Valsiner (eds.), *The Vygotsky Reader* (Oxford: Blackwell, 1994), pp. 27–45.

25. L. S. Vygotsky, "Consciousness as a Problem in the Psychology of Behavior," *Soviet Psychology* 17, 4 (Summer 1979): 3–35. For the original, see K. N. Kornilov (ed.), *Psikhologiia i marksizm* (Moscow-Leningrad: Gosizdat, 1925), pp. 175–198. On Vygotsky's career, see also James V. Wertsch, *Vygotsky and the Social Formation of Mind* (Cambridge, Mass.: Harvard University Press, 1986); Alex Kozulin, *Vygotsky's Psychology: A Biography of Ideas* (Cambridge, Mass.: Harvard University Press, 1990); and G. L. Vygodskaia and T. M. Lifanova, *Lev Semenovich Vygotskii. Zhizn'. Deiatel'nost'. Shtrikhi k portrety* (Moscow: Smysl', 1996), which contains previously unpublished materials.

26. B. D. Fridman, "Osnovnye psikhologicheskie vozzreniia Freida i teoriia istoricheskogo materializma," K. Kornilov (ed.), *Psikhologiia i Marksizm* (1925): 113–159.

27. V. M. Friche, "Freidizm i iskusstvo," *Vestnik kommunisticheskoi akademii,* 12 (1925): 236–264, concludes that psychoanalysis has demonstrated "dilettantism" in its studies on art. I. Grigor'ev, "Psikhoanaliz kak metod issledovaniia khudozhestvennoi literatury," *Krasnaia nov',* 7 (1925): 224–240, includes a critical discussion of Ermakov's psychoanalytic studies of Pushkin and Gogol, as well as of Iolan Neufeld, *Dostoevskii: Psikhoanaliticheskii ocherk* (Leningrad: Izdat. "Petrograd," 1925), recently translated from the German, with a preface by Freud. See also A. Voronskii, "Freidizm i iskusstvo," pp. 241–262, cited above in note 20.

28. I. D. Sapir, "Freidizm i marksizm," *Pod znamenem marksizma,* 11 (1926): 70. Sapir cited Engels's letter to Konrad Schmidt, October 27, 1890 for ideological support.

29. Ibid., p. 76.

30. Ibid., p. 79.

31. Sapir's critique retained its importance for decades in the Soviet Union. The major text on the history of Soviet psychology prior to the Gorbachev era includes an extensive quotation from Sapir in the section of the book devoted to this period of Freudian influences during the postrevolutionary era. See A. V. Petrovskii, *Istoriia sovetskoi psikhologii* (Moscow: Prosveshchenie, 1967), pp. 91–92. Sapir's name, interestingly, does not appear in Petrovskii's footnote reference to the source of his quoted material. Sapir, who was a significant presence in the wider discussions of Soviet psychiatry and mental health during the 1920s, disappeared during the 1930s and was probably a purge victim. Among his works, see I. D. Sapir, *Vysshaia nervnaia deiatel'nost' cheloveka* (Moscow, 1925).

32. "The Russian Psychoanalytic Society," *International Journal of Psychoanalysis,* 7 (1926): 295. See also Marti, "La psychanalyse," p. 232. Among the clinical contributions by psychoanalysts which appeared at this time, see A. S. Griboedov, "Trudnovospituemye deti i psikhoanaliz," *Voprosy izucheniia i vospitaniia lichnosti,* 1–2 (1926): 57–68 in which the delinquency of "problem children" is interpreted psychoanalytically in a lengthy and interesting case history. The author associated these delinquency difficulties with Oedipal and castration complexes as well as inadequate sublimation functions. He concluded that psychoanalysis was an indispensable tool for the study of juvenile crime on the basis of the clinical case studies presented here. Griboedov, who was director of the State Institute for the Study of Children and professor at the State Medical Institute in Leningrad, was familiar with the relevant literature in Germany, England, and America

at a time when fewer and fewer citations from Western sources were appearing in Soviet scientific and medical journals. See also M. V. Wulff, "K psikhoanalizu koketstva," *Sovremennaia psikhonevrologiia*, 3–4 (1925): 33–43; I. A. Perepel, *Opyt primeneniia psikhoanaliza k izucheniiu detskoi defektivnosti* (Leningrad: privately published by the author, 1925); A. M. Khaletskii, "Psikhoanaliz lichnosti i tvorchestva Shevchenko," *Sovremennaia psikhonevrologiia*, 3 (1926): 345–354; and the constructively critical paper by V. M. Gakkebush, "K kritike sovremennogo primeneniia psikhoanaliticheskogo metoda lecheniia," *Sovremennaia psikhonevrologiia*, 8 (1925): 89–96. I am grateful to Prof. V. M. Leibin (Moscow) for these references.

33. Quoted in A. V. Petrovskii, *Psychology in the Soviet Union* (Moscow: Progress, 1990), p. 160.

34. Klara Zetkin, *Reminiscences of Lenin* (London: Modern Books Limited, 1929), pp. 52–53. The memoir was originally published in German in 1925.

35. June 14, 1925, *Pravda*, cited in Petrovskii, *Psychology in the Soviet Union*, pp. 160–161.

36. The evidence for this discussion on Lenin's ties to psychoanalysis has been compiled in Christfried Tögel, "Lenin und die Rezeption der Psychoanalyse in der Sowjetunion der Zwanzigerjahre," *Sigmund Freud House Bulletin*, 13, 1 (1989): 16–27. Most of Tögel's evidence (even more than mentioned here) is circumstantial, but convincing in its comprehensiveness. I am indebted to Lily Feiler (Chapel Hill) for help in translating this article on short notice. There has been little research on most of the individuals discussed here. An exception is the lucid chapter on Pavel Blonskii in Kozulin, *Psychology in Utopia*, pp. 121–136. See also Marti, "La psychanalyse," pp. 212–217, 225–226. On Darkshevich, see James Rice, *Freud's Russia* pp. 26–30, 36–37. For a discussion of the 1925 debate on Freudianism at the Communist Academy, see Helen Gifford Scott (Guest Editor), "V. F. Pereverzev," *Soviet Studies in Literature* 22–23 (Spring–Summer 1986): 19–24, 123–126. I am grateful to Jean Laves Hellie, editor of the journal, for alerting me to this material.

37. Lev Trotsky, *Sochineniia* (Moscow-Leningrad: Gosizdat, 1927), vol. 21, p. 260. Trotsky's experience with Freud undoubtedly came via his comrade in Vienna, A. A. Ioffe, with whom he collaborated in editing the emigre edition of *Pravda*. Ioffe had been in psychoanalytic treatment with Alfred Adler from 1908 to 1912 and had also contributed an article to the journal *Psikhoterapiia* in 1913 (no. 4) while a practicing physician in Russia. He committed suicide in 1927.

38. Leon Trotsky, *Literature and Revolution* (Ann Arbor: University of Michigan Press, 1960), p. 220.

39. Quoted in Isaac Deutscher, *The Prophet Unarmed: Trotsky, 1921–1929* (New York: Random House, 1959), p. 180. For the original, see L. Trotsky, *Sochineniia* (Moscow-Leningrad: Gosizdat, 1927), 21:430–431. See also Alexander Etkind, "Trotsky and Psychoanalysis," *Partisan Review*, 2 (1994): 303–308, and his book *Eros nevozmozhnogo*, pp. 269–310.

40. "Russian Psychoanalytic Society," *International Journal of Psychoanalysis*, 9 (1928): 399. Also see M. W. Wulff, "A Phobia in a Child of 18 Months," *International Journal of Psychoanalysis*, 9 (1928): 354–359. The research was done in Moscow before he emigrated.

41. V. N. Voloshinov, *Freudianism: A Critical Sketch* (Bloomington: Indiana University Press, 1987), p. 77. The original was published in 1927 by the State Publishing House. For the earlier article, see V. Voloshinov, "Po tu storonu sotsial'nogo: o Freidizme," *Zvezda* (Leningrad), 5, 11 (1925): 186–214. There has been a dispute over whether Bakhtin himself was the actual author of the book. See I. R. Titunik's introduction to *Freudianism*, pp. xv–xxv, for the argument that Voloshinov is the author, and Katerina Clark and Michael Holquist, *Mikhail Bakhtin* (Cambridge, Mass.: Harvard University Press, 1984), for the position that Bakhtin was responsible.

42. *Freudianism*, p. 82.

43. Ibid., p. 90. See the chapter on "Freudianism," in Clark and Holquist, *Bakhtin*, pp. 171–185 for a discussion of this book's significance. For an alternative view, see James Rice, *Dostoevsky*, pp. 221–222. For recent scholarship on the points of intersection between Freud and both Bakhtin and Voloshinov, see Gerald Pirog, "The Bakhtin Circle's Freud: From Positivism to Hermeneutics," *Poetics Today*, 8, 3–4 (1987): 591–610, and the same author's "Bakhtin and Freud on the Ego," Daniel Rancour-Laferriere, ed., *Russian Literature and Psychoanalysis* (Amsterdam: John Benjamins, 1988), pp. 401–415.

44. See *Freudianism*, pp. 117–132 for this chapter. The quote is on p. 132.

45. I. A. Perepel, *Sovetskaia psikhonevrologiia i psikhoanaliz: K voprosu o lechenii i profilaktike nevrozov v SSSR* (Leningrad: Izdanie avtora, 1927), pp. 15, 54 (where he takes issue by name with the Commissar of Health, Dr. N. Semashko), 57–60. Also see Perepel's article, "On the Physiology of Hysterical Aphonia and Mutism," *International Journal of Psychoanalysis*, 11 (1930): 185–192.

46. B. D. Fridman, "K dinamike tsikloidnykh zabolevanii," *Zhurnal nevropatologii i psikhiatrii im. Korsakova*, 4 (1928): 367–372. This was also the last year that *Ezhegodnik knigi*, the annual bibliography of publications in the country, included the categories "Psychoanalysis" and "Freudism" as separate headings under the psychology listings. My thanks to Richard Seitz of the Slavic Reference Service at the University of Illinois Library for providing me with photocopies of these materials.

47. See I. B. Galant, "Masturbatsiia i avtokastratsiia v kartine shizofrenicheski-paranoidnogo zabolevaniia: k psikhologii paranoidnoi formy dementia praecoks," ibid., 3 (1928): 307–315; Freud is referred to by name on pp. 310–311, but the entire association, discussed at length in the article, between masturbation and autocastration is, of course, a classic Freudian theme. There is an explicit reference to Freud in N. N. Lavrent'ev, "Dushevnye bolezni i polovye prestupleniia," ibid., 1 (1928): 59–74; Freud is mentioned on p. 61. This article, on sexual crimes, is noteworthy for the statistical data presented, data which would soon be unpublishable. Freud is respectfully appreciated although in a confined and cautious manner, for his pioneering work in applying psychoanalysis to help neurotic disorders, in D. S. Ozeretskovskii, "K kritike psikhoanaliza: o novykh putiakh v lechenii nevrotikov," *Sovremennaia psikhonevrologiia* (Kiev), 8, 1 (1929): 311–319. The author proposes collective psychotherapy as an alternative to an overreliance on, and misuse of "the psychoanalytic method." Several translations of Freud's work appeared in Odessa between 1926 and 1928. See K. V. Mosketi et al. "Materialy po istorii

organizatsii psikhiatricheskoi pomoshchi i razvitiia nauchno-psikhiatricheskoi mysli v
Odesse (1833–1927)," *Zhurnal nevropatologii i psikhiatrii,* 87, 3 (1987): 447.

48. A. V. Petrovskii, *Psychology in the Soviet Union,* p. 165.

49. *International Journal of Psychoanalysis,* 9 (1928): 143.

50. Lev Vygotsky and Alexander Luria, "Introduction to the Russian Translation of Freud's *Beyond the Pleasure Principle,*" van der Veer and Valsiner (eds.), *The Vygotsky Reader,* pp. 9–18.

51. Lobner and Levitin, "Short Account of Freudism," p. 15.

52. On these disagreements, especially in connection with Russia, see Richard Sterba, "Discussions of Sigmund Freud," *Psychoanalytic Quarterly* 47, 2 (1978): 181–184. Reich is discussed in Paul Robinson, *The Freudian Left* (New York: Harper, 1969), pp. 9–73.

53. "Psikhoanaliz kak estestvenno-nauchnaia distsiplina," *Estestvoznanie i marksizm,* 4 (1929): 99–108.

54. Reich, "Psychoanalysis in the Soviet Union," *Sex-Pol. Essays, 1929–1934,* edited by Lee Baxandall (New York: Random House, 1966), p. 81. For the original version, see "Die Stellung der Psychoanalyse in der Sowjetunion: Notizen von einer Studienreise nach Russland," *Die Psychoanalytische Bewegung* 1 (1929): 358. See also Reich's discussion of Freudian theory and Marxism in "Dialekticheskii materializm i psikhoanaliz," *Pod znamenem marksizma,* 7–8 (1929): 180–206. This article is translated in *Sex-Pol: Essays,* pp. 1–74, with some changes.

55. Quoted in Lobner and Levitin, "Short Account of Freudism," pp. 15–16. For the original article, see M. Wulff, "Zur Stellung der Psychoanalyse in der Sowjetunion," *Die Psychoanalytische Bewegung,* 2 (1929): 70–75.

56. See I. Sapir, "Freidizm, sotsiologiia, psikhologiia," *Pod znamenem marksizma,* 7–8 (1929): 207–236, and "Doklady v Komakademii," *Estestvoznanie i marksizm,* 4 (1929): 108–125. The Academy critiques of Reich were written by Sapir, Zalkind, Fridman, V. Ror, and A. N. Zalmanzon. Reich was permitted to respond at the end (pp. 124–125). Zalkind and Fridman, it will be recalled, were former Freudians who had turned into critics of psychoanalysis.

57. See Siegfried Bernfeld, "Die kommunistische Diskussion um die Psychoanalyse und Reichs 'Widerlegung der Todestriebhypothese,'" *Internationale Zeitschrift für Psychoanalyse,* 18, 3 (1932): 352–385. Bernfeld reviewed some of the articles discussed here on Freudian Marxism in addition to Reich's work regarding the Soviet Union. Reich was expelled from the Communist party in 1933 and from the International Psychoanalytic Association one year later. The debates over psychoanalysis in the Soviet Union during the 1920s are discussed in Siegfried Katzel, *Marxismus und Psychoanalyse: eine ideologiegeschichtliche Studie zur Diskussion in Deutschland und der USSR* (Berlin: VEB Deutscher Verlag der Wissenshaften, 1987), pp. 44–49, 108–165. I am grateful to Dr. Norman Elrod (Switzerland) for bringing this book to my attention. See also R. A. Zachepitskii, "Kriticheskii analiz 'Freido-Marksizma'," *Zhurnal nevropatologii i psikhiatrii im. S. S. Korsakova,* 82 (1982): 142–148.

58. "Russian Psychoanalytical Society," *International Journal of Psychoanalysis,* 11 (1930): 521.

59. *The Future of an Illusion* appeared in 1930 as *Budushchnost' odnoi illiuzii,* translated and edited by I. D. Ermakov.

60. Elias Perepel, "The Psychoanalytic Movement in the U.S.S.R.," *Psychoanalytic Review* 26 (1939): 299.

CHAPTER 6. KILLING FREUD

1. A. Kollontai, "Make Way for Winged Eros: A Letter to Working Youth," Alix Holt (ed. and trans.), *Selected Writings of Alexandra Kollontai* (Westport, Conn.: Lawrence Hill and Co., 1977), pp. 291–292. The original appeared in *Molodaia gvardiia* in 1923. See also Stites, *Women's Liberation,* pp. 371–376.

2. See *Upadochnoe nastroenie sredi molodezhi: Eseninshchina,* ed. A. V. Lunacharskii (Moscow: Komakademiia, 1927).

3. See Eric Naiman, "The Case of Chubarov Alley: Collective Rape, Utopian Desire and the Mentality of NEP," *Russian History,* 17, 1 (Spring 1990): 1–30. For the surveys on sex, see Sheila Fitzpatrick, "Sex and Revolution," *The Cultural Front: Power and Culture in Revolutionary Russia* (Ithaca: Cornell University Press, 1992), pp. 65–90.

4. Among Zalkind's works on these themes are the following: *Revoliutsiia i molodezh* (Moscow: 1925); "Polovoi vopros s kommunisticheskoi tochki zreniia," S. M. Kalmanson (ed.), *Polovoi vopros* (Moscow: 1924), pp. 5–16; and, above all his *Ocherki kul'tury revoliutsionnogo vremeni* (Moscow: 1924). One of Zalkind's precepts: "To be sexually attracted to a being who belongs to a different class which is hostile and morally alien to one's own is just as much a perversion as it would be to feel sexual attraction for a crocodile or an ourangutang." Quoted in Mikhail Stern, *Sex in the USSR* (New York: Times Books, 1980), p. 35. For a recent analysis of Zalkind's work at this time, see Eric Naiman, *Sex in Public: The Incarnation of Early Soviet Ideology* (Princeton: Princeton University Press, 1997), pp. 126–138, 147, 169–177, 203–204.

5. Quoted in Laura Engelstein, "Soviet Policy Toward Male Homosexuality: Its Origins and Historical Roots." I have used the manuscript copy of this article, and I am grateful to the author for sharing it with me.

6. "Za partiinost' v filosofii i estestvoznanii," *Estestvoznanie i marksizm,* 2–3 (1930): 111, quoted in V. V. Umrikhin, "'Nachalo kontsa' povedencheskoi psikhologii v SSSR," M. G. Iaroshevskii (ed.), *Repressirovannaia nauka* (Leningrad: Nauka, 1991), p. 137.

7. Quoted in Rene and Eugenie Fischer, "Psychoanalyse in Russland," *Die Psychologie des 20 Jahrhunderts* 3 (1977): 124.

8. Sigmund Freud, *Civilization and its Discontents* (New York: Norton, 1961), pp. 67, 69.

9. Sigmund Freud, "The Question of a Weltanschauung," Peter Gay (ed.), *The Freud Reader* (New York: Norton, 1989), pp. 783–784.

10. Ibid., p. 785.

11. Ibid., p. 790.

12. Ibid., pp. 792–796.

13. See G. Daian, "Vtoroi psikhonevrologicheskii s"ezd," *Krasnaia nov'* 2, 19 (1924): 155–166, and 3, 20 (1924): 223–238.

14. Quoted from the Sixteenth Party Conference resolutions in Daniels, *Conscience of the Revolution*, p. 367.

15. For detailed discussions of these controversies in the field of psychology, which are related but not central to psychoanalysis, see Kozulin, *Psychology in Utopia;* Jaan Valsiner, *Developmental Psychology in the Soviet Union* (Brighton, England: Harvester Press, 1988); Raymond Bauer, *The New Man in Soviet Psychology* (Cambridge, Mass.: Harvard University Press, 1952); Joravsky, "Construction of the Stalinist Psyche," in Sheila Fitzpatrick (ed.), *Cultural Revolution in Russia, 1928–1931* (Bloomington: Indiana University, 1978), pp. 105–128; Petrovskii, *Istoriia sovetskoi psikhologii;* A. A. Smirnov, *Razvitie i sovremennoe sostoianie psikhologicheskoi nauki v SSSR* (Moscow: Pedagogika, 1975), pp. 179–212; E. A. Budilova, *Filosofskie problemy v sovetskoi psikhologii* (Moscow: Nauka, 1972), pp. 30–105; and A. L. Schniermann, "Bekhterev's Reflexological School" and K. N. Kornilov, "Psychology in the Light of Dialectical Materialism," both in Carl Murchison (ed.), *Psychologies of 1930* (Worcester, Mass.: Clark University Press, 1930), pp. 221–278, for firsthand accounts.

16. See A. Zalkind, "I Vsesoiuznyi s"ezd po izucheniiu povedeniia cheloveka," *Zhurnal nevropatologii i psikhiatrii,* 6 (1930): 19–24. The presentations made at the congress included many of the most prominent Soviet figures involved in the study of the mind and human behavior, such as Vygotsky and Luria, as well as V. N. Miasishchev and D. N. Uznadze, who will be discussed in the next chapter.

17. Quoted in Bauer, *New Man,* pp. 99–100. Emphasis is in the original. For Zalkind's original presentation to the congress, see A. B. Zalkind (ed.), *Psikho-nevrologicheskie nauki v SSSR (Materialy I Vsesoiuznogo s"ezda po izucheniiu povedeniia cheloveka)* (Moscow: Gosmedizdat, 1930), pp. 5–12. Another speaker at the 1930 congress stated that "conscious activity as a higher form of correlative [*sootnositel'nyi*] activity includes lower psychic, unconscious forms," meaning that the unconscious was no longer to be perceived as an independent phenomenon of analysis. A. L. Shirman, "O predmete i metode refleksologii kak nauki o sootnositel'noi deiatel'nosti," *Voprosy izucheniia i vospitaniia lichnosti,* ed. V. P. Osipov, nos. 1–2 (Moscow: Gosmedizdat, 130), p. 9. For an evaluative overview of the congress by a participant, see I. F. Kurazov, "Metodologicheskie itogi povedencheskogo s"ezda," ibid., 3–8. The critique of Freud and the associated attack on "idealism" at the congress can be found on pp. 4–5. I am grateful to Jaan Valsiner providing me with these source materials.

18. Zalkind, *Psikho-nevrologicheskie nauki,* pp. 5–9.

19. See B. N. Birman, "Psikhoterapiia, kak sotsiorefleksoterapiia nevropaticheskoi lichnosti," in Zalkind, *Psikho-nevrologicheskie nauki,* pp. 321–322, for the criticism of Freud's "pansexualism." Also, see Iu. V. Kannabikh, "Individual'naia psikhoterapiia Adlera, kak prakticheskii metod psikhoterapii i kak obshchaia teoriia povedeniia," ibid., pp. 319–321, and his *Istoriia psikhiatrii* (Leningrad: Gosmedizdat [1929]), pp. 455–485, one of the finest Soviet histories of psychiatry.

20. Reisner's introduction is in F. Vittels, *Freid* (Moscow: Gosizdat, 1925). Variash was the editor of the Party's main text on modern philosophy, *Istoriia novoi filosofii,* to which he also contributed the introduction and a chapter. Zalkind was attacked for his earlier book, *Ocherki kultury revoliutsionnogo vremeni.* See A. Stoliarov, *Dialekticheskii mate-*

rializm i mekhanisty (Leningrad: Priboi, 1930). It is noteworthy that 30,000 copies of this fifth edition were printed, a clear indication of the government's desire to have the book very widely distributed and read.

21. Joravsky believes that Zalkind may have committed suicide (*Russian Psychology*, p. 237), but Etkind claims that Zalkind died of a heart attack in 1936 (*Eros nevozmozhnogo*, p. 332). The whole field of pedology was criticized and finally abolished by the Central Committee of the Communist party in July 1936. For the original resolution, see *Pravda*, July 5, 1936. It is translated in Wortis, *Soviet Psychiatry*, pp. 242–245. On the links between psychoanalysis and pedology, see A. Etkind, "L'Essor et l'échec du mouvement 'paidologique'," *Cahiers du monde russe et soviétique*, 33, 4 (October–December 1992): 387–418.

22. F. Shemiakin and L. Gershonovich, "Kak Trotskii i Kautskii revizuiut Marksizm v voprosakh psikhologii," *Psikhologiia*, 1–2 (1932): 3–37, especially pp. 3–9. The section of this article which deals with Kautsky is not relevant to our immediate discussion. For Stalin's letter, "O nekotorykh voprosakh istorii bolshevizma," which originally appeared in *Proletarskaia Revoliutsiia* in 1931, see I. V. Stalin, *Sochineniia* (Moscow: Gosizdat, 1951), 13:84–102.

23. A. Talankin, "Protiv men'shevistvuiushchego idealizma v psikhologii," *Psikhologiia*, 1–2 (1932): 38–62, especially pp. 38–43, 55–57, and 60–62. This article contains a critique of the psychological ideas of G. V. Plekhanov, known as the "father of Russian Marxism," whom for years the Bolsheviks had identified pejoratively as one of the leading theoreticians of Menshevism.

24. Cited in Rene van der Veer and Jaan Valsiner, *Understanding Vygotsky: A Quest for Synthesis* (Oxford: Blackwell, 1991), pp. 377–378.

25. A. Luria, "Krizis burzhuaznoi psikhologii," *Psikhologiia*, 1–2 (1932): 63–88, especially pp. 64–73, 84–88. Luria also wrote the article on psychoanalysis for the 1940 edition of the authoritative *Great Soviet Encyclopedia*. Here too, while obediently critical in general, he managed to include a few positive comments. The method of "investigating the repressed unconscious drives of man and their role in the structure of psychic life" was the "scientific importance of psychoanalysis," he wrote. However, generalizing from this data led to the creation of "an erroneous theory." By emphasizing man as a product of instincts, independent of society, psychoanalysis established an "incorrect biological interpretation" which is "hostile to Marxism" and devoid of "a scientific analysis of objective reality." While psychoanalysis retains "importance as a form of treatment for neurotic personalities," it remains outside the framework of "progressive science" because of its denial of the significance of man as a product of historical development and in its reduction of society to a set of forces constraining man's basic drives. See A. Luria, "Psikhoanaliz," *Bolshaia Sovetskaia Entsiklopediia* 47 (1940): 507–510.

26. V. Vnukov, "Psikhoanaliz," *Meditsinskaia Entsiklopediia* 27 (1933): 733.

27. K. Veidemiuller and A. Shcheglov, "Freidizm," *Bolshaia Sovetskaia Entsiklopediia* 59 (1935): 187–193. This article is preceded by a brief but objective biographical article on Freud, who was still in Vienna when this was published. See ibid., pp. 186–187.

28. M. P. Feofanov, writing in the journal *Pedologiia* in 1932, as quoted in Bauer, *New Man*, p. 106.

29. On Rubinstein's career, see T. R. Payne, *S. L. Rubinstein and the Philosophical Foundations of Soviet Psychology* (Dordrecht, Holland: D. Reidel, 1968). For two representative Soviet accounts, see Petrovskii, *Istoriia sovetskoi psikhologii,* especially pp. 215–225, 219–223, 328–333 and E. A. Budilova, *Filosofskie problemy v sovetskoi psikhologii* (Moscow: Nauka, 1972), pp. 151–176.

30. Sergei L. Rubinstein, "Problems of Psychology in the Works of Karl Marx," *Studies in Soviet Thought* 33 (1987): 119. The original can be found in *Sovetskaia psikhotekhnika* 7, 1 (1934): 3–20.

31. Rubinstein, "Problems of Psychology," pp. 123, 126.

32. E. T. Chernakov, "Protiv idealizma i metafiziki v psikhologii," *Voprosy filosofii,* 3 (1948). For a translation, see Wortis, *Soviet Psychiatry,* pp. 261–285. This quotation is from Wortis, p. 266.

33. Wortis, *Soviet Psychiatry,* p. 275. The long series of juxtaposed quotations can be found on pp. 272–275. Rubinstein did devote some attention to psychoanalysis, but made no significant theoretical contributions; see his discussion of Freud in B. F. Lomov (ed.), *Sergei Leonidovich Rubinshtein: Ocherki, Vospominaniia, Materialy* (Moscow: Nauka, 1989), pp. 100, 399.

34. Wortis, *Soviet Psychiatry,* p. 285.

35. A. P. Fomichev, "Concerning the Pedological Distortions in the System of the People's Commissariat of Education," quoted in Wortis, *Soviet Psychiatry,* pp. 119–120.

CHAPTER 7. AFTER STALIN

1. On Spielrein's death, see V. Ovcharenko, "Sud'ba Sabiny Shpil'rein," *Rossiiskii psikhoanaliticheskii vestnik,* 2 (1992): 68–9, which contains the archival evidence that was for decades unavailable. An early piece of evidence for Spielrein's death obtained from family sources by Magnus Ljunggren in 1983 was mentioned in the re-edition of Carotenuto, *A Secret Symmetry* (1984), pp. x–xi, by the editor William McGuire.

2. See Peter Gay, *Freud: A Life for Our Time* (New York: Norton, 1988), pp. 611–651, on the final period of Freud's life.

3. Personal communication to the author from Dr. Irina Dynkin, November 6, 1985. I wish to express my gratitude to Dr. Dynkin for agreeing to an interview with me, and for her long letter recalling her medical training and experience in Moscow.

4. For a detailed study of the psychoanalytic content of Zoshchenko's novel, see Thomas P. Hodge, "Freudian Elements in Zoshchenko's *Pered voskhodom sol'ntsa* (1943)," *Slavonic and East European Review* 67, 1 (January 1989): 1–28. The war metaphor passage is on p. 18. See also, for further details on this subject, Rachel May, "Superego as Literary Subtext: Story and Structure in Mikhail Zoshchenko's *Before Sunrise,*" *Slavic Review,* 55, 1 (Spring 1996): 104–124, and Vera von Wiren-Garczynski, "Zoshchenko's Psychological Interests," *Slavic and East European Journal* 11, 1 (Spring 1967): 3–22. For the novel itself, see Mikhail Zoshchenko, *Pered voskhodom sol'ntsa* (Moscow: Sovetskaia Rossiia, 1976). There has been some discussion of Sergei Eisenstein's interest in psychoanalysis in connection with his work as a major Soviet film director in these years, but there is little in his writings to indicate that this was a serious concern. See Etkind, *Eros nevozmozhnogo,* pp. 381–388.

5. Lobner and Levitin, "Short Account of Freudism," p. 18.

6. See, e.g., N. I. Grashchenkov, "K stoletiiu so dnia rozhdeniia Akademika I. P. Pavlova," *Nevropatologiia i psikhiatriia* 18, 1 (1949): 3–9. The criticism of Freud is on pp. 8–9. Grashchenkov was the chief editor of this journal and also chairman of the main advisory committee in the Ministry of Health.

7. S. I. Vavilov, "Inaugural Address," *Scientific Session on the Physiological Teachings of Academician I. P. Pavlov* (Moscow: Foreign Languages Publishing House, 1951), pp. 9, 15. For the original, see *Nauchnaia sessiia posviashchennaia problemam fiziologicheskogo ucheniia akademika I. P. Pavlova. Stenograficheskii otchet* (Moscow, 1950).

8. *Scientific Session,* pp. 5, 7.

9. Ibid., pp. 17, 20, 23.

10. K. M. Bykov, "Development of the Ideas of I. P. Pavlov," ibid., p. 67. On the conflicts among the pro- and anti-Pavlovians at this conference, see Joravsky, *Russian Psychology,* pp. 404–414.

11. *Scientific Session,* pp. 66, 69, 72. The most extensive argument seeking to demonstrate Bykov's position on the opposition between Freud and Pavlov from the post-Stalin Soviet perspective is Harry K. Wells, *Pavlov and Freud: Toward a Scientific Psychology and Psychiatry,* 2 vols. (New York: International Publishers, 1956). A. S. Chistovich, who had attempted earlier to express some positive interest in psychoanalytic theory, was compelled to apologize at the conference. See Joravsky, *Russian Psychology,* p. 529, n. 21. Needless to say, "reflexological Freudism" did not exist.

12. See Laurence S. Kubie, "Pavlov, Freud and Soviet Psychiatry," *Behavioral Science* 4 (1959): 29–34. For other instances of Pavlov commenting favorably or respectfully on Freud, see Lobner and Levitin, "Short Account of Freudism," p. 17.

13. See the discussion and references in R. Tucker, "Stalin and the Uses of Psychology," *The Soviet Political Mind: Studies in Stalinism and Post-Stalin Change* (New York: Praeger, 1963), pp. 114–116.

14. S. L. Rubinstein, "Voprosy psikhologischeskoi teorii," *Voprosy psikhologii,* 1 (1955): 14. His major book, *Being and Consciousness (Bytie i soznanie),* appeared in 1957.

15. Wortis, *Soviet Psychiatry,* pp. 72, 102.

16. *The Short Philosophical Dictionary,* 4th ed., 1955, p. 527, as cited in Walter Laqueur, "Psychoanalysis in Soviet Perspective," *Soviet Survey,* 7 (1956): 2. A German translation of Laqueur's article can be found in *Psyche* (December 1956), 588–596; the content of the translated version is identical to the original except for an added introductory section.

17. Laqueur, "Psychoanalysis in Soviet Perspective," p. 4, quoted from *Voprosy psikhologii,* 2 (1956). Laqueur's report was one of the first in the West to detect this countertrend in attitudes about psychoanalytic subjects. He also mentioned other Soviet publications in which this current was visible. In addition, he noted that the May 1956 issue of *Neue Deutsche Literatur,* the East German journal, published extracts from Freud's writings together with a positive evaluation of Freud in an article by the novelist Arnold Zweig, who was popular in the Soviet Union as well.

18. *Voprosy psikhologii,* 6 (1956): 72–112.

19. A summary of these awards and honors can be found in Miasishchev's obituary article,

which appeared in *Zhurnal nevropatologii i psikhiatrii* 74, 3 (1974): 467–468. See also the praise accorded Miasishchev by the top echelon of Soviet psychiatrists in Edward Babayan, *The Structure of Psychiatry in the Soviet Union* (New York: International Universities Press, 1985), pp. 200–202.

20. Miasishchev's students and colleagues remained bitter for years about this, as a Western researcher found during a visiting appointment at the Psychoneurological Institute in Leningrad. See W. Lauterbach, *Soviet Psychotherapy* (New York: Pergamon Press, 1984), pp. 94–95. Miasishchev's influence is portrayed as extraordinary in this study.

21. The quote is from the Miasishchev obituary cited above in note 19, p. 467.

22. V. N. Miasishchev, *Personality and Neurosis* (Washington, D.C.: Joint Publication Research Service, 1963), p. v. This is a translation of the author's *Lichnost' i nevrozy* (Moscow: Leningrad University Press, 1960), which won the Bekhterev Prize in 1960. The book contains Miasishchev's most important research papers published between 1935 and 1960. These quotes are on pp. v and 238 of the translated volume.

23. This case is described in Miasishchev, *Personality and Neurosis,* p. 207. For other case summaries, see pp. 238–239.

24. Ibid., p. 45.

25. Ibid., p. 47.

26. Ibid., p. 202.

27. Ibid., p. 155.

28. Ibid., p. 270.

29. Kozulin has drawn attention to these influences on Uznadze, including an article by Uznadze on Bergson published in German in 1926. See *Psychology in Utopia,* pp. 95 and 166, n. 24. For Russian treatments of Uznadze, consult Petrovskii, *Istoriia sovetskoi psikhologii,* pp. 315–318; Budilova, *Filosofskie problemy,* pp. 176–183; and Smirnov, *Razvitie,* pp. 280–282.

30. Hans Lobner, "'The Unconscious' in the Soviet Union," *Sigmund Freud House Bulletin,* 3 (1979): 21.

31. See R. G. Natadze, "Fifty Years of Psychology in Georgia," and A. S. Prangishvili, "The Concept of Set in Soviet Psychology in Light of Research by the Georgia Psychological School," both in *Soviet Psychology* 7, 2 (Winter, 1968–69): 21–32, 33–47.

32. One of Uznadze's important early papers, "On the Problem of the Basic Law of a Change in Set," appeared in Russian in *Psikhologiia* 3 (1930), and another, "On the Weight Illusion and Its Analogue," was published in German in *Psychologische Forschung* (1931). Both of these journals were routinely read by Soviet psychologists at this time.

33. Dmitrii Nikolaevich Uznadze, *The Psychology of Set,* ed. Joseph Wortis and trans. Basil Haigh (New York: Consultants Bureau, 1966), p. 10. This monograph was originally published in Georgia in 1949 and first published in Russian in 1961, together with a companion essay, "The Basic Principles of the Theory of Set." Both are included in the English translation. For an introduction to Uznadze's early experiments, see R. G. Natadze, "Experimental Foundations of Uznadze's Theory of Set," in Michael Cole and Irving Maltzman (eds.), *A Handbook of Contemporary Soviet Psychology* (New York: Basic Books, 1969), pp. 603–624.

34. Uznadze, *The Psychology of Set,* p. 243. Uznadze's theory is far more complex than its

summary here. However, Kozulin's criticism of the discrepancy between Uznadze's "wide theoretical premises" and his "very narrow empirical base" seems fair (Kozulin, *Psychology in Utopia*, p. 97).

35. Uznadze, *Psychology of Set*, pp. 197, 213, 214.

36. Ibid., p. 214.

37. Ibid.

38. D. Fedotov, "The Soviet View of Psychoanalysis," *Monthly Review* 9 (December 1957): 249–254. A response follows, by Dr. Norman Reider, on pp. 254–258, in which Fedotov's argument is refuted. This is, to my knowledge, the first discussion ever published between an American and a Soviet psychiatrist on the subject of psychoanalysis.

39. "Freud and Pavlov: Report of a Soviet Conference," *Soviet Survey*, 29 (July–September 1959): 29–31. For the original report, see P. P. Bondarenko and M. Kh. Rabinovich, "Nauchnoe soveshchanie po voprosam ideologicheskoi bor'by s sovremennym freidizmom," *Voprosy filosofii*, 2 (1959): 164–170.

40. Ibid., pp. 31–33.

41. Ibid., p. 35.

42. Ibid., pp. 35–36. Emphasis in the quoted text is mine. Despite this criticism, Anokhin is best known as one of the major Pavlovian disciple-reformers. On Anokhin's career, see Loren Graham, *Science and Philosophy in the Soviet Union* (New York: A. A. Knopf, 1972), pp. 407–425.

43. "Freud and Pavlov," pp. 36–37.

44. Ibid., p. 37. For an example of the application of this "unmasking" in the case of Freudian influences in contemporary American studies of Russian literature, see L. Zhelianova, "O freidistkom iskazhenii russkoi literatury v sovremennom amerikanskom literaturnovedenii," *Russkaia Literatura*, 2 (1959): 226–234.

45. The original articles can be found in *Voprosy psikhologii*, 5 (1958): 133–145, and 6 (1958): 140–153. There are two partial translations in English which also lack the extensive bibliography of the Russian originals. See F. V. Bassin, "Freudism in the Light of Contemporary Scientific Discussion," *Soviet Survey*, 7 (January–March 1959): 82–87; and F. V. Bassin, "A Critical Analysis of Freudianism," *Soviet Review* 1, 5 (December 1970): 3–14. For responses, see Emanuel Miller, "Freud and Pavlov," *Soviet Survey*, 28 (April–June 1959): 64–65, 80; and "An Answer to F. V. Bassin's Criticism of Freudianism" by Cesare L. Musatti, *Soviet Review* 1, 5 (December 1970): 14–27, followed by Bassin's "Rejoinder to Professor Musatti," pp. 27–44.

46. F. V. Bassin, "A Critical Analysis of Freudianism," *Soviet Review* (December 1970): 3, 7, 10, 14. The response to Bassin's article by Musatti and Bassin's reply, which follow on pp. 14–44, are worth reading in their entirety. Musatti, Italy's leading psychoanalyst at this time, who was familiar with experimental psychology and openly admitted political sympathies with Italian communism, was in an unusual position to respond to Bassin's article.

47. F. Mikhailov and G. Tsaregorodtsev, *Za porogom soznaniia* (Moscow: Gosudarstvennoe izdatel'stvo politicheskoi literatury, 1961), especially pp. 40–66. It is of interest that not only were the number of books and articles explicitly dealing with Freud on the rise at this time, but the quantity of copies printed was also growing. Mikhailov and

Tsaregorodtsev's book, for instance, had a relatively large printing of 42,000 copies, showing that the government publishing house wanted this material to be read. A typical specialized monograph with no official priority attached to it was often printed in an edition of less than 5,000 copies. Mikhailov and Tsaregorodtsev used the Russian translation of Freud's German terminology, such as *Ia* and *Ono* for *Ich* and *Das,* as had been done by the Soviet Freudians in the 1920s. This is in contrast to the far more abstract substitute terms used in English such as "ego" and "id." On this problem, see Bruno Bettelheim, *Freud and Man's Soul* (New York: Knopf, 1983).

48. Graham, *Science and Philosophy in the Soviet Union,* p. 391.

49. F. V. Bassin, "Consciousness and Unconsciousness," Cole and Maltzman (eds.), *A Handbook of Contemporary Soviet Psychology,* especially pp. 401–404.

50. Ivan Terent'evich Kurtsin, *Kritika Freidizma v meditsine i fiziologii* (Moscow-Leningrad: Nauka, 1965). The especially thorough bibliography in Kurtsin's book, pp. 258–294, contains both Russian and Western-language listings.

51. A. M. Khaletskii, "Freudianism, Microsociology and Existentialism," *Soviet Psychology and Psychiatry* 6, 1 (Fall 1965): 45–53. For the original, see *Zhurnal nevropatologii i psikihiatrii* 65, 4 (1965): 624–630.

52. I. S. Kon, *Sotsiologiia lichnosti* (Moscow: Izdatel'stvo politicheskoi literatury, 1967). For the discussion on "Personality Structure According to Freud," see pp. 45–66. Kon's interesting base of sources extends from William James to the poetry of Yevtushenko and Voznesensky. In addition, 55,000 copies of the book were printed, making it the largest printing to date of any social science text on this topic.

53. F. V. Bassin, *Problema bessoznatel'nogo* (Moscow: Meditsina, 1968). The subtitle of the book is "On nonperceived forms of higher nervous activity." A French translation of the book was published in 1973.

54. Ibid., pp. 50–51.

55. Ibid., pp. 90–94. Bassin does not mention it, but this discussion of Freud and his opponents reminds one of the standard Soviet histories of Lenin battling his Marxist opponents.

56. Ibid., pp. 124, 153.

57. Ibid., p. 177.

58. Ibid., pp. 229–233.

59. Ibid., p. 343. See also Nancy Rollins, "The New Soviet Approach to the Unconscious," *American Journal of Psychiatry* 131, 4 (March 1974): 301–304. Before her untimely death, Dr. Rollins was the most knowledgeable American psychiatrist on this subject.

60. Bondarenko and Rabinovich, "Nauchnoe soveshchanie," p. 167.

CHAPTER 8. THE REHABILITATION OF THE UNCONSCIOUS

1. The standard accounts of these developments are by Sidney Bloch and Peter Reddaway: *Soviet Psychiatric Abuse* (Boulder: Westview Press, 1984), and *Psychiatric Terror* (New York: Basic Books, 1977). For another viewpoint, see Martin A. Miller, "The Theory and Practice of Psychiatry in the Soviet Union," *Psychiatry,* 48, 1 (February 1985): 13–24.

2. A. M. Sviadoshch, *Nevrozy i ikh lechenie* (Moscow: Meditsina, 1971), pp. 28–31, 72, 228. Sviadoshch's book was the most comprehensive study on neurosis since Miasishchev's. Regarding Sviadoshch's attitude toward Freud, Levitin wrote that he tried "to smuggle in psychoanalytic concepts" while emphasizing his disagreements with these very ideas." Lobner and Levitin, "Short Account of Freudism," p. 22.

3. A. E. Lichko, "Psikhologiia otnoshenii kak teoreticheskaia kontseptsiia v meditsinskoi psikhologii i psikhoterapii," *Zhurnal nevropatologii i psikhiatrii*, 77, 12 (1977): 1833–8.

4. See Rozhnov's discussion of Soviet psychotherapy in Edward Babayan, *The Structure of Psychiatry in the Soviet Union*, pp. 94–113. Note in particular his critique of Freud and psychoanalysis on pp. 104–105.

5. F. Bassin, V. Rozhnov, M. Rozhnova, "Freidizm: Psevdonauchnaia traktovka psikhicheskikh iavlenii," *Kommunist*, 48 (January 1972): 94–106. This journal, one of the oldest continuously published party organs during the Soviet era, was founded in 1924 as *Bolshevik*. The topic heading under which this article appeared, "The Crisis of Bourgeois Ideology," was a frequent theme in this journal. Bassin and Rozhnov combined on another article, this time published in the country's major philosophical journal, in which they reiterated the psychological importance of the concept of the unconscious in human cognition on the one hand, and, on the other, their claim that the only valid approach to understand this complex subject scientifically was Uznadze's, not Freud's. See F. V. Bassin and V. E. Rozhnov, "O sovremennom podkhode k probleme neosoznavaemoi psikhicheskoi deiatel'nosti (bessoznatel'nogo)," *Voprosy filosofii*, 10 (1975): 94–108. Bassin also continued his dialogues abroad at this time. See F. V. Bassin, "Le conscient, 'l'inconscient' et la maladie: A propos de l'approche moderne du problème psychosomatique," *Revue de Médecine Psychosomatique* 14, 3 (1972): 263–280.

6. A. N. Boiko, *Problema bessoznatel'nogo v filosofii i konkretnykh naukakh* (Kiev: Izdatel'stvo pri Kievskom gosudarstvennom universitete, 1978), p. 131.

7. V. M. Leibin, "Konformizm i respektabel'nost' psikhoanaliza," *Voprosy filosofii*, 4 (1972): 143–147. For an interpretation similar to Leibin's with greater attention to the conformist consequences of the original radicalism in Freud's work, see Russell Jacoby, *The Repression of Psychoanalysis* (New York: Basic Books, 1983).

8. V. I. Dobren'kov, *Kritika neofreidistskoi kontseptsii Erikha Fromma* (Moscow: Znanie, 1972); V. I. Dobren'kov, *Neofreidizm v poiskakh 'istiny'* (Moscow: Mysl', 1974).

9. N. S. Avtonomova, "Psikhoanaliticheskaia kontseptsiia Zhaka Lakana," *Voprosy filosofii*, 11 (1973): 143–150. A related work appeared several years later, a Russian translation of a French Marxist critique of psychoanalysis. See K. B. Klemen, P. Briuno, L. Sev, *Marksistskaia kritika psikhoanaliza*. Translated from the French. Edited, with a foreword, by F. V. Bassin and V. E. Rozhnov (Moscow: Progress, 1976). For the original French edition, see C. B. Clément, P. Bruno, L. Sève, *Pour une critique Marxiste de la théorie psychanalytique* (Paris: Editions sociales, 1973). The content of this interesting book is not discussed here because it was not a Soviet product of the literature on Freudian themes. The authors did, however, deal extensively with topics such as the sources of Freud's theory and the origins of psychoanalysis ("the psychoanalytic revolution"), the transformation of psychoanalysis into a metapsychology and a philosophy of culture, Wilhelm Reich and the efforts to blend Freud with Marx, Lacanian Freudianism, and

the critique of psychoanalysis from the standpoint of Marxist historical materialism. While parts of the book echo earlier Soviet discussions, the French authors included materials and references to Freudian sources which had not appeared in the Soviet literature before.

10. See L. I. Filippov, "Strukturalizm i Freidizm," *Voprosy filosofii,* 3 (1976): 155–163. In addition to Lacan, Filippov discusses the work of Saussure, Derrida, and Lévi-Strauss as well. Also, the completion of Zoshchenko's novel of his self-analysis was published at this time after an interval of four decades. See Mikhail Zoshchenko, *Pered voskhodom solntsa* (Moscow: Sovetskaia Rossiia, 1976).

11. V. M. Leibin, *Psikhoanaliz i filosofiia neofreidizma* (Moscow: Izdatel'stvo politicheskoi literatury, 1977).

12. Nancy Rollins, *Child Psychiatry in the Soviet Union* (Cambridge, Mass.: Harvard University Press, 1972), p. 239.

13. Leon Chertok, "Reinstatement of the Concept of the Unconscious in the Soviet Union," *American Journal of Psychiatry* 138, 5 (May 1981): 575. On Chertok's earlier work in this area, see "Psychiatric Dialogue between East and West," *British Journal of Medical Psychology* 41 (1968): 295–297, and "Psychosomatic Medicine in the West and in Eastern European Countries," *Psychosomatic Medicine* 6 (1969): 510–521.

14. Chertok, "Reinstatement," pp. 575–578.

15. George Pollack, "Psychoanalysis in Russia and the U.S.S.R.: 1908–1972," *Annual of Psychoanalysis,* 10 (1982): 267, 268. Another report on the Tbilisi congress based on reports made by Pollack and other participants from the American Psychiatric Association can be found in "The Unconscious in the USSR: Can Marx and Freud Find Common Ground," *Roche Report: Frontiers of Psychiatry* 11, 9 (October 15, 1981): 12–13. I am grateful to Dr. Pollack for sharing his personal reminiscences of the conference with me.

16. Nancy Rollins, "A Critique of Soviet Concepts of Consciousness and Unconsciousness," *Interaction* 3, 4 (Winter 1980): 225, 226.

17. See Elizabeth Roudinesco, *Jacques Lacan and Co.: A History of Psychoanalysis in France, 1925–1985* (Chicago: University of Chicago Press, 1990), pp. 643–666.

18. A. S. Prangishvili, A. E. Sheroziia, and F. V. Bassin (eds.), *The Unconscious: Nature, Functions, Methods of Study* (Tbilisi: Metsniereba, 1978), vols. I–III. The fourth volume appeared in 1985. The papers were published in their original languages—English, French, German, and Russian. The first three volumes contained 212 papers from submissions prior to the conference, and another 36 appeared in volume IV from discussions held at the conference. This remains the largest collection of papers ever published from a single conference on psychoanalysis and the unconscious.

19. *Unconscious,* I:19–20.

20. Ibid., II:23–24.

21. See, e.g., V. S. Rotenberg's acceptance of the notion of dreams revealing how individuals in treatment "seek ways of reconciling unacceptable motives with the basic norms of behavior" and his use of Freud's concepts in his paper, "Dreaming as an Active Process and the Problem of the Unconscious," ibid., II:99–110; and also A. M. Sviadoshch's positive assessment of Freud in spite of his rejection of the theory of infantile sexuality,

"The Role of Unconscious Motives in the Clinical Picture of Neuroses," ibid., II:361–366. Similarly of interest are the six case studies of defense mechanisms in psychotherapy in the paper by V. E. Rozhnov and M. E. Burno, "The Unconscious and Clinical Psychotherapy: The Problem Posed," ibid., II:346–352.

22. See especially the introductory paper, ibid., III:27–46.

23. Ibid., III:47–55, 156–167.

24. There is one paper by Leon Chertok of Paris, ibid., IV:106–114.

25. N. V. Bakhtadze-Sheroziia, "The International Symposium on the Problem of the Unconscious, Tbilisi, 1979," ibid., IV:147–148. Of the post-Uznadzeans, one of the most representative studies is A. E. Sheroziia's *K probleme soznaniia i bessoznatel'nogo psikhicheskogo*, 2 vols. (Tbilisi: Metsniereba, 1969, 1973). This book contains a lengthy critique of Freud based on a close reading of his works (I:7–169), a reexamination of Uznadze's research (the remainder of vol. I) and Sheroziia's own general theory of consciousness and the unconscious as "an integrated system of relations" of the human personality (all of vol. II). "In light of the proposed new theory," the author concludes in a tone of unwarranted arrogance, "almost all earlier attempts made in this direction in the psychology of consciousness and the unconscious assume the form of mere prehistory" (II:518).

26. See Nancy Rollins, "Consciousness, Unconsciousness and the Concept of Repression," *Unconscious*, I:266–281, and "A Critique of Soviet Concepts of Consciousness and Unconsciousness," *Interaction* 3, 4 (Winter 1980): 225–233.

27. For this attack, see L. Kukuev, "O nekotorykh teoreticheskikh aspektakh nevropatologii i psikhiatrii," *Zhurnal nevropatologii i psikhiatrii* 80, 1:3–8. For the Uznadzeans' response, see A. S. Prangishvili, A. E. Sheroziia, and F. V. Bassin, "Mezhdunarodnyi simpozium po probleme neosoznavaemoi psikhicheskoi deiatel'nosti," *Voprosy psikhologii* 2 (1980): 181–184.

28. *Unconscious*, III:734.

29. Ibid., IV:457. The projected volume did not appear.

30. Chertok, "Reinstatement," p. 582.

31. Lobner, "The 'Unconscious' in the USSR," p. 27.

32. Roudinesco, *Jacques Lacan and Co.*, p. 646.

CHAPTER 9. PSYCHOANALYSIS AND SOVIET HISTORY

1. Andrei Voznesensky, "Sovest' mysli," *Izvestiia*, December 6, 1987, 3. I wish to express my gratitude to Mr. Voznesensky for giving me the reference to his article at the time of its publication, and for confirming the emerging Freud revival in a private conversation at Duke University during his visit to the United States in January 1988.

2. Lobner and Levitin, "Short History of Freudism," p. 26. See also the reports by Leon Chertok, "Sigmund chez Karl," *Le Monde*, September 2–3, 1984; "Philosophie: Les Soviétiques à Paris," *Le Monde Campus*, December 18, 1986; and "L'Etat actuel de la psychanalyse en U.R.S.S.," *Psychanalyse clinique*, 1 (1986): 1–3. For Freud's views on practicing psychoanalysis without approved training, which under certain circumstances he found beneficial to a degree, see S. Freud, "'Wild' Psychoanalysis," *Standard*

Edition of the Complete Psychological Works, ed. James Strachey (London: Hogarth Press, 1957), XI:221–227.

3. See the following examples: B. D. Karvasarskii, *Nevrozy* (Moscow: Meditsina, 1980); B. D. Karvasarskii, *Meditsinskaia psikhologiia* (Leningrad: Meditsina, 1982), which includes a brief discussion of psychoanalysis, p. 141; B. F. Lomov, "Lichnost' v sisteme ob-shchestvennykh otnoshenii," *Psikhologischeskii zhurnal* 2, 1 (1981): 3–17; R. A. Zachepitskii, "Psychotherapy and Psychoanalysis in Neuroses," Jules H. Masserman (ed.), *Current Psychiatric Therapies* 23 (1986): 249–256.

4. G. S. Vasil'chenko, *Obshchaia seksopatologiia* (Moscow: Meditsina, 1977).

5. See L. T. Levchuk, *Psikhoanaliz i khudozhestvennoe tvorchestvo* (Kiev: Izdatel'stvo pri Kievskom universitete, 1980); and A. A. Pruzhinina, "Kritika frantsuzskimi marksistami psikhoanaliza." Avtoreferat dissertatsii kandidata filosofskikh nauk (Moscow: Izdatel'stvo Moskovskogo universiteta, 1984). I wish to thank Dr. L. Chertok (Paris) for providing me with a copy of this latter work.

6. G. N. Veliev, *Problema bessoznatel'nogo v filosofii i psikhologii* (Baku: Elm, 1984).

7. For interesting examples, see L. T. Levchuk, *Psikhoanaliz: ot bessoznatel'nogo k "ustalosti ot soznaniia"* (Kiev: Izdatel'stvo pri Kievskom universitete, 1989); and also K. E. Tarasov and M. S. Kel'ner, *"Freido-Marksizm" o cheloveke* (Moscow: Mysl', 1989).

8. See the debate between Belkin and Chertok in *Literaturnaia gazeta,* November 1, 1989. Also see F. V. Bassin, "Aktual'nost' problemy bessoznatel'nogo na sovremennom etape razvitiia psikhologicheskikh predstavlenii," *Filosofskie nauki,* 3 (1990): 43–53. This article was originally presented as a lecture at the Institute of Psychology in Moscow on the occasion of the fiftieth anniversary of Freud's death. It is far more of a tribute to Freud's work than one finds in Bassin's pre-glasnost publications. His critique of Belkin is on pp. 52–53.

9. See V. M Leibin, *Freid, psikhoanaliz i sovremennaia zapadnaia filosofiia* (Moscow: Politizdat, 1990) as well as the following articles by Leibin: "Vera ili razum," *Voprosy filosofii,* 8 (1988): 126–132; "Iz istorii vozniknoveniia psikhoanaliza (Pis'ma Z. Freida V. Flissu), *Voprosy filosofii,* 4 (1988): 104–117; "Psikhoanaliz i bessoznatel'noe: utochnenie poniatii," *Psikhologicheskii zhurnal* 10, 3 (1989): 17–22.

10. Andrei Zagdansky (director), *Tolkovanie snovedeniia* (1988). I wish to express my gratitude to Dr. Lev Gertsig of the Russian Psychoanalytic Society for drawing my attention to this film and inviting me to view it at his home in Moscow.

11. For a list of many of these publications about Freud in the Soviet press at this time, see I. E. Lalaiants and L. S. Milovanova, "Freid i Freidizm," *Sovetskaia bibliografiia,* 5 (September–October 1990): 59–62. For an example of the return to the media of the politically repressed, see the article on Trotsky under the heading of "bibliographic rehabilitation" compiled by V. V. Krylov, "L. D. Trotskii: Bibliografiia," in the same issue, pp. 78–93.

12. "Zigmund Freid," *Literaturnaia gazeta,* June 1, 1988, p. 15.

13. L. A. Radzikhovskii, "Teoriia Freida: smena ustanovki," *Voprosy psikhologii* 1 (1988): 100–105.

14. See the archival list in A. A. Belkin and A. V. Litvinov, "K istorii psikhoanaliza v Sovetskoi Rossii," *Rossiiskii psikhoanaliticheskii vestnik,* 2 (1992): 24–26.

15. M. G. Iaroshevskii (Yaroshevsky), "Vozvrashchenie Freida," *Psikhologicheskii zhurnal* 9, 6 (1988): 131.

16. On Ermakov, see M. I. Davydova, "Ivan Dmitrievich Ermakov (1875–1942)," *Psikhologicheskii zhurnal,* 10, 2 (1989): 156–159; and M. I. Davydova and A. V. Litvinov, "Ivan Dmitrievich Ermakov," *Rossiiskii psikhoanaliticheskii vestnik,* 1 (1991): 115–127. The Dostoevsky chapter by Ermakov can be found in V. Zelenskii, "Psikhoanaliz v literaturovedenii," *Sovetskaia bibliografiia,* 6 (November–December 1990): 101–111, especially pp. 104–111.

17. A. Belkin, "Mify i realnost'," *Meditsinskaia gazeta,* January 8, 1989, p. 3. This essay appeared as part of a full-page showpiece devoted to Freud, which included excerpts from several documents on Freud by Einstein and Fritz Wittels, and selections from *Future of an Illusion* and *Introductory Lectures on Psychoanalysis.*

18. L. Gozman and A. Etkind, "Ot kul'ta vlasti k vlasti liudei," *Neva* 7 (1989): 156–179. Gozman studied psychoanalysis with Kravtsov in Moscow, according to psychologist Iulia Aleshina (interview at Moscow State University, September 16, 1990).

19. A. I. Belkin, "Zigmund Freid: Vozrozhdenie v SSSR?" S. Freud, *Izbrannoe,* ed A. I. Belkin (Moscow: Vneshtorgizdat, 1989), pp. 5, 7, 9.

20. Ibid., pp. 18–19, 20.

21. Ibid., pp. 21, 29, 31–32.

22. Felicity Barringer, "In the New Soviet Psyche, a Place Is Made for Freud," *New York Times,* July 18, 1988, p. 1. The article also contains a number of errors, such as misnaming Belkin as Ivan instead of Aron, and misdating the Tbilisi International Conference on the Unconscious as 1971 instead of 1979. Similarly, in an American magazine article giving prominent coverage to Belkin's piece in *Literaturnaia gazeta,* the author wrote: "The attempt to rehabilitate Freud can also be viewed as fitting neatly into the context of Mikhail Gorbachev's policies of *glasnost* and *perestroika,* designed to reinvigorate Soviet society." There were also some errors in this article, such as the statement that "Freud's writings disappeared from the intellectual scene, and he remained unmentionable until after Stalin's death in 1953," and a distorted translation of one of Belkin's most important points. Helle Bering-Jenson, "Soviets Curing Their Freud Phobia," *Insight,* September 5, 1988, pp. 50–52.

23. See Geoffrey Cocks, *Psychoanalysis in the Third Reich* (New York: Oxford University Press, 1985). There is a report that Matthias Goering, who headed the Berlin Institute at this time, suggested that the psychoanalysts join the Nazi party "as a birthday present for the Fuehrer." See Edith Kurzweil, *The Freudians* (New Haven: Yale University Press, 1989), p. 322, n. 5. No comparative history of the international psychoanalytic movement has yet been published, but see the special issues of *Social Research* (Winter 1990) on the reception of psychoanalysis, and *Comparative Studies in Society and History* (October 1982) on the origins and development of psychoanalysis worldwide.

24. R. A. Zachepitskii, "Kriticheskii analiz 'Freido–Marksizma'," *Zhurnal nevropatologii i psikhiatrii* (1982): 144.

25. M. Yaroshevskii, *Lev Vygotsky* (Moscow: Progress, 1989), p. 305.

26. P. P. Bondarenko and M. K. Rabinovich, "Nauchnoe soveshchanie po voprosam ideologicheskoi bor'by s sovremennym Freidizmom," *Voprosy filosofii,* 2 (1959): 170.

27. F. V. Bassin, *Problema bessoznatel'nogo* (Moscow: Meditsina, 1968), pp. 77, 78.

28. For contemporary evidence from an unsympathetic observer, see René Fülüp-Miller, *The Mind and Face of Bolshevism* (New York: G. P. Putnam, 1927), especially the visual evidence throughout the book. See also Richard Stites, *Revolutionary Dreams: Utopian Vision and Experimental Life in the Russian Revolution* (New York: Oxford University Press, 1989); William Rosenberg (ed.), *Bolshevik Visions: First Phase of the Cultural Revolution in Soviet Russia* (Ann Arbor: Ardis, 1984); and Katerina Clark, *Petersburg: Crucible of Cultural Revolution* (Cambridge: Harvard University Press, 1995).

APPENDIX

1. On Frieda Teller, see Elke Mühlleitner, *Biographisches Lexikon der Psychoanalyse* (Tübingen: Edition Diskord, 1992), pp. 346–347.

2. A reference to the suicide of the Russian psychoanalyst Tatiana Rosenthal in Petrograd.

3. Published as "Leo Tolstois Seelenleiden," *Imago,* 9 (1923): 495–498.

4. See Osipov's *Tolstois Kindheitserinnerungen: Ein Beitrag zu Freuds Libidotheorie.* Imago-Buecher (Leipzig, Vienna, Zurich: Internat. Psychoanalytische Verlag, 1923).

5. See Oskar Pfister, *Der psychologische und biologische Untergrund expressionistischer Bilder* (Bern, Leipzig: Ernst Bircher, 1920).

6. On Otto Pötzel, see Mühlleitner, *Biographisches Lexikon,* 245–247. Dr. Pollak is probably Ferenczi's former patient, whom he discusses in his letters to Freud. See *The Correspondence of Sigmund Freud and Sandor Ferenczi,* edited by Eva Brabant, Ernst Falzeder, and Patrizia Giampieri-Deutsch (Cambridge, Mass.: Belknap Press of Harvard University Press, 1993), 1:111–113.

7. I. D. Ermakov, Russian psychoanalyst.

8. On Osipov's contribution to the origins of psychoanalysis in Prague, see Eugenia Fischer, "Czechoslovakia," P. Kutter (ed.), *Psychoanalysis International* (Stuttgart: Fromman-Holzborg, 1992), pp. 34–49, and Michael Sebek, "Psychoanalysis in Czechoslovakia," *Psychoanalytic Review,* 80, 3 (Fall 1993): 433–439.

Bibliography

GENERAL WORKS

Annenkov, P. V. *The Extraordinary Decade: Literary Memoirs.* Edited by Arthur P. Mendel. Ann Arbor: University of Michigan Press, 1968.

Artsybashev, Mikhail Petrovich. *Sanin.* New York: Huebsch, 1915.

Bater, James H. *St. Petersburg: Industrialization and Change.* Montreal: McGill–Queen's University Press, 1976.

Belyi, Andrei. *Petersburg.* Translated, annotated, and introduced by Robert A. Maguire and John E. Malmstad. Bloomington: Indiana University Press, 1978.

Briusov, Valerii. "Now That I Have Awakened (Notes of a Psychopath)." *The Silver Age of Russian Culture.* Edited by Carl and Elendea Proffer. Ann Arbor, Mich.: Ardis, 1975, 303–308.

Brower, Daniel. *The Russian City between Tradition and Modernity.* Berkeley: University of California Press, 1990.

Brown, Edward J. "So Much Depends . . . Russian Critics in Search of 'Reality.'" *Russian Review* 48 (1989): 353–381.

Chekhov, Anton P. "A Nervous Breakdown." In *The Oxford Chekhov.* Oxford: Oxford University Press, 1980, 4:157–179.

Clark, Katerina, and Michael Holquist. *Mikhail Bakhtin.* Cambridge: Harvard University Press, 1984.

Crome, Anna Lisa. "Nietzschean, All Too Nietzschean? Rozanov's Anti-Christian

Critique." *Nietzsche in Russia*. Edited by Bernice G. Rosenthal. Princeton: Princeton University Press, 1986, 95–112.

Fauchereau, Serge. *Moscou, 1900–1930*. Fribourg, Switzerland: Mallard Press, 1988.

Filosofov, D. V. "Vesennyi veter." *Slovo i zhizn'*. St. Petersburg: Tipografiia Akts. Obshch. Tip. Dela, 1909, 3–29.

———. "V. V. Rozanov." *Slovo i zhizn'*. St. Petersburg: Tipografiia Akts. Obshch. Tip. Dela, 1909, 148–161.

Fülüp-Miller, René. *The Mind and Face of Bolshevism*. New York: Putnam, 1927.

Ginzburg, Lidiia. *O psikhologicheskoi proze*. Leningrad: Sovetskii pisatel', 1971.

Gorky, Maxim. "Soviet Literature." *Problems of Soviet Literature: Reports and Speeches at the First Writers' Congress*. New York: International Publishers, 1934.

Izgoev, Alexander. "On Educated Youth." *Landmarks*. Edited by Boris Shragin and Albert Todd. New York: Karz Howard, 1977, 88–111. Also reprinted in *Vekhi*. Edited by Marshall S. Shatz and Judith E. Zimmerman. Armonk, N.Y.: M. E. Sharpe, 1994.

Jakobson, Roman. "The Generation that Squandered Its Poets." *Literature and Revolution*. Edited by Jacques Ehrmann. Boston: Beacon Press, 1970.

Jay, Martin. *The Dialectical Imagination*. Boston: Little, Brown, 1973.

Kuprin, A. I. "The Circus Wrestlers." *The Duel and Selected Stories*. New York: Signet, 1961.

Møller, Peter U. *Postlude to the Kreutzer Sonata*. Leiden: Brill, 1988.

Nilus, Pavel. "Summer Heat." *The Silver Age of Russian Culture*. Edited by Carl and Elendea Proffer. Ann Arbor, Mich.: Ardis, 1975, 321–324.

Ostroumov, S. S. *Prestupnost' i ee prichiny v dorevoliutsionnoi Rossii*. Moscow: University Press, 1980.

Perrot, Michelle (ed.). *A History of Private Life*, vol. 4: *From the Fires of Revolution to the Great War*. Cambridge: Harvard University Press, 1990.

Poggioli, Renato. *The Phoenix and the Spider: A Book of Essays on Some Russian Writers and Their View of the Self*. Cambridge: Harvard University Press, 1957.

———. *Rozanov*. New York: Hillary House, 1962.

Roberts, Spencer (ed. and trans.). *Four Faces of Rozanov: Christianity, Sex, Jews and the Russian Revolution*. New York: Philosophical Library, 1978.

Rosenthal, Bernice G. (ed.) *Nietzsche in Russia*. Princeton: Princeton University Press, 1986.

———. *Nietzsche in Soviet Culture*. Cambridge: Cambridge University Press, 1994.

Rozanov, V. V. *O sebe i zhizni svoei*. Moscow: Moskovskii rabochii, 1990.

———. *Solitaria*. London: Wishart, 1927.

Scott, Helen Gifford. "V. F. Pereverzev." *Soviet Studies in Literature*, 22–23 (Spring–Summer 1986): 19–24, 123–126.

Stites, Richard. *Revolutionary Dreams: Utopian Visions and Experimental Life in the Russian Revolution*. New York: Oxford University Press, 1989.

———. *The Women's Liberation Movement in Russia: Feminism, Nihilism and Bolshevism, 1860–1930*. Princeton: Princeton University Press, 1978.

Trotsky, L. *Sochineniia*. Moscow-Leningrad: Gosizdat, 1927. 21 vols.

———. *Literature and Revolution*. Ann Arbor: University of Michigan Press, 1960.

Voznesensky, Andrei. "Sovest' mysli." *Izvestiia*, December 6, 1987: 3.

Walicki, Andrzej. *A History of Russian Thought*. Stanford: Stanford University Press, 1979.

Zetkin, Klara. *Reminiscences of Lenin.* London: Modern Books Limited, 1929. Originally published in 1925.

Zoshchenko, Mikhail. *Pered voskhodom sol'ntsa.* Moscow: Sovetskaia Rossiia, 1976.

HISTORY OF RUSSIAN MEDICINE, PSYCHOLOGY, AND PSYCHIATRY

Babayan, Eduard. *The Structure of Psychiatry in the USSR.* New York: International Universities Press, 1985.

Bauer, Raymond. *The New Man in Soviet Psychology.* Cambridge: Harvard University Press, 1952.

Bazhenov, N. N. *Istoriia moskovskogo dolguaza.* Moscow, 1909.

———. *Psikhiatricheskiia besedy na literaturnyia i obshchestvennyia temy.* Moscow: Tipografiia A. I. Mamontova, 1903.

Bekhterev, V. M. *Avtobiografiia.* Moscow: Gosizdat, 1928.

Belgrave, T. B. "The Asylums for the Insane in St. Petersburg and Copenhagen." *Journal of Mental Science,* 13 (1867): 7–19.

Bogoiavlenskii, N. A. "O dushevnykh i nervnyhk bolezniakh na Rusi epokhi feodalizma (XI–XVII vek)." *Zhurnal nevropatologii i psikhiatrii,* 66 (1966): 1706–1713.

Brown, Julie V. "Heroes and Non-Heroes: Recurring Themes in the Historiography of Russian-Soviet Psychiatry." *Discovering the History of Psychiatry.* Edited by Mark S. Micale and Roy Porter. New York: Oxford University Press, 1994, 304–315.

———. "The Professionalization of Russian Psychiatry: 1857–1911." Ph.D. diss., University of Pennsylvania, 1981.

———. "Revolution and Psychosis: The Mixing of Science and Politics in Russian Psychiatric Medicine, 1905–13." *Russian Review,* 46 (1987): 283–302.

Brown, Mabel W., and Frankwood E. Williams (eds.). *Neuropsychiatry and the War. A Bibliography with Abstracts.* New York: National Committee for Mental Hygiene, 1918.

Budilova, E. A. *Filosofskie problemy v sovetskoi psikhologii.* Moscow: Nauka, 1972.

Bykov, K. M. "Development of the Ideas of I. P. Pavlov." *Scientific Session on the Physiological Teachings of Academician I. P. Pavlov.* Moscow: Foreign Languages Publishing House, 1951, 22–76.

Chernakov, E. T. "Protiv idealizma i metafiziki v psikhologii." *Voprosy filosofii,* 3 (1948): 301–314.

"Diskussii i obsuzhdeniia. Obsuzhdenie dokladov po probleme ustanovki na soveshchanii po psikhologii. 1–6 julia 1955 goda." *Voprosy psikhologii,* 6 (1955): 72–112.

Dix, Kenneth S. "Madness In Russia, 1775–1864: Official Attitudes and Institutions for Its Care." Ph.D. diss., UCLA, 1977.

Dowbiggin, Ian. "Degeneration and Hereditarianism in French Mental Medicine, 1840–1890." *The Anatomy of Madness.* Edited by W. F. Bynum, Roy Porter, and Michael Shepherd. London and New York: Tavistock Publications, 1985, I:188–232.

Fedotov, D. D. *Ocherki po istorii otechestvennoi psikhiatrii.* Moscow: Ministerstvo zdravookhraneniia SSSR, 1957.

Fedotov, D. D., and V. M. Lupandin. "O deiatel'nosti vrachei-psikhiatrov v revoliutsionnom dvizhenii Rossii." *Voprosy psikhopatologii i psikhoterapii,* 40 (1963): 310–320.

Frieden, Nancy Mandelker. *Russian Physicians in an Era of Reform and Revolution.* Princeton: Princeton University Press, 1981.

Galach'yan, A. G. "Soviet Union." *Psychiatry in the Communist World.* Edited by Ari Kiev. New York: Science House, 1968, 29–50.

Graham, Loren. *Science and Philosophy in the Soviet Union.* New York: A. A. Knopf, 1972.

Grashchenkov, N. I. "K stoletiiu so dnia rozhdeniia Akademika I. P. Pavlova." *Nevropatologiia i psikhiatriia,* 18, 1 (1949): 3–9.

Gurevich, S. A. "P. I. Kovalevskii: Osnovatel' pervogo Russkogo zhurnala psikhiatrii." *Zhurnal nevropatologii i psikhiatrii,* 79 (1979): 350–352.

Holquist, Michael. "Bazarov and Sechenov: The Role of Scientific Metaphor in *Fathers and Sons,*" *Russian Literature,* 15 (1984): 359–374.

Hutchinson, John F. "Society, Corporation or Union? Russian Physicians and the Struggle for Professional Unity (1890–1913)." *Jahrbücher für Geschichte Osteuropas,* 30 (1982): 37–53.

———. *Politics and Public Health in Revolutionary Russia, 1890–1918.* Baltimore: Johns Hopkins University Press, 1990.

Iakobii, P. I. *Printsipy administrativnoi psikhiatrii.* Orel: Tip. gub. pravleniia, 1900.

Iaroshevskii, M. G. *Ivan Mikhailovich Sechenov.* Leningrad: Nauka, 1968.

Iudin, T. I. *Ocherki istorii otechestvennoi psikhiatrii.* Moscow: Medgiz, 1951.

Joravsky, David. "The Construction of the Stalinist Psyche." Sheila Fitzpatrick (ed.), *Cultural Revolution in Russia, 1928–1931.* Bloomington: Indiana University, 1978, 105–128.

———. *Russian Psychology.* Oxford: Blackwell, 1989.

Kandinskii, V. Kh. *O psevdogalliutsinatsiiakh.* Edited with an introduction by A. V. Snezhnevskii. Moscow: Gosizdatmedlit, 1952. Originally published in 1890.

Kannabikh, Iu. *Istorii psikhiatrii.* Leningrad: Gosmedizdat, n.d. [1929].

Karvasarskii, B. D. *Meditsinskaia psikhologiia.* Leningrad: Meditsina, 1982.

———. *Nevrozy.* Moscow: Meditsina, 1980.

Kornilov, K. N. "Psychology in the Light of Dialectical Materialism." *Psychologies of 1930.* Edited by Carl Murchison. Worcester, Mass.: Clark University Press, 1930.

Korsakov, S. "Etude medico-psychologique sur une forme des maladies de la mémoire." *Revue philosophique de la France et de l'étranger,* 28, no. 2 (1889): 501–530.

Kozulin, Alex. "Gregory Chelpanov and the Establishment of the Moscow Institute of Psychology." *Journal of the History of the Behavioral Sciences,* 21 (1985): 23–32.

———. *Psychology in Utopia.* Cambridge: MIT Press, 1984.

———. *Vygotsky's Psychology: A Biography of Ideas.* Cambridge: Harvard University Press, 1990.

Krug, John. "The Pirogov Society, 1917–1920." Ph.D. diss., University of Wisconsin, 1979.

Kruglianskii, V. F. *Psikhiatriia: Istoriia, Problemy, Perspektivy.* Minsk: Vysheishaia shkola, 1979.

Kukuev, L. "O nekotorykh teoreticheskikh aspektakh nevropatologii i psikhiatrii." *Zhurnal nevropatologii i psikhiatrii,* 80, no. 1 (1980): 3–8.

Kurazov, I. F. "Metodologicheskie itogi Povedencheskogo s"ezda." V. P. Osipov (ed.), *Voprosy izucheniia i vospitaniia lichnosti,* nos. 1–2. Moscow: Gozmedizdat, 1930.

Leontiev, A. N., and A. R. Luria. "The Psychological Ideas of L. S. Vygotsky." *Historical Roots of Contemporary Psychology.* Edited by Benjamin Wolman. New York: Harper and Row, 1968, 338–367.

Lomov, B. F. "Lichnost' v sisteme obshchestvennykh otnoshenii." *Psikhologicheskii zhurnal,* 2, no. 1 (1981): 3–17.

Lomov, B. F. (ed.). *Sergei Leonidovich Rubinshtein: Ocherki, Vospominaniia, Materialy.* Moscow: Nauka, 1989.

Lotova, E. T. *Russkaia intelligentsia i voprosy obshchestvennoi gigieny.* Moscow: Gosudarstvennoe izdatel'stvo meditsinskoi literatury, 1962.

Lunbeck, Elizabeth. *The Psychiatric Persuasion: Knowledge, Gender and Power in Modern America.* Princeton: Princeton University Press, 1994.

Luria, A. R. "Krizis burzhuaznoi psikhologii." *Psikhologiia,* 1–2 (1032): 63–88.

Miasishchev, V. N. *Personality and Neurosis.* Washington, D.C.: Joint Publication Research Service, 1963. Translation of *Lichnost' i nevrozy.* Moscow: Leningrad State University Press, 1960.

Micale, Marc. *Approaching Hysteria: Disease and Its Interpretations.* Princeton: Princeton University Press, 1995.

Micale, Marc, and Roy Porter (eds.). *Discovering the History of Psychiatry.* New York: Oxford University Press, 1994.

Miller, Martin A. "The Theory and Practice of Psychiatry in the Soviet Union." *Psychiatry,* 48, no. 1 (February 1985): 13–24.

Miller, Martin A., and Ylana N. Miller. "Suicide and Suicidology in the Soviet Union." *Suicide and Life-Threatening Behavior,* 18, no. 4 (Winter 1988): 303–321.

Mosketi, K. V., et al. "Materialy po istorii organizatsii psikhiatricheskoi pomoshchi i razvitiia nauchno-psikhiatricheskoi mysli v Odessa (1833–1927)." *Zhurnal nevropatologii i psikhiatrii,* 87, no. 3 (1987): 442–447.

Natadze, R. G. "Experimental Foundations of Uznadze's Theory of Set." *A Handbook of Contemporary Soviet Psychology.* Edited by Michael Cole and Irving Maltzman. New York: Basic Books, 1969, 603–624.

———. "Fifty Years of Psychology in Georgia." *Soviet Psychology,* 7, no. 2 (Winter 1968–69): 33–47.

Owen, A. R. G. *Hysteria, Hypnosis and Healing: The Work of J.-M. Charcot.* New York: Garett Publications, 1971.

Pavlov, I. P. *Lectures on Conditioned Reflexes.* 2 vols. Edited and translated by W. H. Gantt. New York: International Publishers, 1928–41.

Payne, T. R. *S. L. Rubinstein and the Philosophical Foundations of Soviet Psychology.* Dordrecht, Holland: D. Reidel, 1968.

Petrovskii, A. V. *Istoriia sovetskoi psikhologii.* Moscow: Prosveshchenie, 1967.

———. *Psychology in the Soviet Union.* Moscow: Progress, 1990.

Portnov, A. A., and D. D. Fedotov. *Psychiatry.* Moscow: Mir, 1969.

Prangishvili, A. S. "The Concept of Set in Soviet Psychology in Light of Research by the Georgia Psychological School." *Soviet Psychology,* 7, no. 2 (Winter 1968–69): 21–32.

Raskin, Naomi. "Development of Russian Psychiatry Before the First World War." *American Journal of Psychiatry,* 120, no. 9 (March 1964): 851–855.

Reich, Walter. "Serbsky and Czarist Dissidents." *Archives of General Psychiatry*, 40 (June 1983): 697–698.

Roitel'man, A. G. "Psikhiatricheskie aspekty deiatel'nosti vrachei v meditsinskikh obshchestvakh nezemskikh mestnostei Rossii." *Zhurnal nevropatologii i psikhiatrii*, 86 (1986): 1237–1242.

Rokhlin, L. L. "Les conceptions psychopathologiques de Kandinsky." *L'évolution psychiatrique*, 36, no. 3 (July–September 1971): 475–488.

———. "Filosofskie i psikhologicheskie vozzreniia V. Kh. Kandinskogo." *Zhurnal nevropatologii i psikhiatrii*, 69, no. 5 (1969): 755–761.

Rollins, Nancy. *Child Psychiatry in the Soviet Union*. Cambridge: Harvard University Press, 1972.

Rothman, David. *Discovery of the Asylum*. Boston: Little, Brown, 1971.

Rubinstein, Sergei L. *Bytie i soznanie*. Moscow: Izdatel'stvo Akademii nauk SSSR, 1957.

———. "Problems of Psychology in the Works of Karl Marx." *Studies in Soviet Thought*, 33 (1987): 111–130. Originally published in *Sovetskaia psikhotekhnika*, 7, no. 1 (1934): 3–20.

———. "Voprosy psikhologicheskoi teorii." *Voprosy psikhologii*, 1 (1955): 6–18.

Schniermann, A. L. "Bekhterev's Reflexological School." *Psychologies of 1930*. Edited by Carl Murchison. Worcester, Mass.: Clark University Press, 1930, 221–242.

Shemiakin, F., and L. Gershonovich. "Kak Trotskii i Kautskii revizuiut Marksizm v voprosakh psikhologii." *Psikhologiia*, 1–2 (1932): 3–37.

Shereshevskii, A. M. "Sozdanie v Rossii pervykh spetsial'nykh uchrezhdenii dlia dushevnobol'nykh." *Zhurnal nevropatologii i psikhiatrii*, 78, no. 1 (1978): 131–134.

Shirman, A. L. "O predmete i metode refleksologii kak nauki o sootnositel'noi deiatel'nosti." V. P. Osipov (ed.), *Voprosy izucheniia i vospitaniia lichnosti*, nos. 1–2. Moscow: Gosmedizdat, 1930.

Simon, Bennett. *Mind and Madness in Ancient Greece: The Classical Roots of Modern Psychiatry*. Ithaca: Cornell University Press, 1978.

Sirotkina, I. E. "Psikhologiia v klinike: raboty otechestvennykh psikhiatrov kontsa proshlogo veka." *Voprosy psikhologii*, 6 (1995): 79–92.

Smirnov, A. A. "Vzgliad I. M. Sechenova v razvitie nauchnoi psikhologii v Rossii." *Razvitie i sovremennoe sostoianie psikhologickesoi nauki v SSSR*. Moscow: Pedagogika, 1975, 51–65.

Stoliarov, A. *Dialekticheskii materializm i mekhanisty*. Leningrad: Priboi, 1930.

Surh, Gerald. "A Matter of Life or Death: Politics, Profession and Public Health in St. Petersburg before 1914." *Russian History*, 20, nos. 1–4 (1993): 125–146.

Talankin, A. "Protiv men'shevistvuiushchego idealizma v psikhologii." *Psikhologiia*, 1–2 (1932): 36–62.

Todes, Daniel P. "Biological Psychology and the Tsarist Censor: The Dilemma of Scientific Developments." *Bulletin of the History of Medicine*, 4 (1984): 529–544.

Trudy pervago s"ezda otechestvennykh psikhiatrov. St. Petersburg: Stasiulevich, 1887.

Tucker, Robert. "Stalin and the Uses of Psychology." *The Soviet Political Mind: Studies in Stalinism and Post-Stalin Change*. New York: Praeger, 1963, 91–121.

Umrikhin, V. V. "'Nachalo kontsa' povedencheskoi psikhologii v SSSR." *Repressirovannaia nauka*. Edited by M. G. Iaroshevskii. Leningrad: Nauka, 1991, 136–145.

Uznadze, D. N. *The Psychology of Set.* Edited by Joseph Wortis. Translated by Basil Haigh. New York: Consultants Bureau, 1966.

Vallon, Charles, and Armand Marie. *Les Aliénés en Russie.* Montrevain: Imprimerie Typographique de l'Ecole d'Alembert, 1899.

Valsiner, Jaan. *Developmental Psychology in the Soviet Union.* Brighton, England: Harvester Press, 1988.

Van der Veer, Rene, and Jaan Valsiner. *Understanding Vygotsky: A Quest for Synthesis.* Oxford: Blackwell, 1991.

Vavilov, S. I. "Inaugural Address." *Scientific Session on the Physiological Teachings of Academician I. P. Pavlov.* Moscow: Foreign Languages Publishing House, 1951, 9–15.

Vygotskaia, G. L., and T. M. Lifanova. *Lev Semenovich Vygotskii. Zhizn', Deiatel'nost'. Shtrikhi k Portretu.* Moscow: Smysl', 1996.

Vygotsky, L. S. "Consciousness as a Problem in the Psychology of Behavior." *Soviet Psychology,* 17, no. 4 (Summer 1979): 3–35. Originally published in: *Psikhologiia i Marksizm.* Edited by K. N. Kornilov. Moscow-Leningrad: Gosizdat, 1925, 175–198.

———. "Istoricheskii smysl' psikhologicheskogo krizisa." *Sobranie sochinenii.* Moscow: Pedagogika, 1982, I:291–436.

———. "The Methods of Reflexological and Psychological Investigation." *The Vygotsky Reader.* Edited by Rene Van der Veer and Jaan Valsiner. Oxford: Blackwell, 1994, 27–45.

———. *Thought and Language.* Edited, with an introductory article, by Alex Kozulin. Cambridge: MIT Press, 1986.

Wertsch, James V. *Vygotsky and the Social Formation of Mind.* Cambridge: Harvard University Press, 1986.

Wortis, Joseph. *Soviet Psychiatry.* Baltimore: Williams and Wilkins, 1950.

Yaroshevskii, M. G. "I. M. Sechenov: The Founder of Objective Psychology." In *Historical Roots of Contemporary Psychology.* Edited by Benjamin Wolman. New York: Harper and Row, 1968, 77–110.

———. *Lev Vygotsky.* Moscow: Progress, 1989.

Zilboorg, Gregory. "Russian Psychiatry: Its Historical and Ideological Background." *Bulletin of the New York Academy of Medicine,* 9 (October 1943): 713–728.

PSYCHOANALYSIS, PSYCHOTHERAPY, SEXUALITY, AND THE UNCONSCIOUS

Abraham, Hilda, and Ernst L. Freud (eds.). *A Psychoanalytic Dialogue: The Letters of Sigmund Freud and Karl Abraham, 1907–1926.* New York: Basic Books, 1965.

Asatiani, M. M. "Psikhoanaliz odnogo sluchaia istericheskago psikhoza." *Psikhoterapiia,* 1 (1910): 172–227.

———. "Sovremennoe sostoianie voprosa teoriia i praktiki psikhoanaliza po vzgliadam Jung'a." *Psikhoterapiia,* 1 (1910): 117–125.

Atanasov, A. "Problema katarsisa v nauchnom nasledii N. Krestnikova." *Zhurnal nevropatologii i psikhiatrii,* 86 (1986): 758–760.

Avtonomova, N. S. "Psikhoanaliticheskaia kontseptsiia Zhaka Lakana." *Voprosy filosofii,* 11 (1973): 143–150.

Bakhtadze-Sheroziia, N. V. "The International Symposium on the Problem of the Unconscious, Tbilisi, 1979." *The Unconscious.* Edited by A. S. Prangishvili, A. E. Sherozia, and F. V. Bassin. Tbilisi: Metsniereba, 1985, IV:140–148.

Barringer, Felicity. "In the New Soviet Psyche, A Place Is Made for Freud." *New York Times,* July 18, 1988.

Bassin, F. V. "Aktual'nost' problemy bessoznatel'nogo na sovremennom etape razvitiia psikhologicheskikh predstavlenii." *Filosofskie nauki,* 3 (1990): 43–53.

———. "Le conscient, 'l'inconscient' et la maladie: A propos de l'approche moderne du problème psychosomatique." *Revue de Médecine psychosomatique,* 14, no. 3 (1972): 263–280.

———. "Consciousness and Unconsciousness." *A Handbook of Contemporary Soviet Psychology.* Edited by Michael Cole and I. Maltzman. New York: Basic Books, 1969, 399–420.

———. "A Critical Analysis of Freudianism." *The Soviet Review,* 1, 5 (December 1970): 3–14. Originally in *Voprosy psikhologii,* 6 (1958): 140–153.

———. "Freudism in the Light of Contemporary Scientific Discussion." *Soviet Survey,* 7 (January–March 1959): 82–87. Originally in *Voprosy psikhologii,* 5 (1958): 133–145.

———. *Problema bessoznatel'nogo.* Moscow: Meditsina, 1968.

———. "Rejoinder to Professor Musatti." *The Soviet Review,* 1, 5 (December 1970): 27–44.

Bassin, F. V., and V. E. Rozhnov. "O sovremennom podkhode k probleme neosoznavaemoi psikhicheskoi deiatel'nosti (bessoznatel'nogo)." *Voprosy filosofii,* 10 (1975): 94–108.

Bassin, F., V. Rozhnov, and M. Rozhnova. "Freidizm: Psevdonauchnaia traktovka psikhicheskikh iavlenii." *Kommunist,* 48 (January 1972): 94–106.

Belkin, Aron. "Mify i real'nost'." *Meditsinskaia gazeta,* January 8, 1989: 3.

———. "Svobodnoe issledovanie." *Literaturnaia gazeta,* November 1, 1989.

———. "Zigmund Freid." *Literaturnaia gazeta,* June 1, 1988: 15.

———. "Zigmund Freid: Vozrozhdenie v SSSR?" Sigmund Freud, *Izbrannoe.* Edited by A. I. Belkin. Moscow: Vneshtorgizdat, 1989, 5–35.

Belkin, A. I., and A. V. Litvinov. "K istorii psikhoanaliza v sovetskoi Rossii." *Rossiiskii psikhologicheskii vestnik,* 2 (1992): 9–32.

Bering-Jenson, Helle. "Soviets Curing Their Freud Phobia." *Insight,* September 5, 1988: 50–52.

Bernfeld, Siegfried. "Die kommunistische Diskussion um die Psychoanalyse und Reichs 'Widerlegung der Todestriebhypothese'." *Internationale Zeitschrift für Psychoanalyse,* 18, 3 (1932): 352–385.

Bettelheim, Bruno. *Freud and Man's Soul.* New York: Knopf, 1983.

———. "Scandal in the Family." *New York Review of Books,* June 30, 1983: 39–44.

Birken. Lawrence, *Consuming Desire: Sexual Science and the Emergence of a Culture of Abundance, 1871–1914.* Ithaca: Cornell University Press, 1988.

Birman, B. N. "Psikhoterapiia, kak sotsiorefleksoterapiia nevropaticheskoi lichnosti." In A. B. Zalkind (ed.), *Psikho-nevrologicheskie nauki v SSSR.* Moscow: Gozmedizdat, 1930, 321–322.

Bloch, Iwan. *The Sexual Life of Our Time in Its Relations to Modern Civilization.* New York: Allied Book Co., 1925. Includes: "Appendix: A Contribution to the Psychology of the Russian Revolution (History of the Development of an Algolagnistic Revolutionist)." by N. K.

Boiko, A. N. *Problema bessoznatel'nogo v filosofii i konkretnykh naukakh.* Kiev: Izdatel'stvo pri Kievskom gosudarstvennom universitete, 1978.

Bondarenko, P. P., and M. Kh. Rabinovich. "Nauchnoe soveshchanie po voprosam ideologicheskoi bor'by s sovremennym freidizmom." *Voprosy filosofii,* 2 (1959): 164–70. Translated as "Freud and Pavlov: Report of a Soviet Conference." *Soviet Survey,* 29 (July–September 1959): 29–37.

Buzin, V. N. "Psikhoanaliz v Sovetskom Soiuze: K istorii razgroma." *Puti obnovleniia psikhiatrii.* Edited by Iu. S. Savenko. Moscow: Intermechanics, 1991.

Bykhovskii, Bernard E. "O metodologicheskikh osnovaniiakh psikhoanaliticheskogo ucheniia Freida." *Pod znamenem marksizma,* 11–12 (1923): 158–177.

Carotenuto, Aldo. *A Secret Symmetry: Sabina Spielrein Between Jung and Freud.* New York: Pantheon Books, 1982.

Chertok, Leon. "L'Etat actuel de la psychanalyse en U.R.S.S." *Psychanalyse clinique,* 1 (1986): 1–3.

———. "Psychiatric Dialogue between East and West." *British Journal of Medical Psychology,* 41 (1968): 295–297.

———. "Psychosomatic Medicine in the West and in Eastern European Countries." *Psychosomatic Medicine,* 6 (1969): 510–521.

———. "Reinstatement of the Concept of the Unconscious in the Soviet Union." *American Journal of Psychiatry,* 138, 5 (May 1981): 575–583.

———. "Sigmund chez Karl." *Le Monde.* September 2–3, 1984.

Chertok, Leon, and Raymond de Saussure. *The Therapeutic Revolution.* New York: Brunner-Mazel, 1979.

Cocks, Geoffrey. *Psychoanalysis in the Third Reich.* New York: Oxford University Press, 1985.

Comparative Studies in Society and History. October 1982. Special issue on the historical origins and development of psychoanalysis in a variety of countries.

Crews, Frederick. *Sceptical Engagements.* New York: Oxford University Press, 1986.

Daian, G. "Vtoroi psikhonevrologicheskii s"ezd." *Krasnaia nov',* 2, 19 (1924): 155–166; 3, 20 (1924): 223–238.

Davydova, M. I. "Ivan Dmitrievich Ermakov (1875–1942)." *Psikhologicheskii zhurnal,* 10, 2 (1989): 156–159.

———. "Nezavershennyi zamysel: k istorii izdaniia trudov Z. Freida v SSSR." *Sovetskaia bibliografiia,* 3 (1989): 61–64.

Davydova, M. I., and A. V. Litvinov. "Ivan Dmitrievich Ermakov." *Rossiiskii psikhoanaliticheskii vestnik,* 1 (1991): 115–127.

Decker, Hannah. *Freud in Germany: Revolution and Reaction in Science, 1893–1907.* New York: International Universities Press, 1977.

"Diskussii i obsuzhdeniia. Obsuzhdenie dokladov po probleme ustanovki na soveshchanii po psikhologii. 1–6 iulia 1955 goda." *Voprosy psikhologii,* 6 (1955): 72–112.

Dobren'kov, V. I. *Kritika neofreidistskoi kontseptsii Erikha Fromma.* Moscow: Znanie, 1972.

———. *Neofreidizm v poiskakh 'istiny'.* Moscow: Mysl', 1974.

Domic, Zorka, and Bernard Doray. "Regards sur la psychanalyse en U.R.S.S." *Psychanalytes,* 35 (June 1990): 87–96.

Dosuzhkov, F. N. "Nikolai Evgravovich Osipov kak psikhiatr." *Zhizn' i smert'. Sbornik pamiati D-ra N. E. Osipova.* Edited by A. L. Bem, F. N. Dosuzhkov, and N. O. Losskii. Prague: n.p., 1935, 25–45.

Dubois, Paul. *The Psychic Treatment of Nervous Disorders (The Psychoneuroses and their Moral Treatment).* New York and London: Funk and Wagnalls, 1907. A translation of: *Les psychoneuroses et leur traîtement moral.* Geneva, 1905.

Dynkin, Irina. Memoir letter, Personal communication, November 6, 1985.

Ellenberger, Henri. *The Discovery of the Unconscious.* New York: Basic Books, 1970.

Engelstein, Laura. *The Keys to Happiness: Sex and the Search for Modernity in Fin-de-Siècle Russia.* Ithaca: Cornell University Press, 1992.

———. "Soviet Policy toward Male Homosexuality: Its Origins and Historical Roots." Unpublished paper, 1994.

Ermakov, I. D. "Dvoistvennost'." *Sovetskaia bibliografiia,* 6 (November–December 1990): 104–111.

———. *Etiudy po psikhologii A. S. Pushkina* (Moscow-Petrograd: Gosizdat, 1923).

Etkind, Alexander. *Eros nevozmozhnogo.* St. Petersburg: Meduza, 1993.

———. "L'Essor et l'échec du mouvement 'paidologique'." *Cahiers du monde russe et soviétique,* 23, 4 (October–December 1992): 387–418.

———. "Trotsky and Psychoanalysis." *Partisan Review,* 2 (1994): 303–308.

Fedotov, D. "The Soviet View of Psychoanalysis." *Monthly Review,* 9 (December 1957): 249–254.

Fel'tsman, O. B. "K voprosu o psikhoanalize i psikhoterapii." *Sovremennaia psikhiatriia,* 3 (1909): 214–224, 258–269.

Filippov, L. I. "Strukturalizm i Freidizm." *Voprosy filosofii,* 3 (1976): 155–163.

Fischer, Rene, and Eugenie. "Psychoanalyse in Russland." *Die Psychologie des 20 Jahrhunderts,* 3 (1977): 122–124.

Fitzpatrick, Sheila. "Sex and Revolution." *The Cultural Front: Power and Culture in Revolutionary Russia.* Ithaca: Cornell University Press, 1992, 65–90.

Fout, John C. *Forbidden History: The State, Society and the Regulation of Sexuality in Modern Europe.* Chicago: University of Chicago Press, 1992.

Freud, Sigmund. "An Autobiographical Study." *The Freud Reader.* Edited by Peter Gay. New York: Norton, 1989.

———. *Civilization and Its Discontents.* New York: Norton, 1961.

———. *On the History of the Psychoanalytic Movement.* New York: Norton, 1967.

———. "The Question of a Weltanschauung." *The Freud Reader.* Edited by Peter Gay. New York: Norton, 1989.

———. "Thoughts for the Times on War and Death." *Standard Edition of the Complete Psychological Works of Sigmund Freud.* Edited by James Strachey. (London: Hogarth Press, 1957), XIV:273–302.

———. "'Wild' Psychoanalysis." *Standard Edition of the Complete Psychological Works.* London: Hogarth Press, 1957, XI:221–227.

Freud, Sigmund, and Sandor Ferenczi. *The Correspondence of Sigmund Freud and Sandor Ferenczi.* Volume I, 1908–1914. Edited by Eva Brabant, Ernst Falzeder, and Patrizia Giampieri-Deutsch. Cambridge: Belknap Press of Harvard University Press, 1993.

Freud-Jung Letters: The Correspondence between Sigmund Freud and C. G. Jung. Edited by William McGuire. Princeton: Princeton University Press, 1974.

Friche, V. M. "Freidizm i iskusstvo." *Vestnik kommunisticheskoi akademii,* 12 (1925): 236–264.

Fridman, B. D. "K dinamike tsikloidnykh zabolevanii." *Zhurnal nevropatologii i psikhiatrii,* 4 (1928): 367–372.

———. "Osnovnye psikhologicheskie vozzreniia Freida i teoriia istoricheskogo materializma." *Psikhologiia i marksizm.* Edited by K. N. Kornilov. Leningrad: Gosizdat, 1925, 113–159.

Gakkebush, V. M. "K kritike sovremennogo primeneniia psikhoanaliticheskogo metoda lecheniia." *Sovremennaia psikhonevrologiia,* 8 (1925): 89–96.

Galant, I. B. "Masturbatsiia i avtokastratsiia v kartine shizofrenicheski-paranoidnogo zabolevaniia: k psikhologii paranoidnoi formy dementia praecox." *Zhurnal nevropatologii i psikhiatrii,* 3 (1928): 307–315.

Gellner, Ernest. *The Psychoanalytic Movement or The Coming of Unreason.* London: Paladin-Granada Publishing, 1985.

Gozman, L., and A. Etkind. "Ot kul'ta vlasti k vlasti liudei." *Neva,* 7 (1989): 156–179.

Griboedov, A. S. "Trudnovospituemye deti i psikhoanaliz." *Voprosy izucheniia i vospitaniia lichnosti,* 1–2 (1926): 57–68.

Grigor'ev, I. "Psikhoanaliz kak metod issledovaniia khudozhestvennoi literatury." *Krasnaia nov',* 7 (1925): 224–240.

Grigorov, G., and S. Skotov. "O 'liubvi' i brake." *Staryi i novyi byt.* Moscow-Leningrad: Molodaia gvardia, 1927, 149–181.

Grunbaum, Adolf. *The Foundations of Psychoanalysis.* Berkeley: University of California Press, 1984.

Hale, Nathan. *Freud and the Americans: The Beginnings of Psychoanalysis in the United States,* 1876–1917. Vol. 1. New York: Oxford University Press, 1971.

———. *The Rise and Crisis of Psychoanalysis in the United States: Freud and the Americans,* 1917–1985. Vol 2. New York: Oxford University Press, 1995.

Hodge, Thomas P. "Freudian Elements in Zoshchenko's *Pered voskhodom solntsa,*" *Slavonic and East European Review,* 67, no. 1 (January 1989): 1–28.

Iaroshevskii, M. G. "Vozrashchenie Freida." *Psikhologicheskii zhurnal,* 9, no. 6 (1988): 129–138.

Ioffe, A. A. "Po povodu 'bezsoznatel'nogo' v zhizni individuuma." *Psikhoterapiia,* 4 (1913): 231–238

Iurinets, V. "Freidizm i Marksizm." *Pod znamenem marksizma,* 8–9 (1924): 51–93.

———. "Psychoanalyse und Marxismus." *Unter dem Banner des Marxismus,* 1 (1925): 90–133.

Jaffe, Ruth. Interview with the author, July 8, 1985, Ramat Aviv, Israel.

———. "Moshe Woolf: Pioneering in Russia and Israel." *Psychoanalytic Pioneers.* Edited by F. Alexander. New York: Basic Books, 1966.

Jones, Ernest. *Life and Work of Sigmund Freud.* 3 vols. New York: Basic Books, 1957.

Jung, C. G. "The Freudian Theory of Hysteria." *Collected Works.* Princeton: Princeton University Press, 1979. 20 vols. 4:53–58 (originally published in 1907).

Kannabikh, Iu. V. "Individual'naia psikhoterapiia Adlera, kak prakticheskii metod psikhoterapii i kak obshchaia teoriia povedeniia." A. B. Zalkind (ed.), *Psikho-nevrologicheskie nauki.* Moscow: Gosmedizdat, 1930, 319–321.

Katz, Michael. *Dreams and the Unconscious in Nineteenth-Century Russian Fiction.* Hanover, N.H.: University Press of New England, 1984.

Katzel, Siegfried. *Marxismus und Psychoanalyse: einige ideologiegeschichtliche Studie zur Diskussion in Deutschland und der USSR.* Berlin: VEB Deutscher Verlag der Wissenschaften, 1987.

Kerr, John. *A Most Dangerous Method: The Story of Jung, Freud, and Sabina Spielrein.* New York: Knopf, 1993.

Khaletskii, A. M. "Freudianism, Microsociology and Existentialism." *Soviet Psychology and Psychiatry,* 6, 1 (Fall 1965): 45–53.

———. "Psikhoanaliz lichnosti i tvorchestva Shevchenko." *Sovremennaia psikhonevrologiia,* 3 (1926): 345–354.

Klemen, K. B., P. Bruno, and L. Sev. *Marksistskaia kritika psikhoanaliza.* Translated from the French. Edited, with a foreword, by F. V. Bassin and V. E. Rozhnov. Moscow: Progress, 1976.

Kollantai, Alexandra. "Make Way for Winged Eros: A Letter to Working Youth." *Selected Writings of Alexandra Kollantai.* Edited by Alix Holt. Westport, Conn.: Lawrence Hill, 1977. Originally published in 1923.

Kon, I. S. "Reabilitatsiia Freida." *Moskovskie novosti,* 26 (July 1, 1990): 10.

———. *Sotsiologiia lichnosti.* Moscow: Izdatel'stvo politicheskoi literatury, 1967.

Kon, Igor, and James Riordan. *Sex and Russian Society.* Bloomington: Indiana University Press, 1993.

Kubie, Lawrence S. "Pavlov, Freud and Soviet Psychiatry." *Behavioral Science,* 4 (1959): 29–34.

Kurtsin, I. T. *Kritika Freidizma v meditsine i fiziologii.* Moscow-Leningrad: Nauka, 1965.

Kurzweil, Edith. *The Freudians.* New Haven: Yale University Press, 1989.

Lalaiants, I. E., and L. S. Milovanova. "Freid i Freidizm." *Sovetskaia bibliografiia,* 5 (September–October 1990): 53–62.

Laqueur, Walter. "Psychoanalysis in Soviet Perspective." *Soviet Survey,* 7 (1956): 2–8.

Lauterbach, W. *Soviet Psychotherapy.* New York: Pergamon Press, 1984.

Lavrent'ev, N. N. "Dushevnye bolezni i polovye prestupleniia." *Zhurnal nevropatologii i psikhologii,* 1 (1928): 59–74.

Leibin, V. M. *Freid, psikhoanaliz i sovremennaia zapadnaia filosofiia.* Moscow: Politizdat, 1990.

———. "Iz istorii vozniknoveniia psikhoanaliza (Pis'ma Z. Freida Flissu)." *Voprosy filosofii,* 4 (1988): 104–117.

———. "Konformizm i respektabelnost' psikhoanaliza." *Voprosy filosofii,* 4 (1972): 143–147.

———. "Psikhoanaliz i bessoznatel'noe: utochnenie poniatii." *Psikhologicheskii zhurnal,* 10, 3 (1989): 17–22.

———. *Psikhoanaliz i filosofiia neofreidizma.* Moscow: Izdatel'stvo politicheskoi literatury, 1977.

———. "Repressirovannyi psikhoanaliz: Freid, Trotskii, Stalin." *Rossiiskii psikhoanaliticheskii vestnik,* 1 (1991): 32–55.

———. "Vera ili razum." *Voprosy filosofii,* 8 (1988): 126–132.

Leibin, V. M. (ed.). *Zigmund Freid, psikhoanaliz i russkaia mysl'.* Moscow: Izdatel'stvo "Respublika." 1994.

Levchuk, L. T. *Psikhoanaliz i khudozhestvennoe tvorchestvo.* Kiev: Izdatel'stvo pri Kievskom universiteta, 1980.

———. *Psikhoanaliz: ot bessoznatel'nogo k "ustalosti ot soznaniia."* Kiev: Izdatel'stvo pri Kievskom universitete, 1989.

Lichko, A. E. "Psikhologiia otnoshenii kak teoreticheskaia kontseptsiia v meditsinskoi psikhologii i psikhoterapii." *Zhurnal nevropatologii i psikhiatrii,* 77, 12 (1977): 1833–1838.

Likhnitskii, V. N. "Osnovnyia napravleniia sovremennoi ratsionalisticheskoi psikhoterapii." *Psikhoterapiia,* 3 (1912): 1–11, 103–120.

Ljunggren, Magnus. "The Psychoanalytic Breakthrough in Russia on the Eve of the First World War." *Russian Literature and Psychoanalysis.* Edited by Daniel Rancour-Laferriere. Amsterdam: John Benjamins, 1989.

Lobner, Hans. "'The Unconscious' in the Soviet Union." *Sigmund Freud House Bulletin,* 3 (1979): 20–28.

Lobner, Hans, and Vladimir Levitin. "A Short Account of Freudism: Notes on the History of Psychoanalysis in the USSR." *Sigmund Freud House Bulletin,* 2, 1 (1978): 5–29.

Luria, A. R. *The Making of Mind. A Personal Account of Soviet Psychology.* Edited by Michael and Sheila Cole. Cambridge: Harvard University Press, 1979.

———. "Psikhoanaliz." *Bol'shaia sovetskaia entsiklopediia,* 1940, 40:507–510.

———. "Psikhoanaliz kak sistema monisticheskoi psikhologii." K. N. Kornilov (ed.), *Psikhologiia i marksizm.* Leningrad: Gosizdat, 1925, 47–80. Translated as: "Psychoanalysis as a System of Monistic Psychology." *The Selected Writings of A. R. Luria.* Edited by Michael Cole. White Plains, N.Y.: M. Sharpe, 1978, 3–41.

———. *Psikhoanaliz v svete osnovnykh tendentsii sovremennoi psikhologii.* Kazan: n.p., 1922.

———. "Report of Meetings for the Fourth Quarter, 1923." *International Journal of Psychoanalysis,* 5 (1924): 258–261.

Malis, G. *Psikhoanaliz kommunizma.* Kharkov: Kosmos, 1924.

Manson, Irina. "La psychanalyse en U.R.S.S.: La *perestroika* de la conscience." *Esquisse psychanalytiques,* 11 (Spring 1989): 5–32.

Margetts, Edward L. "The Concept of the Unconscious in the History of Medical Psychology." *Psychiatric Quarterly,* 27 (1953): 116–138.

Marti, Jean. "La psychanalyse en Russie et en Union soviétique de 1909 à 1930." *Critique,* 32, 346 (March 1976): 199–236.

Masson, Jeffrey. *The Assault on Truth: Freud's Suppression of the Seduction Theory.* New York: Penguin Books, 1985.

Masson, Jeffrey (ed.). *The Complete Letters of Sigmund Freud to Wilhelm Fliess, 1887–1904.* Cambridge: Harvard University Press, 1985.

Maximov, Igor. "La psychanalyse russe." *L'Ane,* 10 (1983): 3–5.

Micale, Marc (ed.). *Beyond the Unconscious: Essays of Henri Ellenberger in the History of Psychiatry.* Princeton: Princeton University Press, 1993.

Mikhailov, F., and G. Tsaregorodtsev. *Za porogom soznaniia*. Moscow: Gosizdatpolitlit, 1961.

Miller, Emanuel. "Freud and Pavlov." *Soviet Survey*, 28 (April–June 1959): 64–65, 80.

Miller, Martin A. "Freudian Theory under Bolshevik Rule: The Theoretical Controversy During the 1920s." *Slavic Review*, 44, 4 (Winter 1985): 625–646.

———. "The Origins and Development of Russian Psychoanalysis, 1909–1930." *The Journal of the American Academy of Psychoanalysis*, 14, 1 (January 1986): 125–135.

———. "The Reception of Psychoanalysis and the Problem of the Unconscious in Russia." *Social Research*, 57, 4 (Winter 1990): 875–888.

Musatti, Cesare L. "An Answer to F. V. Bassin's Criticism of Freudianism." *The Soviet Review* 1, 5 (December 1970): 14–27.

Naiman, Eric. "The Case of Chubarov Alley: Collective Rape, Utopian Desire and the Mentality of NEP." *Russian History*, 17, 1 (Spring 1990): 1–30.

———. *Sex in Public: The Incarnation of Early Soviet Ideology*. Princeton: Princeton University Press, 1997.

Neiditsch, Sara. "Über den gegenwärtigen Stand der Freudschen Psychologie in Russland." *Jahrbuch der psychoanalytische und psychopathologische Forschungen*, 2 (1910): 347–348.

Neiditsch, Sara, N. Osipov, and M. Pappenheim. "Psychoanalysis in Russia." *The International Journal of Psychoanalysis* (December 1922): 513–520. Slightly abridged translation of "Die Psychoanalyse in Russland während der letzten Jahre." *International Zeitschrift für ärztliche Psychoanalyse*, 7 (1921): 381–388.

Neufeld, Iolan. *Dostoevskii: Psikhoanaliticheskii ocherk*. Leningrad: Izdatel'stvo "Petrograd," 1925.

Niqueux, Michel. "La critique marxiste face à l'érotisme dans la littérature russe (1908–1928)." *Amour et érotisme dans la littérature russe du XXe siècle*. Edited by Leonid Heller. Bern: Peter Lang, 1992, 83–90.

Nunberg, Herman, and Ernst Federn (eds.). *Minutes of the Vienna Psychoanalytic Society*. New York: International Universities Press, Vol. 1 (1906–1908), 1962. Vol. 2 (1908–1910), 1964. Vol. 3 (1910–1911), 1974. Vol. 4 (1912–1915), 1975.

Obholzer, Karin. *The Wolf Man Sixty Years Later*. New York: Continuum, 1982.

Osipov, N. E. "Eshche o psikhoanalize." *Psikhoterapiia*, 1 (1910): 153–172.

———. "Idealisticheskiia nastroeniia i psikhoterapiia." *Psikhoterapiia*, 1 (1910): 244–255.

———. "Mysli i somneniia po povodu odnogo sluchaia 'degenerativnoi psikhopatii'." *Psikhoterapiia*, 3 (1912): 189–215, 299–306.

———. "O bol'noi dushe." *Zhurnal nevropatologii i psikhiatrii*, 13 (1913): 657–673.

———. "O naviazchivoi ulybke." *Zhurnal nevropatologii i psikhiatrii*, 12 (1912): 570–578.

———. "O nevroze boiazni (*Angstneurose*)." *Zhurnal nevropatologii i psikhiatrii*, 9, nos. 1–2 (1909): 783–805.

———. "O 'panseksualizme' Freud'a." *Zhurnal nevropatologii i psikhiatrii*, 11, 1 (1911): 749–760.

———. "O psikhoanalize." *Psikhoterapiia*, 1 (1910): 11–28, 106–116.

———. "Posledniia raboty Freud'ovskoi shkoly." *Zhurnal nevropatologii i psikhiatrii*, 9 (1909): 526–586.

———. "Psikhologicheskie i psikhpatologicheskie vzgliady Sigm. Freud'a v nementskoi literature 1907 goda." *Zhurnal nevropatologii i psikhiatrii*, 8, nos. 1–2 (1908): 564–584.

————. "Psikhologiia kompleksov i assotsiativnyi eksperiment po rabotam tsiurikhskoi kliniki." *Zhurnal nevropatologii i psikhiatrii*, 8, no. 1 (1908): 1021–1074.

————. "Psikhoterapiia v literaturnykh proizvedeniiakh L. N. Tolstogo." *Psikhoterapiia*, 2 (1911): 1–21.

————. "Zapiski sumashedshago." *Psikhoterapiia*, 3 (1913): 141–158.

Ovcharenko, V. I. "Sud'ba Sabiny Shpil'rein." *Rossiiskii psikhoanaliticheskii vestnik*, 2 (1992): 64–69.

Ozeretskovskii, D. S. "K kritike psikhoanaliza: o novykh putiakh v lechenii nevrotikov." *Sovremennaia psikhonevrologiia*, 8, no. 1 (1929): 311–319.

Perepel, Elias. "On the Physiology of Hysterical Aphonia and Mutism." *International Journal of Psychoanalysis*, 11 (1930): 185–192.

————. "The Psychoanalytic Movement in the U.S.S.R." *Psychoanalytic Review*, 26 (1939): 291–299.

Perepel, I. A. *Opyt primeneniia psikhoanaliza k izucheniiu detskoi defektivnosti.* Leningrad: Izdanie avtora, 1925.

————. *Sovetskaia psikhonevrologiia i psikhoanaliz: K voprosu o lechenii i profilaktike nevrozov v SSSR.* Leningrad: Izdanie avtora, 1927.

Pevnitskii, A. A. "Neskol'ko sluchaev psikhoanalizma." *Psikhoterapiia*, 2 (1910): 51–62.

Pirog, Gerald. "Bakhtin and Freud on the Ego." *Russian Literature and Psychoanalysis.* Edited by Daniel Rancour-Laferriere. Amsterdam: John Benjamins, 1988, 401–415.

————. "The Bakhtin Circle's Freud: From Positivism to Hermeneutics." *Poetics Today*, 8 (1987): 591–610.

Pokrovskii, A. "Sushchestvuiut-li bezsoznatel'nye psikhicheskie protsessy i esli sushchestvuiut, to kakova ikh deistvitel'naia priroda?" *Vera i razum* (Kharkov), 11 (1912): 640–655.

Pollack, George. "Psychoanalysis in Russia and the U.S.S.R.: 1908–1979." *Annual of Psychoanalysis*, 10 (1982): 267–279.

Polosin, M. P. "Dr. Med. N. E. Osipov." *Zhizn' i smert'. Sbornik pamiati D-ra N. E. Osipova.* Edited by A. L. Bem, F. N. Dosuzhkov, and N. O. Losskii. Prague, 1935, 5–15.

Porter, Roy, and Mikulas Teich (eds.). *Sexual Knowledge, Sexual Science: A History of Attitudes to Sexuality.* Cambridge: Cambridge University Press, 1994.

Prangishvili, A. S., A. E. Sherozia, and F. V. Bassin (eds.). "Mezhdunarodnyi simpozium po probleme neosoznavaemoi psikhicheskoi deiatel'nosti." *Voprosy psikhologii*, 2 (1980): 181–184.

————. *The Unconscious: Nature, Functions, Methods of Study.* Tbilisi: Metsniereba, 1978. 3 vols.

Pruzhinina, A. A. *Kritika frantsuzskimi Marksistami psikhoanaliza.* Moscow: Izdatel'stvo Moskovskogo universiteta, 1984.

Radzikhovskii, L. A. "Teoriia Freida: smena ustanovki." *Voprosy psikhologii*, 6 (1988): 100–105.

Reich, Wilhelm. "Dialekticheskii materializm i psikhoanaliz." *Pod znamenem marksizma*, 7–8 (1929): 180–206.

————. "Psikhoanaliz kak estestvenno-nauchnaia distsiplina." *Estestvoznanie i marksizm*, 4 (1929): 99–108.

————. "Psychoanalysis in the Soviet Union." *Sex-Pol. Essays, 1929–1934*. Edited by Lee Baxandall. New York: Random House, 1966, 75–88. Originally published as: "Die Stellung der Psychoanalyse in der Sowjetunion: Notizen von einer Studienreise nach Russland." *Die Psychoanalytische Bewegung*, 1 (1929): 358–368.

Reisner, M. A. "Freid i ego shkola o religii." *Pechat' i revoliutsiia*, 1 (January–February 1924): 40–60; 3 (May–June 1924): 81–106.

————. "Sotsial'naia psikhologiia i uchenie Freida." *Pechat' i revoliutsiia*, 3 (May 1925): 54–69; 4 (June 1925): 88–100; 5–6 (July–September 1925): 133–150.

Rice, James. *Dostoevsky and the Healing Art*. Ann Arbor: Ardis, 1985.

————. *Freud's Russia: National Identity in the Evolution of Psychoanalysis*. New Brunswick, N.J.: Transaction, 1993.

————. "Russian Stereotypes in the Freud-Jung Correspondence." *Slavic Review*, 41, 1 (Spring 1982): 19–34.

Robinson, Paul. *The Freudian Left*. New York: Harper and Row, 1969.

Rollins, Nancy. "Consciousness, Unconsciousness and the Concept of Repression." *The Unconscious*. Edited by A. S. Prangishvili, A. E. Sherozia, and F. V. Bassin. Tbilisi: Metsniereba, 1978. I:266–281.

————. "A Critique of Soviet Concepts of Consciousness and Unconsciousness." *Interaction*, 3, 4 (Winter 1980): 225–233.

————. "The New Soviet Approach to the Unconscious." *American Journal of Psychiatry*, 131, 4 (March 1974): 301–304.

Rotenberg, V. S. "Aktivnost' snovidenii i problema bessoznatel'nogo." *The Unconscious*. Edited by A. S. Prangishvili, A. E Sherozia, and F. V. Bassin. Tbilisi: Metsniereba, 1978. II:99–110.

Roudinesco, Elisabeth. *Jacques Lacan and Co.: A History of Psychoanalysis in France, 1925–1985*. Translated by Jeffrey Mehlman. Chicago: University of Chicago Press, 1990. Originally published as *La bataille de cent ans: Histoire de la psychanalyse en France*. Paris: Editions du Seuil, 1986, 2 vols.

Rozental, Tatiana. "'Opasnyi vozrast' Karin Mikhaelis v svete psikhoanaliza." *Psikhoterapiia*, (1911): 189–194, 273–289.

————. "Stradanie i tvorchestvo Dostoevskogo. Psikhologicheskoe issledovanie." *Voprosy izucheniia i vospitaniia lichnosti*, 1 (1919): 88–107.

Rozhnov, V. E., and M. E. Burno. "Uchenie o bessoznatel'nom i klinicheskaia psikhoterapiia: postanovka voprosa." *The Unconscious*. Edited by A. S. Prangishvili, A. E. Sherozia, and F. V. Bassin. Tbilisi: Metsniereba, 1978. II:346–352.

"Russian Psychoanalytic Society." *International Journal of Psychoanalysis*. Selected reports throughout the 1920s.

Rutkovskii, Leonid. "Gipoteza bezsoznatel'nykh dushevnykh iiavlenii." *Zhurnal ministerstva narodnago prosveshcheniia* (1895): 323–371.

Sapir, I. D. "Doklad v Komakademii." *Estestvoznanie i marksizm*, 4 (1929): 108–125.

————. "Freidizm i marksizm." *Pod znamenem marksizma*, 11 (1926): 57–87.

————. "Freidizm, sotsiologiia, psikhologiia." *Pod znamenem marksizma*, 7–8 (1929): 207–236.

————. *Vysshaia nervnaia deiatel'nost' cheloveka*. Moscow: Gosizdat, 1925.

Schmidt, Vera. "Education psychanalytique en Russie soviétique." *Les temps modernes,* 273 (March 1969): 1626–1647.

———. *Psychoanalytische Erziehung in Sowjetrussland. Bericht über das Kinderheim-Laboratorium in Moskau.* Leipzig: Internationaler Psychoanalytischer Verlag, 1924.

Sharp, Jane A. "Redrawing the Margins of Russian Vanguard Art: Natalia Goncharova's Trial for Pornography." *Sexuality and the Body in Russian Culture.* Edited by Jane T. Coslow, Stephanie Sandler, and Judith Vowels. Stanford: Stanford University Press, 1993.

Sheroziia, A. E. *K probleme soznaniia i bessoznatel'nogo psikhicheskogo.* 2 vols. Tbilisi: Metsniereba, 1969, 1973.

Sirotkina, I. E. "Is istorii russkoi psikhoterapii: N. E. Osipov v Moskve i v Prage." *Voprosy psikhologii,* 1 (1995): 74–83.

Smirnov, A. I. *O soznanii i bezsoznatel'nykh dukhovnykh iiavleniiakh.* Kazan: Univ. tipograf., 1875.

Spielrein, Sabina. "Beiträge zur Kenntnis der kindliche Seele." *Zentralblatt für Psychoanalyse,* 3 (1912): 57–72.

———. "Die Destruktion als Ursache des Werdens" *Jahrbuch für psychoanalytische und psychologische Forschungen,* IV (1912): 465–503.

———. "Über den psychologischen Inhalt eines Falles von Schizophrenie." *Jahrbuch für psychoanalytische und psychologische Forschungen,* III (1911): 329–400.

———. "Russische Literatur." *Bericht über die Fortschritte der Psychoanalyse in den Jahren* 1914–1919. Leipzig: Internationaler Psychoanalytischer Verlag, 1921, 356–365.

Sterba, Richard. "Discussions of Sigmund Freud." *Psychoanalytic Quarterly,* 47, 2 (1978): 181–184.

Stern, Mikhail. *Sex in the USSR.* New York: Times Books, 1980.

Sullaway, Frank. *Freud: Biologist of the Mind.* New York: Basic Books, 1979.

Sviadoshch, A. M. *Nevrozy i ikh lechenie.* Moscow: Meditsina, 1971.

———. "Rol' neosoznavaemykh motivov v klinike nevrozov." *The Unconscious.* Edited by A. S. Prangishvili, A. E. Sherozia, and F. V. Bassin. Tbilisi: Metsniereba, 1978. II:361–366.

Tarasov, K. E., and M. S. Kel'ner. *"Freido-Marksizm" o cheloveke.* Moscow: Mysl', 1989.

Tögel, Christfried. "Lenin und die Rezeption der Psychoanalyse in der Sowjetunion der Zwanzigerjahre." *Sigmund Freud House Bulletin,* 13, 1 (1989): 16–27.

Tsentral'nyi gosudarstvennyi arkhiv RSFSR (Moscow). Fondy 298, 2306, 2307.

"The Unconscious in the USSR: Can Marx and Freud Find Common Ground." *Roche Report: Frontiers of Psychiatry,* 11, 9 (October 15, 1981): 12–19.

Upadochnoe nastroenie sredi molodezhi: Eseninshchina. Edited by A. V. Lunacharskii. Moscow: Kommunisticheskaia akademiia, 1927.

Vasil'chenko, G. S. *Obshchaia seksopatologiia.* Moscow: Meditsina, 1977.

Veidemiuller, K., and A. Shcheglov. "Freidizm." *Bol'shaia sovetskaia entsiklopediia,* 1935, 59: 187–193.

Veliev, G. N. *Problema bessoznatel'nogo v filosofii i pskihologii.* Baku: Elm, 1984.

Vittels, F. *Freid.* With an introduction by M. A. Reisner. Moscow: Gosizdat, 1925. Russian translation of Fritz Wittels, *Sigmund Freud, der Mann, die Lehre, die Schule.* Leipzig: E. P. Tal, 1924.

Vnukov, V. A. "Psikhoanaliz," *Meditsinskaia entsiklopediia,* 1933, 27: 733.

Voloshinov, V. N. *Freudianism: A Critical Sketch*. Bloomington: Indiana University Press, 1987. Originally published in 1927 as *Freidizm: Kriticheskii ocherk*. Reprinted in *Zigmund Freid, psikhoanaliz i russkaia mysl'*. Edited by V. M. Leibin. Moscow: Izdatel'stvo "Respublika," 1994, 269–346.

———. "Po tu storonu sotsial'nogo: o Freidizme." *Zvezda*, 5, 11 (1925): 186–214.

Von Wiren-Garczynski, Vera. "Zoshchenko's Psychological Interests." *Slavic and East European Journal*, 11, 1 (Spring 1967): 3–22.

Voronskii, A. "Freidizm i iskusstvo." *Krasnaia nov'*, 7 (1925): 241–262.

Vyrubov, N. A. "K voprosu o geneze i lechenii nevroza trevogi kombinirovannym gipno-analiticheskim metodom." *Psikhoterapiia*, 1 (1910): 29–41.

Waning, Adeline Van. "The Works of Pioneering Psychoanalyst, Sabina Spielrein." *International Review of Psychoanalysis*, 19 (1992): 399–414.

Wells, Harry K. *Pavlov and Freud: Toward a Scientific Psychology and Psychiatry*. 2 vols. New York: International Publishers, 1956.

White, Lancelot Law. *The Unconscious before Freud*. New York: Basic Books, 1960.

Wolf Man. *The Wolf Man*. Edited by Muriel Gardiner. New York: Basic Books, 1971.

Wolff, Larry. *Postcards from the End of the World: Child Abuse in Freud's Vienna*. New York: Atheneum, 1988.

Wood, Elizabeth. "Prostitution Unbound." *Sexuality and the Body in Russian Culture*. Edited by Jane T. Coslow, Stephanie Sandler, and Judith Vowels. Stanford: Stanford University Press, 1993, 124–135.

Wulff, Moshe. "Beiträge zur infantilen Sexualität." *Zentralblatt für Psychoanalyse*, 2 (1912): 6–17.

———. "Bemerkungen über einige Ergebnisse bei einer psychiatrisch-neurologischen Untersuchung von Chauffeuren." *Internationale Zeitschrift für Psychoanalyse*, 14 (1928): 237–242.

———, "Die russische psychoanalytische Literatur bis zum Jahre 1911." *Zentralblatt für Psychoanalyse*, 7–8 (April–May 1911): 364–371.

———. "Eine interessanter Zusammenhang von Traum Symbolhandlung und Krankheitssymptom." *Internationale Zeitschrift für arztlich Psychoanalyse*, 1 (1913): 559–560.

———. "K psikhoanalizu koketstva." *Sovremennaia psikhonevrologiia*, 3–4 (1925): 33–43.

———. "Kleine Beiträge aus der psychoanalytischen Praxis." *Zentralblatt für Psychoanalyse*, 1 (1911): 337–341.

———. "Opyt' psikhoanaliticheskago razbora sluchaia psikhonevroticheskago zabolevaniia." *Sovremennaia psikhiatriia*. 3 (March 1914): 197–224.

———. "A Phobia in a Child of 18 Months." *International Journal of Psychoanalysis*, 9 (1928): 354–359.

———. "Zur Stellung der Psychoanalyse in der Sowjetunion." *Die Psychoanalytische Bewegung*, 2 (1929): 70–75.

Young, Donald. "Ermakov and Psychoanalytic Criticism in Russia." *Slavic and East European Journal*, 23, 1 (Spring 1979): 72–86.

Zachepitskii, R. A. "Kriticheskii analiz 'Freido-Marksizma'." *Zhurnal nevropatologii i psikhiatrii*, 82 (1982): 142–148.

———. "Psychotherapy and Psychoanalysis in Neuroses." Jules H. Masserman (ed.), *Current Psychiatric Therapies,* 23 (1986): 249–256.

Zagdanskii, Andrei. Director of the film *Tolkovanie snovedeniia* (1988).

Zalkind, A. B. "Freidizm i Marksizm." *Krasnaia nov',* 4, 21 (1924): 163–186.

———. *Ocherki kul'tury revoliutsionnogo vremeni.* Moscow: Gosizdat, 1924.

———. "Pervyi vsesoiuznyi s"ezd po izucheniiu povedeniia cheloveka." *Zhurnal nevropatologii i psikhiatrii,* 6 (1930): 19–24.

———. "Polovoi vopros s kommunisticheskoi tochki zreniia." *Polovoi vopros.* Edited by S. M. Kalmanson. Moscow: Gosizdat, 1924, 5–16.

———. *Polovoi vopros v usloviiakh sovetskoi obshchestvennosti.* Leningrad: Gosizdat, 1926.

Zalkind, A. B. (ed.). *Psikho-nevrologicheskie nauki v SSR (Materialy I Vsesoiuznogo s"ezda po izucheniiu povedeniia cheloveka).* Moscow: Gosmedizdat, 1930.

———. *Revoliutsiia i molodezh.* Moscow: Gosizdat, 1925.

Zelenskii, V. "Psikhoanaliz v literaturovedenii." *Sovetskaia bibliografiia,* 6 (November–December 1990): 101–111.

Zhelianova, L. "O freidistskom iskazhenii russkoi literatury v sovremennom amerikanskom literaturovedenii." *Russkaia literatura,* 2 (1959): 226–234.

FIRST REPUBLICATIONS OF FREUD'S WORKS DURING THE GORBACHEV ERA

Izbrannoe. Edited and with an introduction by A. I. Belkin. Moscow: Vneshtorgizdat, 1989.

Psikhologiia bessoznatel'nogo. Edited and with an introduction by M. G. Iaroshevskii. Moscow: Prosveshchenie, 1989.

Vvedenie v psikhoanaliz. Edited by M. G. Iaroshevskii. With an essay by F. V. Bassin and M. G. Iaroshevskii. Moscow: Nauka, 1989.

Index

Abraham, Karl, xi, 24, 27, 32, 35, 66, 165

Academic Society for Psychiatry and Neurobiology (Moscow), 34, 37, 46

Academy of Medical Sciences, 116, 121, 128, 130, 131

Academy of Sciences (Azerbaizhan), 155

Academy of Sciences (Georgia), 147, 149

Academy of Sciences (Russian-Soviet), 5, 116

Adler, Alfred, xii, 32–57 passim, 104, 119, 121, 137, 142, 146, 150, 165

Aichhorn, August, 64

Alexander, Franz, 129

All-Mourners Hospital (St. Petersburg), 7

"All-Russian" Psychoanalytic Society, 61, 84, 88, 92, 104

All-Union Congress of Psychologists (*1930*), 92

Althusser, Louis, 150

Anokhin, P. K., 130, 139

Arieti, Silvano, 151

Arnold, Matthew, 30

Asatiani, M. M., 33, 34

Asnaurov, F., 34

Assagioli, R., 34

Asylum system: origins of, 5–6, 7, 8; taken over by zemstvos, 9

Averbukh, R. A., 58, 60

Avtonomova, N. S., 146, 155

Bakhtin, Mikhail, 88

Balinskii, Ivan, 8, 10

Bassin, F. V., 144, 145, 155; quoted, 93; on Freud's theory, 129, 131–33, 135, 142–43; book on the Unconscious, 136–38, 141; organizer of International Conference on the Unconscious, 147

Bazhenov, N. N., 22, 25, 47
Bekhterev, V. M., 10, 11, 37, 39, 48, 55,
    58, 70, 72, 75, 81, 110, 120
Bekhterev Psychoneurological Institute
    (Leningrad), 120, 142
Belkin, Aaron, 156, 157, 158, 159–61
Berg, F., 33
Bergson, H., 78, 103, 108, 124, 146
Berlin-Lankwitz Sanatorium, 32
Berlin Psychoanalytic Institute, 59, 162
Bernfeld, Siegfried, 61, 64
Bernheim, Hippolyte, 25
Bernshtein, A. N., 34
Bernstein, Nikolai, 56
Birman, B. N., 104
Bloch, Iwan, 17
Blonskii, Pavel, 57, 66, 87
Boiko, A. N., 144
Bolshevik/Communist party: seizure of
    power by, 53; expanding control by, in
    society, 54, 56; Freudians' efforts to-
    ward approval by, 62–64; growing po-
    litical influence on psychoanalytic
    work, 66–68, 70; and potential for a
    Marxist psychology, 70; and journalis-
    tic debate over Freudian-Marxist
    theory, 72; and creation of term
    Freudism, 77; attacks on Freudianism,
    82, 95–96; and end of debate, 94, 95;
    and politicized science, 101; use of
    Pavlov against Freud, 117–18; use of
    psychiatry as a weapon against dissi-
    dents, 140; discussion of problem of
    Freud by leadership, 143, 164. *See also
    names of individuals*
Bondarenko, P. P., 130–31
Brentano, Franz, 22
Breuer, Josef, 25, 32, 132
Brezhnev, Leonid, 140
Briusov, Valerii, 16
Brücke, Ernst, 130
Bukharin, Nikolai, 62, 76, 154
Burghölzli Clinic (Zurich), 27, 33
Burghölzli Hospital (Zurich), 26

Bykhovskii, B., 71, 72, 77, 78, 87, 89
Bykov, K. M., 117

Catherine the Great, 5, 6–7
Centre de Médecine Psychosomatique
    (Paris), 147
Charasov, G. A., 67
Charcot, Jean-Martin, 25, 130
Chekhov, Anton, 15
Chernakov, E. T., 111
Chertok, Leon, 147, 150, 152
Commissariat of Enlightenment and Ed-
    ucation, 62, 64, 65, 66, 72
Communist Academy, 83, 87, 91, 92,
    102, 104
Communist Academy of Science, 105
Communist Party Conference: Six-
    teenth, 101
Communist Party Congress: Sixteenth,
    106; Twentieth, 118, 120, 128, 140
"Compulsive Smile," 38–40
Conference on "Problems of Ideological
    Struggle with Modern Freudism,"
    128–31
Congress of Russian Psychiatrists (1887),
    10, 12
Congress on Human Behavior (*1930*), xii,
    100, 101–02, 104

Darkshevich, L. O., 86
Dobren'kov, V. N., 145, 155
Dostoevsky, Fedor, 55, 158
Drosnes, Leonid, 24, 27, 40, 48
Dubois, Paul, 26, 33, 35, 43, 48, 165

Ehrenburg, Ilya, 118
Ellenberger, Henri, xi
Ellis, Havelock, 16
Engels, Friedrich, 73, 83
Eppelbaum, Vera, 34
Erikson, Erik, 145
Ermakov, Ivan, 165, 173; and founding of
    psychoanalytic society, 56, 57; and
    founding of psychoanalytic institute,

59; and International Psychoanalytic Association, 61, 63; and publication of Psychoanalytic Library series, 63, 67, 84, 90, 109; and Children's Home, 64; literary work of, 158

Esenin, Sergei, 95

Existentialism, 135, 136

Fedotov, D. D., 126–28, 145, 150

Fel'tsman, O. B., 33, 34, 46

Fenichel, Otto, 61

Ferenczi, Sandor, 24, 48; translations of, 60, 165

Frankfurt Institute for Social Research, 144

Frankfurt School, 79

Freud, Anna, x, 165

Freud, Sigmund, 14, 20, 21, 23, 30, 114; and psychoanalysis in Russia, ix–xiii; Russian translations of, 24, 46, 60, 67, 86, 90, 104; and Osipov, 25–29, 36, 38, 56, 169–73; and Russian psychiatry, 31; early Russian followers of, 32–35, 40, 43, 44, 47, 165, 168; and Rosenthal, 41, 55; and Spielrein, 45–46, 59; and Wulff, 45; on Russia and the Soviet Union, 46, 60–61, 94, 97–100; and Wolf Man, 47–49; and Luria, 57–58, 80–81, 108; and Soviet followers, 61, 66, 79–82, 84, 86–87, 89–90; and Schmidt, 66; and Zalkind, 76–77, 102–03; Bolshevik attacks on, in 1920s, 77–79, 83–84, 88–90, 92, 102–04; and Lenin, 85–86; and Trotsky, 87, 106; and Reich, 91–92; on Marxism, 98–100; and counter-revolution, 105–06; communist attacks on, in 1930s, 108–09, 111–13, 118, 119; and Rubinstein, 111–13; death of, 115; and Zoshchenko, 115-16; and Pavlov, 116–18; and Miasishchev, 120–23; and Uznadze, 124–26; post-Stalin revival of interest in, 126–35, 141–42, 143–44; and Bassin, 129, 131–33, 137–

38, 142–43; and Soviet studies of Fromm, 144–45; and the International Conference on the Unconscious, 146, 150–52; and perestroika, 154–55, 157–58; and Zagdansky's film, 156; and Belkin, 156–57, 159–61; and anti-Soviet criticism, 159–61; as threat to the Soviet Union, 163–64

Freze, A. U., 22

Fridman, B. D., 58, 82, 89, 90, 92

Fromm, Erich, 119, 144–45, 146

Gabrichevsky, A. G., 56

Gannushkin, Petr, 11

Gershonovich, L., 105–06

Gertsog, F. I., 7

Giliarovskii, Vasilii, 11

Gogol, Nikolai, 60

Gorbachev, Mikhail, 153, 153, 166

Gorky, Maxim, 96

Grashchenkov, N. I., 130

Griboedov, Alexander, 60

Helmholtz, Hermann, 22

Horney, Karen, 119, 129, 145, 146

Iakobii, P. I., 13, 25

Iakovlenko, Vladimir, 25

Iarotskii, A. I., 36

Il'in, Ivan, 47, 56

Institute of Brain Pathology (St. Petersburg-Leningrad), 55, 58

Institute of Psychology (Moscow), 58, 71, 81, 88, 105, 106

Institute of Psychology (Tbilisi), 123

International Congress of Psychoanalysis, First (1909), 24.

International Psychoanalytic Association (IPA), 24, 60, 61, 69, 90

Ioffe, A. A., 46, 62

Israel Psychoanalytic Society, 88

Iurinets, V., 77, 78, 79

Ivanov, Nikolai, 160

Izgoev, Alexander, 16

Jacobson, Edith, 142
Jakobson, Roman, 147, 151
James, William, 22, 39, 73, 81
Janet, Pierre, 25, 39, 150
Jarvis, Edward, 12
Jones, Ernest, x, 47, 61
Juliusburger, Otto, 32
Jung, Carl, 24; influence of, in Russia, xi, xii, 33–34, 43, 46, 73, 137, 146, 150, 165; and Osipov, 26, 27, 32, 36, 38; and Rosenthal, 41; and Spielrein, 45; and differences with Freud, 47; translations of, 60

Kandinskii, Viktor, 23
Kannabikh, Iu. B., 34, 88, 104
Kautsky, Karl, 105
Kavelin, Konstantin, 11
Kazan Psychoanalytic Society, 57, 58, 71, 82
Kerbikov, O. V., 129
Khaletskii, A. M., 135
Khrushchev, Nikita, 118, 139, 140
Kibal'chich, Z. I., 7
Kierkegaard, Soren, 146
Kirkbride, Thomas, 10, 75, 110
Klein, Melanie, 60, 165
Kollontai, Alexandra, 94–95
Kon, I. S., 136
Kornilov, K. N., 58
Korsakov, Sergei, 10, 11, 14, 23
Kovalevskii, P. I., 10, 12, 13
Kozhevnikov, I. I., 10
Kozhevnikov Prize, 34
Kraepelin, Emil, 48
Krafft-Ebing, Richard, 16
Krupskaia, Nadezhda, 75, 85, 86
Krylenko, Nikolai, 96
Kurtsin, I. T., 135
Kurzweil, Edith, x

Lacan, J., 144, 145–46, 147, 150, 165
Leibin, V. M., 144–45, 146, 150, 155, 156
Lenin, Vladimir, 54, 62, 72, 77, 83; on

psychoanalysis, 85–87, 100, 106, 113, 136
Lévy-Bruhl, Lucien, 73
Lichko, A. E., 142, 150
Likhnitskii, V. N., 34
Little Friday psychiatric group, 36
Ludwig, Carl, 11
Lunacharsky, Anatoly, 62, 64, 66, 72, 101, 162
Luria, Alexander R., 82, 84, 143, 158; quoted, 53; and establishment of psychoanalytic group in Kazan, 57–58; position at Institute of Psychology, 58; involvement in Psychoanalytic Institute, 60, 66; on psychoanalytic theory, 71, 80–81, 107–08; resignation as secretary of Psychoanalytic Institute, 88; attacked, 89

McLuhan, Marshall, 146
Magnan, Valentine, 10
Mandelstam, Nadezhda, 158
Mandelstam, Osip, 114, 154
Marcuse, Herbert, 145
Marx, Karl, 73, 79, 82; criticism of, by Freud, 98, 107, 129
Maudsley, Henry, 22
Medical Encyclopedia, 91, 108
Medical-Surgical Academy (St. Petersburg), 8, 10
Merzheevskii, I. P., 10, 12
Meynert, Theodor, 130
Miasishchev, V. N., 120–22, 130, 136, 142
Michaelis, Karen, 41–42, 43
Mikhailov, F., 134
Military Hospital, First (St. Petersburg), 9
Moscow Psychiatric Clinic, 24, 25, 26, 28

Nechaev, A. P., 75
New Economic Policy (NEP), 54, 67, 94, 95, 100, 165, 166
Newton, Isaac, 22, 158
Nicholas I (tsar of Russia), 7

Nicholas II (tsar of Russia), 54
Nietzsche, F., 3, 17, 78, 108, 130
Nilus, Pavel, 16

Orshanskii, I. G., 22, 23
Osipov, E. A., 8–9, 25
Osipov, Nikolai E., 165; review of
    Freud's work, 24–25, 27, 32, 36, 46;
    early career of, 25–26, 35; first psycho-
    analytic case studies by, 28–29, 31, 36,
    38–40, 43–44; and creation of the
    journal *Psychotherapy*, 34; and Freud,
    35, 56, 97, 98, 169–73; on Tolstoy, 37;
    emigration to Prague, 54, 56, 88

Pankeev, Sergei. *See* Wolf Man
Pappenheim, Martin, 54, 56
Pasternak, Boris, 154
Pavlov, Ivan: as Soviet scientific model,
    70, 117, 141, 157; compatibility with
    Freud's work, 72, 76, 84; and clashes
    among psychological schools, 75; and
    Trotsky, 87, 106; and Zoshchenko,
    115; Pavlov Conference, 116–17; on
    Freud, 118; Rubinstein on, 119; Mia-
    sishchev on, 121; compared with
    Uznadze, 124; opposition to Freud,
    131; Bassin on, 132, 133
"Pavlov Conference" (*1950*), 116, 141
Pedology, 103
Perepel, I. A., 89
Peter I (tsar of Russia), 4–5, 6–7
Peter III (tsar of Russia), 5, 6, 7
Pevnitskii, A. A., 43
Piaget, Jean, 46
Pinel, Philippe, 10
Pollack, George, 148
Popov, E. A., 129
Prangishvili, A. S., 147, 151
Preobrazhenskii Hospital (Moscow), 7–
    8, 25
Psychiatry (prerevolutionary): accepted
    as a science, 19; contrasted with psy-
    chology, 19–20

Psychoanalysis, in the USSR: Stalinist
    attacks on, 108; Rubinstein's alterna-
    tive to, 110–11; during World War II,
    115; renewed postwar attacks on, 116;
    association with American capitalism
    and imperialism during Cold War,
    117; rebirth of interest in, during the
    1950s, 125–26; revival of, through criti-
    cal discourse, 126; as subject of new
    attacks, 128–29; and criticism of Stali-
    nism, 131; increasing legitimacy of,
    136; confusion over prominence of, in
    1970s, 141; further erosion of hostility
    toward, 146; Western and Uznadzian
    orientations of, at Tbilisi conference,
    148–50; Tbilisi conference as turning
    point for, 151; increased interest in,
    during perestroika, 154; used to rein-
    terpret Soviet history, 155; as weapon
    against the Soviet government, 159;
    symbolic value of, for Soviet regime,
    164, 166; role in collapse of Soviet re-
    gime, 169
Psychoanalytic Library, 34, 46
Psychological and Psychoanalytic Li-
    brary, 60, 84, 90, 92
Psychoneurological Congress, 75; of
    1924, 81; of *1923*, 100
Psychoneurological Institute (Moscow),
    57, 64
Psychotherapy (Psikhoterapiia), 34; and
    first systematic explanation of psycho-
    analysis, 36, 40, 43, 44, 46, 54
Pushkin, Alexander, 67

Radek, Karl, 62, 76
Radzikhovskii, L. A., 157–58
Rank, Otto, 27, 45, 66, 73, 109, 171, 172,
    173
Reich, W., 61, 90–92, 109, 119, 146
Reik, Theodore, 73
Reisner, M. A., 72–74, 75, 77, 79, 87,
    104, 105
Riul', Ivan F., 7

Rollins, Nancy, 147, 148, 150

Rosenthal (Rozental'), Tatiana, 47; at meetings of Vienna Psychoanalytic Society, 24; training of, 41; research of, using literature and psychoanalysis, 41–43; psychoanalytic work under Bekhterev, 55, 58; study of Dostoevsky's novels, 56; death, 56, 171; psychoanalytic children's school in Petrograd, 57

Rozanov, Vasilii, 16

Rozhnov, V. E., 143

Rubinstein, Sergei, 110–12, 113, 119, 143

Russian Care Committee for Backward Children, 55

Russian Psychoanalytic Institute (Moscow), 59–69 passim, 88, 162

Russian Psychoanalytic Society (Moscow), 40, 57, 58, 59, 63, 64, 162. See also Russian Psychoanalytic Institute

Sabler, V. F., 7–8

Sanin, 16

Sapir, I. D., 83, 84

Sarkisov, S. A., 128

Sartre, Jean-Paul, 146, 156–57

Schmidt, Otto, 56, 57, 60, 66, 86

Schmidt, Vera, 64, 65, 66, 84, 86, 88, 92

Schopenhauer, A., 30, 108, 111, 130

Sechenov, Ivan, 10, 11

Serbskii, Vladimir, 11, 18, 25, 26, 35, 36, 44, 56

Serbskii Institute of Forensic and General Psychiatry (Moscow), 140

Sexual anxieties, 45; before the Revolution, 15–18; among children, 65, 90; and Kollontai, 94–95; and Zalkind, 95–96

Shatskii, Stanislav, 57, 65, 86

Shemiakin, F., 105–06, 107

Sheroziia, A. E., 147, 151, 152

Siderov, A. A., 56

Snezhnevskii, A. V., 130

Society for Petersburg Doctors for the Insane, 8

Society of Materialist Psychoneurologists, 101, 105

Society of Neuropathologists and Psychiatrists, 37, 44

Soloviev, Vladimir, 123

Solzhenitsyn, Alexander, 118, 140

Sorel, Georges, 78

Spencer, Herbert, 22, 73

Spielrein, Sabina, 27, 44, 49, 66, 165; at psychoanalytic meetings in Vienna, 24, 41; early psychoanalytic contributions of, 45–46; return to Soviet Russia, 59; clinical work in Moscow, 67; death, 114

Spinoza, Baruch, 136

Stalin, Joseph, 100, 106, 113, 115, 117, 118, 131, 158, 159, 163; Stalinism, 94, 105; height of Stalinization of psychology and psychiatry, 112

State Administration for Scientific Institutions, 63

State Publishing House, 62, 63, 67, 80, 89

State Scientific Soviet, 62

Stekel, W., 27, 34, 36, 42, 43, 165

Stoliarov, A., 104, 105

Strachey, James, 47

Sukharova, G. E., 115

Sullivan, Harry Stack, 119, 121, 129, 145, 146

Sumbaev, Igor, 160

Sviadoshch, A. M., 141, 150

Talankin, A., 106–07

Teller, Frieda, 170, 173

Tolstoi, Lev, 16, 37, 39, 171, 172

Trotsky, L. D., 62, 76, 86; on Freud and psychoanalysis, 87–88, 100; attacks on, 105–06, 153, 154, 162

Tsaregorodtsev, G., 134

Tsuladze, Sergei, 147

Union of Russian Psychiatrists and Neu-
    ropathologists, 14, 44
University Hospital (Berlin), 32
University Psychiatric Clinic (Moscow),
    10, 26
Uspensky, N. E., 56
Uznadze, Dmitry: early work of, 120,
    144; and "set" experiments with the
    unconscious, 124–25; followers of, 126,
    150; and Bassin, 133, 137–38, 142–43

Variash, A., 104, 105
Vavilov, S. I., 116
Verbitskaia, Anastasia, 16
Vienna Psychoanalytic Institute, 59
Vienna Psychoanalytic Society, x, 24, 40,
    41, 42, 44, 54, 56, 90
Vnukov, V., 108–09
Voloshinov, V. N., 88–89, 107
Voznesensky, Andrei, 153–54, 155
Vygotsky, Lev, 143, 150, 151; quoted, 53;
    at Psychoanalytic Society meetings,
    57, 67, 88; and Luria, 81; on the un-
    conscious, 82; under attack, 107, 112
Vyrubov, N. A., 32, 34, 40

Wednesday Psychological Society, 24
Witte, Sergei, 15
Wittels, Franz, 104
Wolf Man (Sergei K. Pankeev), 47–49
World Congress of Psychiatry: Third
    (*1961*), 135

World Psychiatric Association, 140
Wulff, Moshe, 165, 173; work with Karl
    Abraham, 32; at Vienna Psychoanaly-
    tic Society meetings, 34; translations
    of Freud, 34, 67, 109; review of
    psychoanalysis in Russia, 35; clinical
    research of, 44–45; founding of
    Psychoanalytic Society, 56–57; found-
    ing of Psychoanalytic Institute, 59–60,
    61, 63; and Children's Home, 64;
    member of editorial board of Freud's
    journal, 84; and departure from
    Russia, 88; and critique of Reich, 91–
    92
Wundt, Wilhelm, 22

Yaroshevsky (Iaroshevskii), M. G., 158

Zagdansky, Andrei, 156
Zalkind, A. B.: involvement with psy-
    choanalysis, 75–77; Bolshevik critique
    of, 78, 89, 104, 105; sexual theory of,
    95–96; attack on psychoanalysis, 102–
    03
Zemstvo, 8, 9
Zetkin, Klara, 85, 86, 106
Zhenotdel, 94
Ziehen, Theodor, 48
Zinoviev, Gregory, 76
Zoshchenko, Mikhail, 115–16